The Experience Economy

The Experience Economy

Work Is Theatre &
Every Business a Stage

B. JOSEPH PINE II
JAMES H. GILMORE

HARVARD BUSINESS SCHOOL PRESS
BOSTON, MASSACHUSETTS

Library of Congress Cataloging-in-Publication Data

Pine, B. Joseph
    The experience economy : work is theatre & every business a stage
    : goods & services are no longer enough / B. Joseph Pine II and
    James H. Gilmore.
        p.   cm.
    Includes index.
    ISBN 0-87584-819-2
    1. Product management. 2. Diversification in industry.
    3. Customer services.   I. Gilmore, James H., 1959– . II. Title.
    HF5415.15.P56 1999   98-33202
    658.5'6—dc21   CIP

The paper used in this publication meets the requirements of the
American National Standard for Permanence of Paper for Printed Library Materials
Z39.49-1984

To the Author and Perfecter of our faith.

Contents

Step Right Up

● ●

OVERSTOCKED! UNDERSOLD. Ten, 20, 30, 40 percent discounts. Half off everything! Buy one, get one free. Free financing for a year. Guaranteed lowest prices! Going out of business sale. . . . In a word: Commoditized.

This book offers an escape from the all-too-easy practice of competing on the basis of price. While customers love a sale, businesses perish from relying on low prices as a means of hawking their offerings. That approach worked for years, indeed decades, as economies of scale associated with mass producing goods and services resulted in a corresponding cost savings with every successive price reduction. But in industry after industry, that system of competition no longer sustains growth and profitability. You know it; we all know it. But what do we do about it?

We wrote this book for those searching for new ways to add value to their enterprises—fully aware that executives and managers have been bombarded with business books with the same aim. We've all been continuously improved, reengineered, and downsized. We've embraced time-based competition and the one-to-one future. We're now demassified, informationalized, digitized, and, yes, even mass customized—perhaps self-organizing and thriving on chaos to boot. Every business competing for the future is customer-centric, customer-driven, customer-focused, customer-yadda-yadda-yadda. So what's new?

This is new: Experiences represent an existing but previously unarticulated *genre of economic output*. Decoupling experiences from services in accounting for what businesses create opens up possibilities for extraordinary economic expansion—just as recognizing services as a distinct and legitimate offering led to a vibrant economic foundation in the face of a declining industrial base. And a new base is emerging. Ignore the familiar hype: Information is *not* the foundation of the "New Economy," for information is not an economic offering. As our friend John Perry Barlow likes to say, information wants to be free. Only when companies constitute it in the form of information *services*—or informational *goods* and informing *experiences*—do they create economic value. Economic offerings, not forms of intelligence, comprise the substance of buying and selling.

Recognizing experiences as a distinct economic offering provides the key to future economic growth, as shown in Chapter 1. Economic pessimist Jeremy Rifkin is right to suggest that businesses will need fewer workers to deliver services in the future, just as in the past due to innovations and higher productivity they needed fewer factory workers to produce goods, and before that fewer farm workers to harvest agricultural commodities. But those who decry the loss of agricultural and manufacturing jobs are wrong in asserting that the total number of jobs available will soon go down. Future waves of economic activity based on new economic offerings will provide ample opportunities to generate more wealth and create new jobs—if only businesses remain free to compete, unencumbered by government's view of what constitutes appropriate economic offerings to promote or protect.

Those businesses that recognize this dramatic shift and respond to it effectively—both are required—will forestall the forces of commoditization and create new economic value. (That is not to say that all companies must stage experiences to be profitable. Commodity companies can make money, at least on the up cycles. But watch out for those downturns!) Chapters 2 and 3 show how to stage engaging and compelling experiences using two frameworks we've gleaned from studying companies that have already successfully shifted to the Experience Economy. For those not yet ready to do so directly, a second route is provided by understanding that mass customizing automatically turns goods into services and services into experiences. Embracing the principles of Mass Customization articulated in Chapters 4 and 5—and thereby helping customers experience less sacrifice in their interactions with you and your offerings—may first be required for many goods manufacturers and service providers to enter the Experience Economy. (And don't neglect to read the short Intermission for an extension of this route.)

This new economy also demands new models for work. At every level in any company, workers need to understand that in the Experience Economy every business is a stage, and therefore work is theatre. That may sound strange, but it is true: Chapter 6 makes the case that whenever a customer happens across your bare stage of business, the workers are acting. It then introduces techniques for performing accordingly. Chapter 7 goes through four forms of theatre and in what situations each should be applied, while Chapter 8 sets down basic guidelines for those taking on each of the various roles required for any enterprise to stage experiences. All workers—from boardroom executives to front-line staffers—should be able to see themselves anew in this chapter, and those in human resource and organizational development departments should read it particularly closely to gain insight into changes required in the new economy.

Of course, not everyone will agree that we are shifting to an Experience Economy or that such a development is a good thing. Consider Las Vegas, the experience capital of America (although Orlando, Los Angeles, Manhattan, and even Branson, Missouri, would win their share of votes in any poll). Virtually *everything* about Vegas is a designed experience, from the slot machines at the airport to the gambling casinos that line the Strip; from the themed hotels and restaurants to the singing, circus, and magic shows; and from the Forum Shops mall that recreates ancient Rome to the amusement parks, thrill rides, video arcades, and carnival-style games that attract the twentysomethings and give older parents a reason to bring their kids in tow.

Of course, there is another side to the Vegas experience: the readily available alcohol, drugs, nudity-filled nightclubs, and prostitution. Unfortunately, these are every bit as much a part of the Experience Economy as any other entertainment or escapist fare. True, as we shift to this new economy, some people (perhaps more people) will make unwise and immoral choices due to the ready availability and slicker staging of prurient experiences. And most of the experiences mentioned above, while engaging and memorable, are certainly not virtuous. Further, many people object, with reason, to the artificiality of Disney World, the simulated nature of various motion-based attractions, and the techno-centric remoteness of the Internet (although these "artificial" experiences are counterbalanced to some degree by the concatenate rise of such "real" experiences as camping at Yellowstone National Park, donkey-riding down the Grand Canyon, kayaking on the Colorado River, and, more recently, a host of such "extreme sports" as rollerblading, snowboarding, skysurfing, and the like).

Despite the great improvements in working conditions, health, life expectancy, and the standard of living associated with every previous economic shift, those shifts were not without their dislocations and negative effects; we should not expect otherwise in the shift from the Service to the Experience Economy. All the issues mentioned above are legitimate and worthy of debate. But it is clear that we cannot retreat from the impending reality of the Experience Economy already surrounding us. Commendable or deleterious, virtuous or immoral, natural or artificial—these are all choices we make as together we create this new economy.

Those who decried previous economic shifts—two centuries ago to the Industrial Economy and in the past twenty years to the Service Economy—failed to stop the progression of economic value to higher-echelon offerings. It happened despite their protestations. Therefore, we believe that the moral emphasis should not lie on whether commerce should shift to experiential offerings. If societies are to seek continued economic prosperity, they must stage experiences to add sufficient value to their economies to employ the masses (goods and services are no longer enough). The moral emphasis must be placed instead on *what kinds of experiences will be staged.* The business executive, like everyone else, must in the end concern himself with the ultimate aims of man. That will be our focus in Chapters 9 and 10, as we explore the business world when experiences become commoditized, and the fifth, and final, economic offering—transformations—comes to the fore. You won't want to miss these last two chapters, nor the encore, for the implications for your business, whatever it is today, may be profound. And we won't back away from stating what we believe when it is the right thing to do.

We hope all readers discover a clear and compelling articulation of the new competitive landscape for the strategic options facing their enterprises. But even more, we hope you personally find the tools to begin staging compelling experiences and guiding vital transformations for your customers, present and future.

JOE PINE   DECEMBER 1998   JIM GILMORE
Dellwood, Minnesota   Shaker Heights, Ohio

STRATEGIC HORIZONS LLP
P.O. Box 548
Aurora, OH 44202-0548 U.S.A.
+1 (330) 995-4680
pine&gilmore@customization.com

The Experience Economy

1 *Welcome to the Experience Economy*

● ●

COMMODITIZED. No company wants that word applied to its goods or services. Merely mentioning *commoditization* sends shivers down the spines of executives and entrepreneurs alike. Differentiation disappears, margins fall through the floor, and customers buy solely on the basis of price, price, price.

Consider, however, a true commodity: the coffee bean. Companies that harvest coffee or trade it on the futures market receive—at the time of this writing—a little more than $1 per pound, which translates into one or two cents a cup. When a manufacturer grinds, packages, and sells those same beans in a grocery store, turning them into a good, the price to a consumer jumps to between 5 and 25 cents a cup (depending on brand and package size). Brew the ground beans in a run-of-the-mill diner, corner coffee shop, or bodega and that service now sells for 50 cents to a dollar per cup.

So depending on what a business does with it, coffee can be any of three economic offerings—commodity, good, or service—with three distinct ranges of value customers attach to the offering. But wait: Serve that same coffee in a five-star restaurant or espresso bar, where the ordering, creation, and consumption of the cup embodies a heightened ambience or sense of theatre, and consumers gladly pay anywhere from $2 to $5 for each cup. Businesses that ascend to this fourth level of value (see Figure 1-1) establish a distinctive experience that envelops the purchase of coffee, increasing its value (and therefore its price) by two orders of magnitude over the original commodity.

1

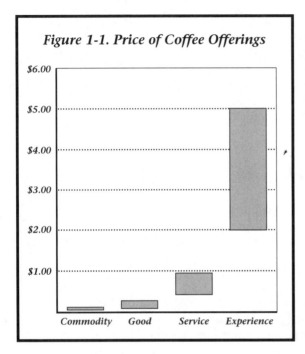

Figure 1-1. Price of Coffee Offerings

Or more. Immediately upon arriving in Venice, Italy, a friend asked a hotel concierge where he and his wife could go to enjoy the city's best. Without hesitation they were directed to the Cafe Florian in St. Mark's Square. The two of them were soon at the cafe in the crisp morning air, sipping cups of steaming coffee, fully immersed in the sights and sounds of the most remarkable of Old World cities. More than an hour later, our friend received the bill and discovered the experience had cost more than $15 a cup. Was the coffee worth it, we asked? "*Assolutamente!*" he replied.

A NEW SOURCE OF VALUE

Experiences are a fourth economic offering, as distinct from services as services are from goods, but one that has until now gone largely unrecognized. Experiences have always been around, but consumers, businesses, and economists lumped them into the service sector along with such uneventful activities as dry cleaning, auto repair, wholesale distribution, and telephone access. When a person buys a service, he purchases a set of intangible activities carried out on his behalf. But when he buys an experience, he pays to spend time enjoying a series of memorable events that a company stages—as in a theatrical play—to engage him in a personal way.

Experiences have always been at the heart of entertainment, from plays and concerts to movies and TV shows. Over the past few decades, however, the number of entertainment options has exploded to encompass many, many new experiences. We trace the beginnings of this experience expansion to one man and the company he founded: Walt Disney. After making his name by continually layering new levels of experiential effects onto cartoons (he innovated synchronized sound, color, three-dimensional backgrounds, stereophonic sound, audio-animatronics, and so forth), Disney capped his career in 1955 by opening Disneyland—a living, immersive cartoon world—in California. Before his death in 1966, Disney had also envisioned Walt Disney World, which opened in Florida in 1971. Rather than creating another amusement park, Disney created the world's first *theme* parks, which immerse guests (never "customers" or "clients") in rides that not only entertain but involve them in an unfolding story. For every guest, cast members (never "employees") stage a complete production of sights, sounds, tastes, aromas, and textures to create a unique experience.[1] Today, The Walt Disney Company carries on its founder's heritage by continually "imagineering"

Experiences are as distinct from services as services are from goods

new offerings to apply its experiential expertise, from the Disney Institute to Club Disney play centers, and from Broadway shows to the Disney Cruise Line, complete with its own Carribean island.

Where Disney used to be the only theme park proprietor, it now faces scores of competitors in every line of business, both traditional and experimental. New technologies encourage whole new genres of experience, such as interactive games, World Wide Web sites, "motion-based attractions," 3-D movies, and virtual reality. Desire for ever-greater processing power to render ever-more immersive experiences now drives demand for the goods and services of the computer industry. In a speech at the November 1996 Comdex computer show, Intel Chairman Andrew Grove declared, "We need to look at our business as more than simply the building and selling of personal computers [that is, goods]. Our business is the delivery of information [that is, services] and lifelike interactive experiences." Exactly.

Many traditional service industries, now competing for the same dollar with these new experiences, are becoming more experiential themselves. At theme restaurants such as the Hard Rock Cafe, Planet Hollywood, Dive! and the Bubba Gump Shrimp Co., the food functions as a prop for what's known in the industry as an "eatertainment" experience. And stores such as FAO Schwarz, Jordan's Furniture, and Niketown draw consumers through fun activities and promotional events (sometimes called "shoppertainment" or "entertailing").

But this doesn't mean that experiences rely exclusively on entertainment; entertainment is only one aspect of an experience. Rather, companies stage an experience whenever they *engage* customers, connecting with them in a personal, memorable way. Many dining experiences have less to do with the entertainment motif or celebrity of the financial backers than with the merging of dining with comedy, art, architecture, history, or nature, as happens at such restaurants as Pomp Duck and Circumstance,

Iridium, the Cypress Club, Medieval Times, and the Rainforest Cafe, respectively.[2] In each place, the food service provides a stage for layering on a larger feast of sensations that enchants consumers.

The "commodity mind-set," according to former British Airways chairman Sir Colin Marshall, means mistakenly thinking "that a business is merely performing a function—in our case, transporting people from point A to point B on time and at the lowest possible price." What British Airways does, he continued, "is to go beyond the function and compete on the basis of providing an experience."[3] The company uses its base service (the travel itself) as a stage for a distinctive en route experience, one that gives the traveler a respite from the inevitable stress and strain of a long trip.

Even the most mundane transactions can be turned into memorable experiences. Standard Parking of Chicago plays a signature song on each level of its parking garage at O'Hare Airport and decorates walls with icons of a local sports franchise—the Bulls on one floor, the White Sox on another, and so forth. As one Chicago resident told us, "You never forget where you parked!" Trips to the grocery store, so often a burden for families, become exciting events at places such as Bristol Farms Gourmet Specialty Foods Markets in Southern California. This upscale chain "operates its stores as if they were theatres," according to *Stores* magazine, featuring "music, live entertainment, exotic scenery, free refreshments, a video-equipped amphitheater, famous-name guest stars and full audience participation."[4] Russell Vernon, owner of West Point Market in Akron, Ohio—where fresh flowers decorate the aisles, restrooms feature original artwork, and classical music wafts down the aisles—describes his store as "a stage for the products we sell. Our ceiling heights, lighting and color create a theatrical shopping environment."[5]

Companies stage an experience when they engage customers in a memorable way

Consumers aren't the only ones to benefit from experiences. Businesses are made up of people, and business-to-business settings also present stages for experiences. A computer installation and repair firm in Minneapolis dubs itself the Geek Squad. Its "special agents" costume themselves in white shirts with thin black ties and pocket protectors, carry badges, and drive around in old cars, turning a normally humdrum service call into a memorable encounter. Similarly, many companies hire theatre troupes to turn otherwise ordinary meetings into improvisational events (an example is the Minneapolis-based Interactive Personalities, Inc., which stages rehearsed plays and "spontaneous scenes" with audience members and displays computer-generated characters that interact in real time).[6] And business-to-business marketers increasingly orchestrate elaborate venues for selling. In June 1996, Silicon Graphics, for example, opened its "VISIONAR-IUM Reality Center" at its corporate headquarters in Mountain View, California, to bring customers and engineers together in an environment where they could interact with real-time, three-dimensional product visualizations. Attendees view, hear, and touch as well as drive, walk, or fly through myriad product development simulations. As former chairman and CEO Edward R. McCracken related at the time, "This is experiential computing at its ultimate, where our customers can know what their products will look like, sound like, feel like before manufacturing."

VALUABLE DISTINCTIONS

The above examples—from consumer to business customer, theme restaurant to computer repair service—only hint at the newfound prominence of such experiences within the U.S. economy and, increasingly, that of other developed nations as well. They are heralds of the emerging Experience Economy.

Why now? Part of the answer lies with technology, which powers so many experiences, and part with increasing competitive intensity, which drives the ongoing search for differentiation. But the most encompassing answer resides in the nature of economic value and its natural progression—like that of the coffee bean—from commodities to goods to services and then to experiences. An additional reason for the rise of the Experience Economy is, of course, rising affluence. Economist Tibor Scitovsky notes that "man's main response to increasing affluence seems to be an increase in the frequency of festive meals; he adds to the number of special occasions and holidays considered worthy of them and, ultimately, he makes them routine—in the form, say, of Sunday dinners."[7] The same is true of experiences we pay for. We are going out to eat more frequently at increasingly experiential venues, and even drinking more "festive" types of coffee. As summarized in Table 1-1, each economic offering differs from the others in fundamental ways, including just what, exactly, it is. These distinctions demonstrate how each successive offering creates greater economic value. All too often some manager claims a company is "in a commodity business" when in fact the product sold is *not* a true commodity. The perception results in part from a self-fulfilling commoditization that occurs whenever an organization fails to fully recognize the distinctions between higher-value offerings and pure commodities. (And if an analyst or pundit says your company sells a commodity when you don't, you've been insulted, as well as challenged to shift up to a higher stage in economic value.) If you fear that your offerings are being commoditized, read

Table 1-1. Economic Distinctions

Economic Offering	Commodities	Goods	Services	Experiences
Economy	Agrarian	Industrial	Service	Experience
Economic function	Extract	Make	Deliver	Stage
Nature of offering	Fungible	Tangible	Intangible	Memorable
Key attribute	Natural	Standardized	Customized	Personal
Method of supply	Stored in bulk	Inventoried after production	Delivered on demand	Revealed over a duration
Seller	Trader	Manufacturer	Provider	Stager
Buyer	Market	User	Client	Guest
Factors of demand	Characteristics	Features	Benefits	Sensations

the simple descriptions given below. And if you think your offerings could never be commoditized—think again. A haughty spirit goes before a great fall (in prices).

Commodities

True commodities are materials extracted from the natural world: animal, mineral, vegetable. People raise them on the ground, dig for them under the ground, or grow them in the ground. After slaughtering, mining, or harvesting the commodity, companies generally process or refine it to yield certain characteristics and then store it in bulk before transporting to market. By definition, commodities are *fungible*—they are what they are. Because commodities cannot be differentiated, commodity traders sell them largely into nameless markets where some company purchases them for a price determined simply by supply and demand. (Companies do of course supply gradations in categories of commodities, such as different varieties of coffee beans or different grades of oil, but within each grade the commodity is purely fungible.) Every commodity trader commands the same price as everyone else selling the same stuff, but when demand greatly exceeds supply, handsome profits ensue. When supply outstrips demand, however, profits may be hard to come by. Over the short term, the cost of extracting the commodity bears no relationship to its price, and over the long term price is determined by the invisible hand of the market as it encourages companies to move in or out of commodity businesses.

Agricultural commodities formed the basis of the Agrarian Economy, which provided a subsistence level of existence for families and small communities for millennia. At the Agrarian Economy's zenith in eighteenth-century United States, more than 80 percent of the workforce was employed on farms. Today, less than 3 percent of the population work on farms.[8]

Commodities are fungible materials extracted from the natural world

What happened? The tremendous productivity improvements that became known as the Industrial Revolution drastically altered this way of life, beginning on the farm but quickly extending into the factory (such as the pin-making factory made famous by Adam Smith in his 1776 book *The Wealth of Nations*). Building on the success of companies in England from the 1750s onward, flourishing U.S. factories developed their own production innovations that in the 1850s collectively became known as the American System of Manufactures.[9] As manufacturers the world over copied and learned these techniques, automating millions of craft jobs in the process, the foundation for all advanced economies irrevocably shifted to goods.

Goods

Using commodities as their raw materials, companies make and then inventory goods—tangible items sold to largely anonymous customers who buy them off the shelf, from the lot, out of the catalog, and so on. Because manufacturing processes actually convert the raw materials in making a variety of goods, leeway exists to set prices based on the costs of production as well as product differentiation. Today significant differences exist in the features of different makes of automobiles, computers, soft drinks, and, to some degree, even lowly pins. And because they can be put to immediate use—to get places, write reports, quench thirsts, fasten things together—their users value them more highly than the commodities from whence they came.

Although people have turned commodities into useful goods throughout history,[10] the time-intensive means of extracting commodities and the high-cost methods of craft producing goods long prevented manufacturing from dominating the economy. This changed when companies learned to standardize goods for economies of scale. People came off the farm in droves to work in factories, and by the 1880s the United States had overtaken England as the world's leading manufacturer.[11] With the advent of Mass Production, brought about in the first assembly line at Henry Ford's Highland Park, Michigan, plant on April 1, 1913,[12] the United States solidified its position as the number one economic power in the world.

Goods are tangible products that companies standardize and then inventory

As continued process innovations gradually reduced the number of workers required to produce a given output, the need for manufacturing workers leveled off and eventually began to decline. Simultaneously, the vast wealth generated by the manufacturing sector, as well as the sheer number of physical goods accumulated, drove a greatly increased demand for services and, as a result, service workers. It was in the 1950s, when services first employed more than 50 percent of the U.S. population, that the Service Economy overtook the Industrial (although this was not recognized until long after the fact). Today, manufacturing jobs employ a mere 17 percent of the population.[13] What economists today categorize as services makes up the remaining 80 percent.

Services

Services are intangible activities customized to the individual request of known clients. Service providers use goods to perform operations on a particular client (such as haircuts or eye exams) or on his property or possessions (such as lawn care or computer repair). Clients generally value the benefits of services more highly than the goods required to provide them. Services accomplish specific tasks they want done but don't want to do themselves; goods merely supply the means.

Just as gray areas lie between commodities and goods (extensive processing or refining sometimes merges into making), the line between goods and services can be blurry. Even though restaurants deliver tangible food, for example, economists place them in the service sector because their offerings aren't standardized and inventoried but rather delivered on demand in response to an individual patron's order. While fast-food restaurants that make the food in advance share fewer of these attributes and so lie closer to the realm of goods than others, economists are not mistaken when they count those employed at McDonald's, for instance, in the service sector.

While employment in services now dominates the economy, output in the commodity and goods sectors has not abated. Today, fewer farmers harvest far more than their ancestors ever conceived possible, and the sheer quantity of goods rolling off assembly lines would shock even Adam Smith. Thanks to continued technological and operational innovations, extracting commodities from the ground and making goods in factories simply takes fewer and fewer people. Still, the percentage of gross domestic product (GDP) devoted to the service sector today dwarfs the other offerings. After fearing for so many years the hollowing of America's industrial base, most pundits now recognize it as a positive development that the United States, along with most advanced countries, has shifted full-bore to a Service Economy.

With this shift comes another little realized or discussed dynamic: In a Service Economy, *individuals desire service.* Whether consumers or businesses, they scrimp and save on goods (buying at Wal-Mart, squeezing suppliers) in order to purchase services (eating out, managing the cafeteria) they value more highly. That's precisely why so many manufacturers today find their goods commoditized. In a Service Economy, the lack of differentiation in customers' minds causes goods to face the constant price pressure indelibly associated with commodities. As a result, customers more and more purchase goods solely on price and availability.

To escape this commoditization trap, manufacturers often deliver services wrapped around their core goods. This provides fuller, more complete economic offerings that better meet customer desires.[14] So automakers increase the range and length of their warranties and offer to lease cars, consumer goods manufacturers manage inventory for grocery stores, and so forth. Initially, manufacturers almost always give away these services to enhance selling their goods. Many later realize that customers value the services so highly that the companies can charge separately for them. Eventually, astute manufacturers shift away from a goods mentality to become predominantly service providers. For example, who buys cellular telephones anymore? Except for those who absolutely must have the latest and greatest techno-goodies, most everyone just waits until one of the paging service providers offers it for a nominal fee as little as one cent as incentive to sign up for its service.

> **Services are intangible activities performed for a particular client**

Look at IBM. In its heyday in the 1960s and 1970s the hardware manufacturer's well-earned slogan was "IBM Means Service," as it lavished services—at no cost—on any company that would buy its hardware goods. It planned facilities, programmed code, integrated other companies' equipment, and repaired its own machines so prodigiously as to overwhelm nearly all competitors. But as time went on and the industry matured, customer demand for service surpassed the company's ability to give it away (not to mention the Justice Department suit that forced IBM to unbundle its hardware and software), and it began to charge explicitly for its services. Company executives later discovered that the services it once provided free were, in fact, its most valued offerings. Today, with its mainframe computers long since commoditized, IBM's Global Services unit grows at double-digit rates. The company no longer gives away its services to sell its goods. Indeed, the deal is reversed: IBM will *buy* its clients' hardware if they'll contract with Global Services to manage its information systems. IBM still manufactures computers, but it's now in the *business* of providing services. Similarly, General Electric's highest-profit contributor is GE Capital, and the Big Three automakers actually make more money from their financial arms than they do from manufacturing cars.

Giving away or buying goods to sell services is a harbinger that the Service Economy has reached a level once thought unimaginable and by many undesirable. Indeed, until just a few short years ago one could still hear the voices of academics and pundits decrying that services were taking over as the engine of economic growth, that no economic power could afford to lose its industrial base, and that an economy based so overwhelmingly on services would become ephemeral, destined to lose its prowess and its place among nations. That is now obviously untrue.

Even more so, the commoditization trap that forced manufacturers to add services to the mix now attacks services with the same vengeance. Telephone companies sell long-distance service solely on price, price, price. Airplanes resemble cattle cars, with a significant number of passengers flying on free awards. Fast-food restaurants all stress "value" pricing. (Indeed, McDonald's now finds itself so commoditized that the *Economist* created the Big Mac Index to compare the price levels in different countries based on the price of a local Big Mac.[15])

The Internet is the greatest force for commoditization known to man

And a price war looms in the financial services industry as first discount and then Internet-based brokers constantly drive down commissions, in some cases charging as little as $8 for what a full-service broker would charge more than $100. The chairman of AmeriTrade Holding Corp., J. Joe Ricketts, even told *Business Week* this: "I can see a time when, for a customer with a certain size margin account, we won't charge commissions. We might even pay a customer, on a per trade basis, to bring the account to us."[16] An absurdity? Only if one fails to recognize that any shift up to a new, higher-value offering entails giving away the old, lower-value offering.

Indeed, the Internet is the greatest force of commoditization ever known to man, for both goods and services. It eliminates much of the human element in traditional buying and selling. Its capability for friction-free trans-actions enables instant price comparisons across myriad sources. And its ability to quickly execute these transactions allows customers to benefit from time as well as cost savings. In today's world of time-starved con-sumers and speed-obsessed businesses, the Internet increasingly turns transactions for goods and services into a virtual commodity pit.[17] Web-based businesses busy commoditizing both consumer and business-to-busi-ness industries include the following:

- www.appliances.com (appliances)
- www.priceline.com (airline travel)
- www.narrowline.com (advertising space)
- www.necx.com (computer components)
- www.getsmart.com (financial services)
- www.insweb.com (insurance)
- www.compare.net (consumer goods)
- www.energymarket.com (natural gas and electricity)
- www.netmarket.com (virtually all goods and services households buy)

In addition to such commoditization, service providers face a second adverse trend unknown to goods manufacturers: *disintermediation.* Compa-nies such as Dell Computer, Streamline, USAA, and Southwest Airlines increasingly go around retailers, distributors, and agents to connect directly with their end-buyers. Decreased employment in these intermediaries, as well as bankruptcies and consolidations, invariably results. And a third trend further curtails service sector employment: that old boogeyman *automation,* which today hits many service jobs (telephone operators, bank clerks, and the like) with the same force and intensity that technological progress hit employment in the goods sector during the twentieth century. Today, even professional service providers increasingly discover that their offerings have been "productized"—embedded into software, such as tax preparation programs.[18]

All this points to an inevitable conclusion: The Service Economy is peaking. A new, emerging economy is coming to the fore, one based on a distinct kind of economic output. Goods and services are no longer enough.

Experiences

The newly identified offering of experiences occurs whenever a company intentionally uses services as the stage and goods as props to engage an individual. While commodities are fungible, goods tangible, and services intangible, experiences are *memorable*. Buyers of experiences—we'll follow Disney's lead and call them *guests*—value being engaged by what the company reveals over a duration of time. Just as people have cut back on goods to spend more money on services, now they also scrutinize the time and money they spend on services to make way for more memorable—and more highly valued—experiences.

The company—we'll call it an *experience stager*—no longer offers goods or services alone but the resulting experience, rich with sensations, created within the customer. All prior economic offerings remain at arms-length, outside the buyer, while experiences are inherently personal. They actually occur within any individual who has been engaged on an emotional, physical, intellectual, or even spiritual level. The result? No two people can have the same experience—period. Each experience derives from the interaction between the staged event and the individual's prior state of mind and being.

Even so, some may still argue that experiences are just a subclass of services, merely the latest twist required in today's fast-paced world to get people to buy certain services. Interestingly, the esteemed Adam Smith made the same argument about the relationship between goods and services more than two hundred years ago in *The Wealth of Nations*. He regarded services almost as a necessary evil—what he called "unproductive labour"—not as an economic offering in itself, precisely because services cannot be physically inventoried and therefore create no tangible testament that any work has been done. Smith did not limit his view of unproductive activity to such commoners as household servants. He included the "sovereign" and other "servants of the public," the "protection, security, and defence of the commonwealth," and a number of occupations ("churchmen, lawyers, physicians, men of letters of all kinds") whose work the market has today determined to be of far more value than that of most laborers. He then singled out the experience stagers of his day ("players, buffoons, musicians, opera-singers, opera-dancers, &c.") and concluded:

> **Experiences are events that engage individuals in a personal way**

> The labour of the meanest of these has a certain value, regulated by the very same principles which regulate that of every other sort of labour; and that of the noblest and most useful, produces nothing which could afterwards purchase or procure an equal quantity of labour. Like the declamation of the actor, the harangue of the orator, or the tune of the musician, the work of all of them perishes in the very instant of its production.[19]

However, while the *work* of the experience stager perishes upon its performance (precisely the right word), the *value* of the experience lingers in the memory of any individual who was engaged by the event.[20] Most parents don't take their kids to Walt Disney World just for the event itself but rather to make that shared experience part of everyday family conversations for months, and even years, afterward. While the experience itself lacks tangibility, people greatly value the offering because its value lies within them, where it remains long afterward.

While the work of the experience stager perishes, the value of the experience lingers

Those companies which capture this economic value will not only earn a place in the hearts of consumers, they will capture their dollars. Indeed, the notion of inflation as purely the result of companies passing on increased costs to consumers simply is not valid. The shift in consumer (and business) demand from commodities to goods to services and now to experiences should shift the prototypical "market basket" to these higher-valued offerings, but the federal government is behind the times; as of 1997 services made up only a little more than 57% of its Consumer Price Index (CPI)[21]—services weren't even included in the Producer Price Index until 1995. But if we examine the CPI statistics, as shown in Figure 1-2, we see that the CPI for commodities increases less than that for goods (using new cars as the prototypical Industrial Economy good), which increases less than the CPI for services, which in turn increases less than the CPI for the one prototypical experience that

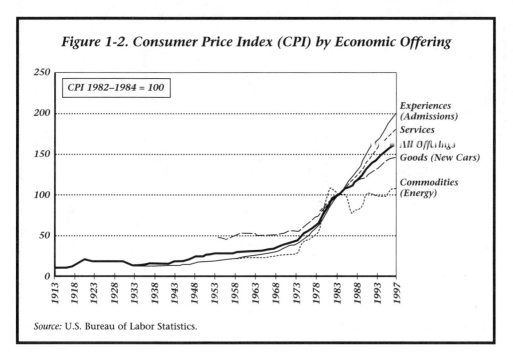

Figure 1-2. Consumer Price Index (CPI) by Economic Offering

CPI 1982–1984 = 100

Experiences (Admissions)
Services
All Offerings
Goods (New Cars)
Commodities (Energy)

Source: U.S. Bureau of Labor Statistics.

can be found in the government statistics: admissions to recreational events (movies, concerts, sports, etc.).[22] Note, too, the volatility of the CPI for energy commodities relative to the other offerings. Increased price volatility as market forces take over awaits the sellers of all *commoditized* goods and services.[23] Companies that stage experiences, on the other hand, increase the price of their offerings much faster than the rate of inflation simply because consumers value experiences more highly.

The employment and nominal gross domestic product statistics show the same effect as the CPI, as Figure 1-3 makes clear.[24] Using the period 1959 to 1996, where the data remains consistent across the offerings, we see the same relative position of each successive offering. While commodity output produced in the United States increased by a compound annual growth rate (CAGR) of more than 5 percent from 1959 to 1996, employment in

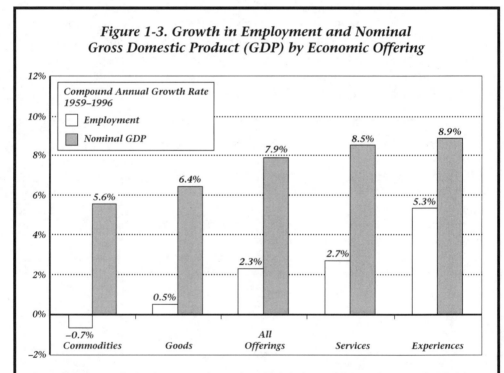

Figure 1-3. Growth in Employment and Nominal Gross Domestic Product (GDP) by Economic Offering

Source: U.S. Bureau of Labor Statistics, Labstat; *The Statistical History of the United States: Colonial Times to 1970,* United States Bureau of the Census; U.S. Census, Bureau of Economic Analysis, National Income and Product Accounts, unpublished detail; Strategic Horizons LLP and Diamond Technology Partners, analysis.

commodity industries actually *decreased.* Manufacturing output increased more than commodity output, while employment increased slightly (although the relative number of people employed in the manufacturing sector decreased greatly in this time period). Services dominated the statistics with a 2.7 percent CAGR in employment and more than 8 percent in GDP. But those industries which could be pulled out of the government's service sector statistics as clearly experiential grew even faster: almost twice the annual growth in employment with a slightly higher GDP growth rate.[25] Why such a disparity in employment growth between services and experiences? Previously because the Experience Economy is still in its infancy and has not yet undergone the automation now endemic to much of the service sector.

No wonder so many companies today wrap experiences around their existing goods and services to differentiate their offerings. Service providers clearly have an edge in this regard, as they are not wedded to tangible offerings. They can enhance the environment in which clients purchase and/or receive the service, layer on inviting sensations encountered while in that company-controlled environment, and otherwise figure out how to better engage clients to turn the service into a memorable event.

ING THE THING

So what's a manufacturer to do? Short of leapfrogging into the experience business itself—quite a stretch for most diehard manufacturers—manufacturers must focus on the experience customers have while *using* their goods.[26] Most product designers focus primarily on the internal mechanics of the good itself: how *it* performs. What if the attention centered instead on the individual's use of the good? The focus would then shift to the user: how the individual performs while *using* the good.

In the Experience Economy, people seek to perform a wide variety of activities. Fodor's Travel Publications, which issues vacation guides for scores of places around the world, recently published Peter Guttman's "escapist scrapbook," which describes twenty-eight adventures in which potential travelers can immerse themselves. Consider the diversity of activities—some old, some new, but all very intense experiences: houseboating, portaging, mountain biking, cattle driving, bobsledding, tall-ship sailing, tornado chasing, canyoneering, wagon training, seal viewing, iceberg tracking, puffin birding, race-car driving, hot-air ballooning, rock climbing, spelunking, white-water rafting, canoeing, heli-hiking, hut-to-hut hiking, whale kissing, llama trekking, barnstorming, land yachting, historic battle reenacting, iceboating, polar bearing, and dogsledding.[27]

Retailers like Bass Pro Shops Outdoor World, Recreational Equipment, Inc., (REI), and Cabela's sell goods as tools for use in these types of experiences, and lead the way in making their retail space an experience itself. Bass Pro Shops brings the outdoor environment indoors, REI erected a fifty-five-foot mountain that customers can climb to test out gear, and Cabela's displays a thirty-five-foot dioramic mountain filled with stuffed wild animals. Manufacturers must explicitly design their goods to enhance the user's experience as well—essentially *experientializing* the goods— even when customers pursue less adventurous activities. Automakers do this when they focus on enhancing the *driving experience.* But what could a valve manufacturer do to improve the *pumping experience,* a furniture producer the *sitting experience,* a publisher the *reading experience*? What changes could an appliance manufacturer make to its white goods that would enhance the *washing experience,* the *drying experience,* and the *cooking experience*?

Executives at one appliance maker already think this way. At Maytag, William Beer, president of the company's appliances unit, implores his people to create innovations that "wow" the customer. He told *Industry Week,* "The eating experience is now wherever a person is at the moment. We have people eating in the car on the way back and forth to work, in front of the TV." This leads Beer to deduce that "People may need a refrigerated compartment in an automobile or in the arm of a chair,"[28] innovations that would greatly enhance the eating experience but would never be considered within the framework of the industry's old mindset, which focuses on how appliances perform rather than on what users do when eating.

Manufacturers must experientialize their goods

Many goods encompass more than one experiential aspect, opening up areas for differentiation. Apparel manufacturers, for instance, could focus on the *wearing experience,* the *cleaning experience,* and perhaps even the *hanging* or *drawering experience.* (And, like the people at Fodor's, they should not be afraid to make up new nouns whenever needed.) Other industries might create the *briefcasing experience,* the *wastebasketing experience,* or the *mask-taping experience.* If you as a manufacturer start thinking in these terms—*ing*ing your things—you'll soon be surrounding your goods with services that add value to the activity of using them and then perhaps surrounding those services with experiences that make using them more memorable.

Any good can be *ing*ed. Consider a simple baseball. The Rawlings Sporting Goods Company of St. Louis, Missouri, exclusive baseball manufacturer to the Major Leagues, introduced a ball that makes *play-catching* more engaging. This "radar ball" has a microchip in it that digitally displays how fast the ball has been thrown after each toss. Retailing for more than $30, consumers pay much more for radar balls than regular baseballs, which generally go for less than five dollars each. Information about a ball's physical speed has long been available via radar guns, but those cost around $1,000 and few little league, high school, or American Legion teams own one. The radar ball makes it affordable to know a kid's throwing velocity. But the real value lies in the new social interaction generated between two people playing catch. Rawlings used simple information technology to make playing catch a richer experience. The thrower must rely on the catcher—the other person sharing the same experience—not some third party on the sidelines with a radar gun, to know his speed. Thanks to Rawlings, right now somewhere in a backyard, some child is asking, "Hey, Dad, how fast was that one?"

One can imagine more sophisticated balls in the future able to capture the spin and drop of breaking balls (curves, sliders, split-finger fastballs), the height from ground when released from the hand, the height from ground when caught, and so forth. (Someday some kid will ask, "How much did that one curve?") Such higher-tech enhancements would further enhance the play-catching experience. The more technologically sophisticated the readings and the higher the price, the more likely that you would not own a radar ball yourself but would go to an experiential place to use one (much like aspiring athletes and weekend wannabees don't own their own pitching machines and batting cages but go to places like Swings'n'Things to indulge in those experiences).

Information technology provides but one means to *ing* a thing, to experientialize the good. Manufacturers can also avail themselves of a number of other related possibilities for creating demand via *ing*ed things in the Experience Economy.

Embedding Goods in an Experiential Brand

Create a brand image emphasizing the experience customers can have surrounding the purchase, use, or ownership of a good.[29] Nike's ability to turn $20 sneakers into $100 cross-training tools is a prime example, as is Intel's "Intel Inside" marketing of its computing capability (complete with a melodious signature tone and multicolored multimedia characters). Coca-Cola and Pepsi-Cola continually try to outdo each other in advertising to convince consumers that the people who drink their soda have better drinking experiences. Meanwhile, every beer company in America tries to outdo them both. Automakers excel at experientializing their vehicles. After all, in this case the customer immerses himself in the good. Infiniti has even trademarked the phrase "Total Ownership Experience," while the new nostalgia-laden Beetle from Volkswagen appears to be a big hit—owners report heads turning on every street. But the company that is perhaps most successful in embedding its goods into a total experience is Harley-Davidson. How many other company logos do you find tattooed on users' bodies?

Producing Goods Experience Stagers Need

As the demand for experiences grows, so too will the demand for those goods which enable experiences. This includes goods affecting the senses (for example, textured materials, lights and lighting controls, audio equipment, flavor ingredients, and fragrances) as well as those "propping" the event, such as the audio-animatronic animals at the Rainforest Cafe, the baseball-glove booths at the All Star Cafe, and the skimpy costumes at Hooters. And don't forget perhaps the largest, most important category of goods that experience stagers require: memorabilia. After all, someone has to make all those hats, T-shirts, mugs, stuffed animals, key chains, toys, pens, and all assorted manner of knickknacks, novelties, and souvenirs guests scoop up to extend the memory of their experiences. You don't make any of these items? Good news! Many of the goods traditionally used for memorabilia are boringly overabundant. You have the opportunity to make your goods an appealing alternative to the pedestrian merchandise generally available.

Sensorializing Goods

Perhaps the most straightforward approach to making goods more experiential is to add elements that enhance the customer's *sensory interaction* with them. Some goods richly engage the senses by their very nature: toys, cotton candy, home videos, CDs, cigars, wine, and so forth. While the very use of these goods creates a sensory experience, companies can *sensorialize* any good by accentuating the sensations created from its use.[30] Doing so requires awareness of which senses most affect customers, focus on those senses and the sensations they experience, and the consequent redesign of the good to make it more appealing. Automakers, for example, now spend millions of dollars on every model to make sure that car doors sound *just so* when they close. Publishers greatly enhance the covers and interiors of books and magazines with a number of tactile innovations (embossed lettering; scratchy, bumpy, or ultrasmooth surfaces) and sight sensations (translucent covers, funky fonts, clever photographs, three-dimensional graphics). Even presentation markers aren't just colored anymore; Sanford scents them as well (licorice for black, cherry for red, etc.).

Making Goods Scarce

When a company limits the availability of a hot item, it can turn mere ownership of the good into an experience. Think Beanie Babies. The privately held Oakbrook, Illinois, company that makes them, Ty, Inc., takes a number of steps to ensure the scarcity of these stuffed animals. It limits the total production of each cuddly creature, "retires" certain favorites, and restricts the availability of any single character at any single store or outlet. By making its goods scarce, Ty heightens the experience of *having* one. Other goods can exploit the same approach. What if, when the next design in Nike's Air Jordan series comes out, the company numbered each pair as it came off the production line: #1, #2, #3, etc.? And why not let a secondary market develop to buy and sell those at higher prices, so Nike could variably price the items as they come off the line? (Used Air Jordans already fetch up to $400 in Japan.) Nike and other manufacturers could institute a whole new pricing model to maximize the value created from a single production run. (How much might Air Jordan pair #23 fetch?)

Forming a Goods Club

Exclusivity is the economic sibling of scarcity. By forming a club, companies can charge customers for the experience of *getting* their goods. This goods club should not, however, be modeled after many of the book or music clubs that have been around for decades. These businesses entice people with free or low-cost merchandise to sign up and then offer a featured selection that can be accepted or rejected until a minimum quantity of goods have been purchased. The club is just a mechanism for pushing goods customers may or may not want.

One company, Merchant Direct of Lake Bluff, Illinois, has adopted a new model to sell alcohol and other experiential goods with a much more subtle and sophisticated effect. The company's first and largest club, Beer Across America, ships two six-packs of microbrewed beer each month to members along with an issue of its newsletter, *Something's Brewin'*. Members also receive a quarterly lifestyle magazine called *DRINK*. Merchant Direct focuses solely on those goods which directly enable experiences. It also offers the Big Brew 22 club (for dark beer lovers), the International Wine Cellers and Prestige Wine Program clubs, the Cigar Affair club, the Coffee Quest club, and, the most experiential of all, the Spa Discoveries club. Monthly fees range from $16.95 to $39.95 in open-ended memberships.

The key to successfully launching such clubs is packaging and promoting the experience in such a way that makes the sale of the goods automatic as the buyer wants (and pays for) an expert to enhance his private experience. The next step? Connecting the people in a club, physically or virtually, to share reactions to selections or ideas on how to best experience the goods. Such discussions could be used to improve selections, perhaps even to customize them to individual members.

Staging a Goods Event

Many manufacturers stage their own experiences, although generally still as a sideline, when they add museums, amusement parks, or other attractions to their factory output. Hershey's Chocolate World, where else but in Hershey, Pennsylvania, is perhaps the most famous, but there are others, including Spamtown USA (Hormel Foods, Austin, Minnesota), Goodyear World of Rubber (Akron, Ohio), Crayola Factory Museum (Binney & Smith, Easton, Pennsylvania), and Cereal City USA (Kellogg, Battle Creek, Michigan).[31] Not every manufacturer can turn extra space into a ticket-taking museum, but any company can recast production as a miniaturized plant tour, thus turning the everyday acquisition and consumption of a candy bar, box of cereal, bottle of vitamins, or any other good into a memorable event. The goal is to draw the customer into the process of designing, producing, packaging, and/or delivering the item. Customers often value the way in which they obtain something as much as the good itself: Witness the great feeling with which new Saturn car owners leave the lot after every employee in the place gathers around to clap and celebrate their purchase. (To say nothing of how Volkswagen customers will feel when they pick up their cars at the company's Autostadt theme park, opening in the year 2000 next to the VW plant in Wolfsburg, Germany.) Bazaars, auctions, flea markets, and similar endeavors where prices aren't fixed have always created a distinctive experience around the purchase of goods, appealing to some while turning off others. Companies such as AUCNET, OnSale, Internet Shopping Network, and eBay have moved this time-honored format to the Internet. They may be commoditizing the goods, but at least their customers have a good time buying them!

THE PROGRESSION OF ECONOMIC VALUE

As the placard Rebecca Pine gave to her father for his birthday says, "The best things in life are not things." Consider that common event everyone experiences growing up: the birthday party. Most baby boomers can remember back to childhood birthday parties when Mom would bake a cake from scratch. Which meant what, exactly? That she actually *touched* such commodities as butter, sugar, eggs, flour, milk, and cocoa. And how much did these ingredients cost back then? A dime or two, maybe three.

Such commodities became less and less relevant to the needs of consumers when companies such as General Mills with its Betty Crocker brand and Procter & Gamble with Duncan Hines packaged most of the necessary ingredients into cake mixes and canned frostings. And how much did these goods cost as they increasingly flew off the supermarket shelf in the 1960s and 1970s? Not much, perhaps a dollar or two at most, but still quite a bit more than the cost of the basic commodities. The higher cost was recompense for the increased value of the goods in terms of flavor and texture consistency, ease of mixing, and overall time savings.

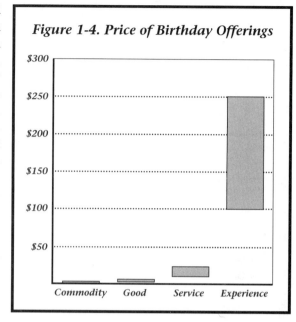

Figure 1-4. Price of Birthday Offerings

In the 1980s, many parents stopped baking cakes at all. Mom or Dad simply called the supermarket or local bakery and ordered a cake, specifying the exact type of cake and frosting, when it would be picked up, and the specific words and designs desired on top. At $10 to $20 this custom service cost ten times the goods needed to make the cake at home and still involved less than a dollar's worth of ingredients. Many parents thought this a great bargain, however, enabling them to focus their time and energy on planning and throwing the actual party.

What do families do at the dawn of the twenty-first century? They outsource the entire party to companies such as Chuck E. Cheese's, the Discovery Zone, Club Disney, and Creativities. These companies stage a birthday experience for family and friends for costs between $100 and $250, as depicted in Figure 1-4. For Elizabeth Pine's seventh birthday, the Pine family went to an old-time farm called New Pond Farm where she and fourteen of her friends experienced a taste of the old Agrarian Economy by brushing

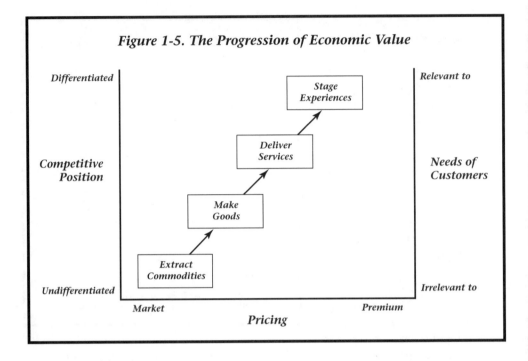

Figure 1-5. The Progression of Economic Value

cows, petting sheep, feeding chickens, making their own apple cider, and taking a hay ride over the hill and through the woods.[32] When the last guest had left after opening the presents, Elizabeth's mom, Julie, got out her checkbook. When Dad asked how much the party had cost, Julie replied, "A hundred and forty-six dollars—not including the cake"!

The simple saga of the birthday party illustrates the Progression of Economic Value depicted in Figure 1-5.[33] Each successive offering—pure ingredients (commodities), packaged mixes (goods), finished cakes (services), and thrown parties (experiences)—greatly increases in value because the buyer finds each more *relevant* to what he truly wants (in this case, the giving of a fun and effortless birthday party). And because companies stage so many different kinds of experiences, they more easily differentiate their offerings and thereby charge a premium price based on the distinctive value provided, not the market price of the competition. Those moms who baked from scratch paid out only a few dimes worth of ingredients. Likewise, the old-time farm accrues relatively little marginal cost (a few dollars for labor, a little feed, and an hour or two's worth of depreciation) to turn a nice profit.[34]

One company that well illustrates the concept of the Progression of Economic Value is Ogden Corporation. This multibillion dollar firm traces its origins to two companies.[35] The first, Allied, was founded in 1888 when two Danish immigrants began working for a railroad terminal, tending the facility's kerosene lamps (cleaning, refueling, and trimming the wicks). From this humble beginning delivering one of the key commodities of the nineteenth century, Allied moved into contract cleaning services (for homes, office buildings, churches, and playhouses), inventing and manufacturing a number of cleaning goods along the way. The second company, Ogden, began in 1939 as a public utilities holding company, producing one of the key commodities of the twentieth century. It later moved into waste-water treatment facilities (yet another key commodity). Like Allied, Ogden began operating contract services, specializing in supporting experience offerings such as facility cleaning, food service, ticket taking, and public address announcements at Yankee Stadium. (It even made a lasting contribution to movie experiences when it first sold popcorn in cinemas back in 1940.) These two companies merged in 1982 as a highly diversified service support organization.

In the 1990s, Ogden Corporation feared the increasing commoditization of its service businesses. Realizing that consumers themselves (not the companies that Ogden supplied) increasingly drove demand for new and varied experiences, Ogden decided to forge its own experience offerings. It started owning and operating sports, performing arts, and entertainment arenas and theaters, often through joint ventures. It even signed artists to management contracts, promoted concerts, and produced TV specials, Broadway shows, and musical recordings. The company also entered the business of managing location-based entertainment complexes, such as the Top of the World at the World Trade Center, where guests can experience an aerial sightseeing tour of New York City. In 1996 it purchased two nature-based theme parks, Silver Springs and Wild Waters in Ocala, Florida, and through a consortium began constructing a theme park in Seville, Spain.

To cap its full-fledged entrance into these experience businesses, in 1996 Ogden committed $100 million to create eight attractions called the American Wilderness Experience. There it immerses guests in nature scenes that feature the live animals, foliage, scents, and climates indigenous to various locales.[36] The company's first American Wilderness Experience opened in late 1997 in the Ontario Mills Mall in San Bernardino, California. The company charges an admission fee of $9.95 for adults to take in five "biomes" depicting different aspects of California's natural environment: Redwoods, Sierras, deserts, coasts, and valleys. These exhibits are inhabited by 160 wild animals, across 60 distinct species, including snakes, bobcats, scorpions, jellyfish, and porcupines. Guests begin their journey with a motion-based attraction, called the Wild Ride Theater, that lets them experience the world through the eyes of various animals—running like a mountain lion, buzzing like a bee—and then tour live animal exhibits and enjoy nature discussions with costumed Wilderness rangers. Of course, once guests pay to participate in the American Wilderness Experience, Ogden also makes money on the food service at its Wilderness Grill and the memorabilia at its Naturally Untamed retail store.

LET THE ACTION BEGIN

Managing such a far-flung enterprise as the American Wilderness Experience always proves difficult, particularly making the transition from business-to-business selling to consumer marketing, and time will tell how successful Ogden will be. A shopping mall remains unexplored territory for such an intensive and expensive experience, and getting the right mix of sensory cues from faux surroundings with live animals is not an easy task. (Although with the need to keep the smells of the grill away from the animals, and vice-versa, perhaps the American Wilderness Experience isn't quite so far afield from the company's waste management business after all.) But Ogden, like the many companies entering the Experience Economy, realizes that staging experiences forestalls the commoditization that is rapidly driving down the differentiation, relevancy, and price of so many goods and services.

Of course, no one repealed the laws of supply and demand. Companies that fail to provide consistently engaging experiences, overprice their experiences relative to the value received, or overbuild their capacity to stage them will of course see demand and/or pricing pressure. For example, one stalwart of the birthday party circuit, Discovery Zone, has had a few rough years because of inconsistently staged events, poorly maintained games, and little consideration of the experience received by the adults, who, after all, pay for the event.[37] More recently, same-store sales went down at the Rainforest Cafe and Planet Hollywood because they failed to refresh their experiences. Repeat guests see or do little different from what they saw and did on previous visits. Even Disney succumbed to this problem when it let Tomorrowland grow horribly out of date over the past couple of decades. But it did manage to refresh the Orlando complex in April 1998 by opening its fourth and largest theme park at Disney World, Animal Kingdom.

As the Experience Economy unfolds into the twenty-first century, more than a few experience stagers will find the going too tough to stay in business. It's hard to imagine, for example, how each and every one of the scores of theme-based restaurants in business today will survive into the new millennium. But such dislocations occur as the result of any economic shift. Once there were more than a hundred automakers in eastern Michigan and more than forty cereal manufacturers in western Michigan. Now there are only the Big Three in Detroit and the Kellogg Company in Battle Creek, all stalwarts of the Industrial Economy.

As the experience economy unfolds, many experience stagers won't stay in business

The growth of both the Industrial Economy and the Service Economy brought with it a proliferation of offerings that didn't exist before imaginative companies invented and developed them. That's also how the Experience Economy will grow, as companies tough out what economist Joseph Schumpeter termed the "gales of creative destruction" that comprise business innovation. Those businesses that relegate themselves to the diminishing world of goods and services will be rendered irrelevant. To avoid this fate, you must learn to stage a rich, compelling experience.

2 *Setting the Stage*

● ●

ON A HOT AUGUST NIGHT you find yourself in Evanston, Illinois, at the corner of Dempster and Elmwood. You spy a storefront named "LAN Arena" and, wondering what it might be, step inside. Some T-shirted gen-xer with "Commander Francisco" printed on his badge looks your way and mouths some words of greeting from atop his elevated platform. You nod in that general direction but decline his offer to explain the strange surroundings as you take a few more paces inside.

The walls are bare, the floor sparse. A faint odor of cement after a summer rain wafts its way into your nostrils. The tonal range looks decidedly grey. The sights and sounds soon draw your focus to the very heart of the place, in front of the Commander's platform, where you finally behold the domain he rules: Fourteen PCs with large monitors, standard keyboards, and assorted gadgetry, half of them tethered to obviously quick-moving and presumably quick-witted people. You now identify the background noise that has been omnipresent from the moment you opened the door: the clicking and clacking of fingers on keys combined with the smooth sliding of joysticks. A yelp goes up from one of the six souls whose eyes focus on the screens before them: "Go away you greasy-haired piece of monkey brains!" he yells, as you reflexively jump behind a pillar. Feeling foolish, you realize the taunt was aimed not at you but some unseen combatant sparring with the truly greasy-haired piece of animated humanity before you. Another person mutters: "Who's in there? Careful! You're not getting off that easy!" A third shouts mild obscenities, punctuated by the occasional repeatable word.

As you walk around, desiring a closer look at both the human beings and their cybernetic appendages, you see that every PC has a nameplate: Toby, Fergie, Grape Ape, and—somehow you knew this was coming—Larry, Moe, and Curly. The screamer bangs away at Eastwood, the mutterer at one named Buddha. You glance back at Commander Francisco and notice for the first time that behind him are a number of shelves filled with row upon row of software boxes. Here, more names greet you: Diablo, Red Alert, Warcraft II, Command & Conquer. Ah! That's it! They're all playing some computer-based game against each other. "It's called Quake," the Commander announces, having watched your exploration of the place and now sensing your need to know. "It's sort of an electronic version of capture the flag."

You finally understand the attraction of this place and soon gain vicarious enjoyment from watching the players play. Three on three, virtual opponents physically less than twenty feet away from each other battle in a virtual arena by means of a local area network, or LAN. You see the excitement in each player's face, the fluidity of human and machine working as one, and finally the joy that resounds in the one final cry of the victor as he vanquishes his last opponent. While disappointed in their loss, the also-rans all too happily begin anew. Hesitantly, anxiously, eagerly, you inform the Commander that you wish to join them. You sit down at a station and begin to experience the play for yourself.

THIS NARRATIVE, written in the second-person style endemic to certain kinds of computer games, more or less describes the real-life LAN Arena as we first experienced it. It's a new kind of place, one like many others dotting the urban landscape in the late 1990s, where for a fee people play computer-based games against like-minded competitors. Commander Francisco Ramirez, who, in addition to being our host, was also one of three co-owners, explained that he charges $5 to $6 per hour and that regulars can select annual membership plans ranging between $25 and $100 to receive discounted rates, reserve a spot in the LAN Arena Directory, and play in occasional tournaments as well. He also related that the company, which opened its storefront in October 1996 with equipment that was mostly leased, was already profitable by the end of 1997 and planned to open more locations.

Despite its profitability, we couldn't help but get the feeling that the LAN Arena resembled all the mom-and-pop video stores that mom-and-popped up across the country fifteen or twenty years ago. The self-owned and -run local video store is now largely a historical curiosity—an interim solution—thanks to the creative destruction of alternative formats and innovative distribution and merchandising programs created by bigger enterprises. Not to mention industry consolidations, culminating in the wide swath Blockbuster Video cut across the countryside to gain the lion's share of the nascent industry's revenues.

Similarly, the LAN Arena format, with players physically seated together at a common site, may be just an interim solution between the play-at-home games of the past and the play-in-cyberspace games of the future. Today, LAN Arena offers a ready-to-play gaming environment that's less costly and cumbersome than setup of the same at home. It provides faster play than that generally available on the Internet. Today, multiple players already participate in the same Quake game online. As bandwidth expands inexorably toward becoming plentiful and free, the competitive landscape for gaming experiences will literally know no boundaries.[1]

Surely a direct, online, from-home approach epitomizes the future of the gaming experience. Or does it? What about the social interaction, the game outside of the game, so important to our enjoyment of all of the old table-top contests, and obviously important to the vociferous competitors at LAN Arena? Won't this need enable businesses like it to maintain a gaming role? Certainly for a while, and perhaps forever, but real-time audio, video, and tactile technologies continue to advance toward the point where in a few years we'll be able to experience all interactions—yells and glares, teases and taunts, perhaps even pushes and shoves—*virtually* as well. Like the chat rooms and instant messages on America Online, no cybergame experience will be complete without its attendant virtual social experience.[2]

Still, will that be enough to wipe out site-based, interactive gaming establishments like the LAN Arena? Or will some future Blockbuster-like enterprise come along to consolidate this gaming industry, design a more inviting social interface to mask the raw technological network, and give it staying power? The answers are, of course, unclear. What is clear is that not every company that stages these new experiences will be successful in the short term, much less the long term. Only a few will survive. What we don't know are which ones. Those which thrive will do so because they treat their economic offering as a rich experience, not a glorified good or celebrated service, staged in a way that engages the individual and leaves behind a memory. That means not making the mistake we see time and time again: equating experiences with entertainment.

ENRICHING THE EXPERIENCE

Because so many exemplars of staged experiences come from what the popular press loosely calls the entertainment industry, it's easy to conclude that shifting up the Progression of Economic Value to stage experiences

Staging experiences is not about entertaining customers; it's about *engaging* them

simply means adding entertainment to existing offerings. That would be a gross understatement. Remember that staging experiences is not about entertaining customers, it's about *engaging* them.

An experience may engage guests on any number of dimensions. Consider two of the most important, as depicted in the axes of Figure 2-1. The first (on the horizontal axis) corresponds to the level of *guest participation.* At one end of the spectrum lies *passive* participation, where customers do not directly affect or influence the performance. Such participants include symphony goers, who experience the event as pure observers or listeners. At the other end of the spectrum lies *active* participation, in which customers personally affect the performance or event that yields the experience. These participants include skiers, who actively participate in creating their own experience. But even people who turn out to watch a ski race are not completely passive; simply by being there, they contribute to the visual and aural event that others experience.

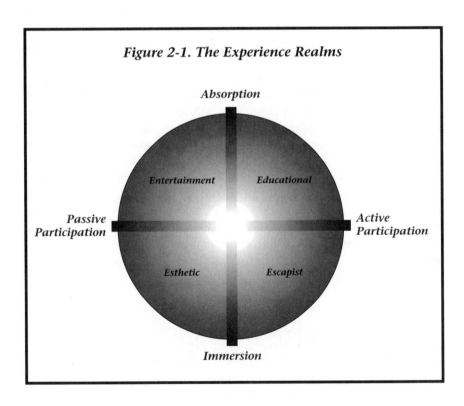

Figure 2-1. The Experience Realms

Absorption

Entertainment   *Educational*

Passive Participation   *Active Participation*

Esthetic   *Escapist*

Immersion

The second (vertical) dimension of experience describes the kind of *connection,* or *environmental relationship,* that unites customers with the event or performance. At one end of this spectrum lies *absorption*—occupying a person's attention by bringing the experience into the mind—at the other end *immersion*—becoming physically (or virtually) a part of the experience itself. In other words, if the experience "goes into" the guest, as when watching TV, then he is absorbing the experience. If, on the other hand, the guest "goes into" the experience, as when playing a virtual reality game, then he is immersed in the experience.

People viewing the Kentucky Derby from the grandstand absorb the event taking place before them from a distance. Meanwhile, people standing right up against the rails in the infield are immersed in the sights, sounds, and smells of the race itself as well as the activities of the other revelers around them. A student inside a lab during a physics experiment is immersed more than when he just listens to a lecture; seeing a film at the theatre with an audience, large screen, and stereophonic sound will immerse a person in the experience far more than if he were watching the same film at home on video.

The coupling of these dimensions defines the four "realms" of an experience—entertainment, education, escape, and estheticism, as shown in Figure 2-1—mutually compatible domains that often comingle to form uniquely personal encounters. The kind of experiences most people think of as *entertainment* occur when they *passively absorb* the experiences through their senses, as generally occurs when viewing a performance, listening to music, or reading for pleasure. But while many experiences entertain, they are not all, strictly speaking, *entertainment,* defined by the *Oxford English Dictionary* as "the action of occupying a person's attention agreeably; amusement."[3] Entertainment provides not only one of the oldest forms of experience (surely jokes have been around at least since the beginning of humankind) but also one of the most developed and, today, the most commonplace and familiar. (The "unproductive labourers" Adam Smith singled out were all entertainers: "players, buffoons, musicians, opera-singers, opera-dancers, &c.") As the Experience Economy gears up, people will look in new and different directions for more unusual experiences. At the same time, few of these experiences will exclude at least some momentary entertainment by making people

Entertainment is passively absorbed through the senses

smile, laugh, or otherwise enjoy themselves. But there will also be an opportunity for those enterprises staging these experiences to add to the mix components of the other three realms of experience: the educational, the escapist, and the esthetic.

The Educational

As with entertainment experiences, with education experiences the guest (or student, if you prefer) absorbs the events unfolding before him. Unlike entertainment, however, education involves the active participation of the individual. To truly inform a person and increase his knowledge and/or skills, educational events must actively engage the mind (for intellectual education) and/or the body (for physical training). As Stan Davis and Jim Botkin recognize in *The Monster Under the Bed:*

> The industrial approach to education . . . [made] teachers the actors and students the passive recipients. In contrast, the emerging new model [of business-led education] takes the market perspective by making students the active players. The active focus will shift from the provider to the user, from educat-*ors* (teachers) to learn-*ors* (students), and *the educating act will reside increasingly in the active learner, rather than the teacher-manager.* In the new learning marketplace, customers, employees, and students are all active learners or, even more accurately, interactive learners.[4]

Judith Rodin, the seventh president of the University of Pennsylvania, also recognizes the active nature of education, as well as the fact that learning occurs not just in the classroom. In her 1994 inaugural address she proclaimed, "We will design a new Penn undergraduate experience. It will involve not only curriculum, but new types of housing, student services, and mentoring, to create a seamless experience between the classroom and the residence, from the playing field to the laboratory. I am committed to having this in place for students entering Penn in the fall of 1997. That class—the Class of 2001—will be our first class to have an entirely new experience—the Penn Education of the Twenty-First Century."[5]

While education is serious business, that doesn't mean that educational experiences can't be fun. The term *edutainment* was coined to connote an experience straddling the realms of education and entertainment.[6] Bamboola, a 28,000-square-foot facility in San Jose, California, stages an education experience for children ten years of age or younger by giving them the wherewithal to engage in "developmentally appropriate" spontaneous play. For an $8.95 admission fee ($3.95 for toddlers and only $1.95 for accompanying adults), kids dig for fossils, artifacts, and even a full-scale dinosaur skeleton in the outdoor jungle garden and sand pit. They prepare their own food in an interactive kitchen and dress up in playclothes in Grandmother's Attic. They can also climb rocks and boulders and play dozens of skill-based games.[7] Randy White, head of the firm that designed Bam-

With education experiences a guest absorbs the events unfolding before him while actively participating

boola, White Hutchinson Leisure & Learning Group in Kansas City, Missouri, told us that "while Bamboola is a lot of fun, it's really about helping kids learn in a way that exercises their creative muscles. Each play area provides multiple learning experiences, including math concepts at the playhouse, mapping skills from the maze, and even principles of physics with the water table."

The Escapist

Memorable encounters of the third kind, *escapist experiences,* involve much greater immersion than entertainment or education experiences. In fact, they are the polar opposite of pure entertainment experiences. The guest of the escapist experience is completely immersed in it, an actively involved participant.[8] Examples of environments that are essentially escapist include theme parks, casinos, virtual reality headsets, chat rooms, or even a game of paintball played in the local woods. Rather than playing the passive role of couch potato, watching others act, the individual becomes an actor, able to affect the actual performance.

> **The guest of an escapist experience actively participates in an immersive environment**

Enhancing the inherent entertainment value of a movie, for example, might be accomplished not only with larger screens, bigger sound, cushier chairs, VIP rooms and so forth, but also by having customers actually *participate* in the thrill of movement. Myriad companies now bring such experiences to a neighborhood near you via motion-based attractions. One such attraction is part of the American Wilderness Experience in California, where a film that presents the world from an animal's point of view is supplemented by the sensation of flowing forward and backward, pitching and yawing, shuddering, lurching, and sometimes even rotating 360 degrees.[9]

Early stars of this genre include Tour of the Universe, a group flight through outer space from SimEx of Toronto; Magic Edge, a simulation of a military dogfight for multiple players in Mountain View, California, and Tokyo; and Disney's Star Tours, a simulation of a heroic battle for galactic domination based loosely on the Star Wars movies.

Most such escapist experiences are essentially motion simulator rides based on popular adventure or science fiction movies. Additional examples include "Back to the Future: The Ride" and "Terminator 2: Battle Across Time" hosted at Universal Studios in Orlando, "Aladdin's Magic Carpet" at Walt Disney World, and "Robocop" and "Days of Thunder" of Iwerks Entertainment of Burbank.[10] These rides perfectly express the shift from Service to Experience Economy. It used to be, "You've read the book, now go see the movie!" Today, it's "Now that you've seen the movie, go experience the ride!"[11]

Despite the appellation, guests participating in escapist experiences do not just embark *from* but also voyage *to* some specific place and activity worthy of their time. For example, some vacationers, no longer content to bask in the sun go rollerblading, snowboarding, skysurfing, white-water kayaking, mountain climbing, sports-car racing or take part in other extreme sports.[12] Others try their hand at the time-honored art of gambling—to the tune of more than $500 billion a year in the United States alone—not just to forget all their troubles and forget all their woes but because they really enjoy the visceral experience of risking their money in opulent surroundings for a chance at greater fortune. Others want to escape their already-made fortune to see what it's like conversing with the common man. Dallas Cowboys quarterback Troy Aikman, for instance, told *Sports Illustrated* why he frequently visits America Online: "I like to go to the Texas Room and chat with people. It puts us on the same level. It's nice, too, having a normal conversation with somebody without them knowing who I am."[13] While a celebrity may value an experience that turns him into an ordinary Joe, many escapist experiences, such as computer-based sports games, let the average person feel what it's like to be a superstar.

> **Escapist experiences are not just about embarking *from* but voyaging *to***

Cyberspace is a great place for such experiences, but many businesses still don't get it. They're heading into the commoditization trap, trying to figure out how to better sell their company's goods and services over the World Wide Web, when in fact most individuals surf the Net for the experience itself. Surprisingly, Pete Higgins, vice president of Microsoft's Interactive Media Group, told *Business Week,* "So far, the Internet isn't a place for truly mindless entertainment."[14] But who wants it to be? The Internet is an inherently *active* medium—not passive, like television—that provides a *social* experience for many. Interactive entertainment is an oxymoron. The value people find online derives from actively connecting, conversing, and forming communities.

Once the domain of mom-and-pop outfits like The Well, it took Prodigy, CompuServe, and America Online (mistakenly dubbed online "service" providers), to bring cyberspace to the masses. AOL won the battle for members primarily because it understood that they wanted a social experience, where they could actively participate in the online environment growing up around them. While Prodigy at one point limited the amount of e-mail its members could send and CompuServe limited member identities to a string of impersonal numbers, AOL allowed its members to pick up to five screen names (to suit the several moods or roles they might want to portray online[15]) and actively encouraged the use of features that connect people: e-mail, chat rooms, instant messages, personal profiles, and "buddy lists," which let users know when their friends are also online. Even before AOL went to a flat-rate pricing scheme in late 1996, more than 25 percent of its 40 million connect-hours each month were spent in chat rooms, where members interacted with each other.[16]

For many, cyberspace provides a welcome respite from real life, an escape from the humdrum routine and the harried rush. But it is unclear whether the near ubiquity of the Internet obviates the need most people have for a physical place set apart from home and work, a "third place," in the words of sociologist Ray Oldenburg, where a person can interact with others he has come to know as members of the same community.[17] These places—pubs, taverns, cafes, coffee houses, and the like—once seemed to be on every street corner of every city, but the suburbanization of society has all too often left people too far apart to commune in this way. Some people now look for community in cyberspace while others use vacations at themed attractions to connect with large masses of people.[18] Still others find a middle ground at Starbucks or other espresso, water, or cigar bars. Or even at a Barnes & Noble, where the innovation of bringing books and coffee together creates a place worth escaping to, for hanging out, browsing, sipping, and talking.

The Esthetic

The fourth and last experiential realm we'll explore is the esthetic. In such experiences, individuals immerse themselves in an event or environment but themselves have little or no effect on it, leaving the environment (but not themselves) essentially untouched. Esthetic experiences include standing on the rim of the Grand Canyon, visiting an art gallery or museum, and sitting at the Café Florian in Old World Venice. Sitting in the grandstand at the Kentucky Derby would also qualify. While guests partaking of an educational experience may want to *learn,* of an escapist experience to *do,* of an entertainment experience want to—well, *sense* might be the best term—those partaking of an esthetic experience just want to *be* there.[19]

At the Rainforest Cafe, for example, diners find themselves in the midst of dense vegetation, rising mist, cascading waterfalls, and even startling lightning and thunder. They encounter live tropical birds and fish as well as artificial butterflies, spiders, gorillas, and, if you look closely, a

In esthetic experiences, individuals immerse themselves but remain passive

snapping baby crocodile.[20] Note that the Rainforest Cafe, which combines the dining room with a retail shop and bills itself as "A Wild Place to Shop and Eat," is not out to *simulate* the actual experience of being in a rain forest. Rather it aims to stage an authentic—and esthetic—experience of the Rainforest Cafe.

Another wild place to shop can be found in Owatonna, Minnesota, at Cabela's, a 150,000-square-foot outfitter of hunting, fishing, and other outdoor gear. Rather than add elements of entertainment to the store, Dick and Jim Cabela turned it into an esthetic experience, centered (literally) around a thirty-five-foot-high mountain with a waterfall and featuring more than a hundred stuffed taxidermic animals, many of them shot by the two brothers or other family members. This part of the store represents four different North American ecosystems. Elsewhere, two huge dioramas depict African scenes that include the so-called Big Five big-game targets: the elephant, lion, leopard, rhinoceros, and cape buffalo. Three aquariums hold a number of varieties of prized fish, while almost seven hundred different kinds of animals in total are mounted in and around every department of the store. Truly, as Dick Cabela told the *St. Paul Pioneer Press,* "We're selling an experience."[21] So much so that more than 35,000 people visited the refurbished store on the day it opened, and the company expects more than one million visitors every year.

The esthetics of an experience may be completely natural, as when touring a national park, primarily man-made, as when dining at the Rainforest Cafe, or somewhere in between, as when shopping at Cabela's. There's no such thing as an artificial experience. Every experience created within the individual is real, whether the stimuli be natural or simulated. Extending this view, renowned architect Michael Benedikt discusses the role he believes architects play in connecting people to a "realness" within their created environments:

> Such experiences, such privileged moments, can be profoundly moving; and precisely from such moments, I believe, we build our best and necessary sense of an independent yet meaningful reality. I should like to call them *direct esthetic experiences of the real* and to suggest the following: in our media-saturated times it falls to architecture to have the direct esthetic experience of the real at the center of its concerns.[22]

While architects may lead, it really falls to everyone involved in the staging of esthetic experiences to connect individuals and the (immersive) reality they directly (albeit passively) experience, even when the environment seems less than "real." Benedikt would likely call the Rainforest Cafe and similar venues "non-real," and insist that its architects address "the issue of authenticity by framing [displaying the inauthentic as inauthentic], by making fakery honest, as it were."[23] To stage compelling esthetic experiences, designers must acknowledge that any environment designed to create an experience is *not* real (the Rainforest Cafe, for instance, is *not* the rain forest). They should not try to fool their guests into believing it's something it is not.

Architecture critic Ada Louise Huxtable makes a similar distinction when she says "it is becoming increasingly difficult to tell the real fake from the fake fake. All fakes are clearly not equal; there are good fakes and bad fakes. The standard is no longer real versus phony, but the relative merits of the imitation. What makes the good ones better is their improvement on reality."[24] To illustrate the difference, we'll consider two invented environments Huxtable spends considerable time critiquing: Universal City Walk and just about anyplace Disney.

City Walk in Los Angeles is a collection of retail shops, restaurants, movie theatres, high-tech rides, and low-tech kiosks, each with a distinctive facade. Controlled exaggeration abounds, as in the four-story guitar adorning the Hard Rock Cafe. Visitors lazily stroll through a water fountain that shoots up at well-timed intervals. Guests pay an entrance fee for parking (nobody walks to anything in L.A., but here they pay admission to walk around) that's reimbursed only if they spend money at a dining or movie experience (purchases of goods merit no reimbursement). Part theme park and part public square, City Walk primarily imparts an esthetic experience, Huxtable confirms, as it "is being used for its own sake."[25] The realness of its fakery evidences itself from the very moment you park your car in the ungarnished lot. The back of the buildings greet arriving guests, who thus see the unadorned undersides of the facades as they walk in. Outside you see the inside of the mask; inside you see its outside. Adjacent buildings, unassociated with City Walk, remain visible through alleys and other off-shoots to the main drag. Its esthetic acknowledges its fakeness. Through framing, it's truly a *real* fake.

There's no such thing as an artificial experience

The esthetic of most Disney experiences, on the other hand, seeks to hide all things fake: No one gets to see behind the curtain. Parking lots smoothly flow into shuttle buses, welcoming booths, and turnstiles. Facades seamlessly integrate into one another, lest some guest detect the trickery in the dimensional downsizing. Mickey Mouse never takes off his mask, lest we see the pimply faced kid inside. It's the fake fake that Huxtable and other critics decry, not being true to what they deem it really is.

Or is it *real* fake fake? Other critics laud Disney for creating wholly immersive environments, consistent and engaging within themselves. One writes "that from whatever angle, *nothing looks fake.* Fabricated, yes— fake, no. Disneyland isn't the mimicry of a thing; it's a thing. . . . I'm convinced the genius of Disneyland isn't its fancifulness, but its literalism."[26] On the subject of Disney theme parks many people (including coauthors) disagree. But one thing remains clear: an esthetic experience must be true to itself and come off as real to its guests.

EXPERIENCING THE RICHNESS

Companies can enhance the realness of any experience by blurring the boundaries between realms. While many experiences engage primarily through one of the four realms outlined above, most in fact cross boundaries. British Airways, for example, stages a primarily esthetic experience: personnel pamper guests in an environment where they don't have to do anything for themselves. According to Sir Colin Marshall's successor as CEO, Robert Ayling, the company is now working on enhancing in-flight entertainment systems and integrating them with the overall flying esthetic. He believes that eventually more people will see movies in the air than in cinemas. "Long-haul airlines," he says, "will increasingly be seen not only as transport systems but as entertainment systems."[27]

American Express often mixes esthetic and educational elements in the Unique Experiences (AmEx's capitalization) it offers those enrolled in its Membership Rewards program.[28] In one such offer, "Images of the Rain Forest—Photo Safari in Costa Rica," the company invited cardmembers to join "celebrated nature photographers Jay Ireland and Georgienne Bradly for an unforgettable five-day photography workshop in Costa Rica's flourishing rain forest" and tempted them with the following description:

> Surrounded by wildlife, you'll learn techniques and professional secrets that will enable you to capture astounding images. From cuddly Three-toed Sloths to majestic Great Egrets and comical Red-eyed Tree Frogs, you'll have countless opportunities to shoot professional quality images of exotic animals. You'll also enjoy enchanting views of the canals from the balcony surrounding your hotel, and be served first-class meals in the comfortable jungle setting. No matter what your photographic experience, this adventure promises to be unforgettable.

To make retailing more unforgettable, most store executives and shopping mall developers talk about making the shopping experience more entertaining, but leading-edge companies also incorporate elements from the other experiential realms. For example, to engage the locals and tourists at the six-block retail and entertainment district Bugis Junction in Singapore, design firm CommArts of Boulder, Colorado, mined the historical trading culture of Singapore to create what cochairman Henry Beer calls "an esthetically pleasing built environment designed to connect the project deeply to the resident culture of Singapore." Seaside architecture, sails, chronometers, and kindred elements fulfill the dominant motif, while bright signage informs and educates guests on the history of the native seafaring merchants known as the Bugis people. Similarly, for the Ontario Mills retail project, CommArts laid out streets and neighborhoods that provide a distinctive esthetic experience drawn from the rich heritage of Southern California. It's not traditionally anchored by large department stores selling goods but by businesses staging large experiences—a thirty-screen AMC movie house, Dave & Buster's arcade/restaurant, and a 3-D UltraScreen theatre. One of its wings houses Steven Spielberg's Gameworks across from the escapist adventures of the American Wilderness Experience. As Beer related to us, "Competition for the retail dollar demands that we create a rich retail theatre that turns products into experiences."

> **The richest experiences encompass aspects of all four realms**

The richest experiences encompass aspects of all four realms. These center around the "sweet spot" in the middle of the framework.[29] America Online's success results not from any one element but from the collective experience it allows each member to enjoy as he sifts through the available options—and crosses the boundaries of the realms of experience. As Steve Case, president and CEO, said in a response to a question about which online areas would generate AOL's future growth, "We don't break it out into separate areas or applications. We see online as a whole packaged experience that we want to bring to consumers. This package increasingly includes some new areas, and more of what we already have—multiplayer games, shopping, and financial services. But what's really going to drive this is the overall experience."[30]

To design a rich, compelling, and engaging experience, you don't want to select and then stay in just one realm. Instead you want to use the experiential framework (depicted in Figure 2-1) as a set of prompts that help you to creatively explore the aspects of each realm that might enhance the particular experience you wish to stage. When designing your experience, you should consider the following questions:

- What can be done to improve the *esthetics* of the experience? The esthetics are what make your guests want to come in, sit down, and hang out. Think about what you can do to make the environment more inviting, interesting, or comfortable. You want to create an atmosphere in which your guests feel free "to be."

- Once there, what should your guests do? The *escapist* aspect of an experience draws your guests further, immersing them in activities. Focus on what you should encourage guests "to do" if they are to become active participants in the experience.

- The *educational* aspect of an experience, like the escapist, is essentially active. Learning, as it is now largely understood, requires the full participation of the learner. What do you want your guests "to learn" from the experience? What information or activities will help to engage them in the exploration of knowledge and skills?

- *Entertainment,* like esthetics, is a passive aspect of an experience. When your guests are entertained, they're not really doing anything but responding to (enjoying, laughing at, etc.) the experience. Professional speakers lace their speeches with jokes to hold the attention of their audience, to get them to listen to the ideas. What can you do by way of entertainment to get your guests "to stay"? How can you make the experience more fun and more enjoyable?

Addressing these design issues sets the stage for service providers to begin competing on the basis of an experience. Those which have already forayed into the world of experiences will gain from further enriching their offerings in light of these four realms.

For instance, while the American Wilderness Experience provides a great stage for three of the realms, its educational aspects could be strengthened to further enrich the experience. Watching playful sea otters behind glass truly entertains, the Wild Ride Theatre enables guests to experience what it would be like to see through the eyes of a frog, owl, or dolphin— pure escapism—and guests can immerse themselves in five California ecosystems, one right after the other, all esthetically pleasing. But there's a noticeable lack of educational instruction integrated into the mix. Signs provide short descriptions of each species of animal on display, but this quickly begets museum-like monotony. Guests encounter no specially designed places set aside for curators to bring animals out into the open so children can examine and discuss them. On occasion, particularly for school field trips, a curator will bring an animal or two out from behind the glass, but even then the guests' experience is not distinctly educational. All

Set the stage by exploring the possibilities of each realm

of this is surprising, given that the current integration of the entertainment, escapist, and esthetic realms actually create a desire to learn more about various species—a prime reason many families go to the American Wilderness Experience. Strengthening the educational element would make this already praiseworthy experience even better.

Such oversights can be prevented at the outset by systematically exploring the possibilities intrinsic to each of the four realms.

A rich mix of all four realms marks Club Disney, a new playsite experience for children age ten and under. Disney opened the first site in February 1997 in Thousand Oaks, California, as a free-standing building adjacent to an ordinary strip mall. At Club Disney, guests pay to play. Both adults and children pay $8 to roam any of nine play-area modules: Enchanted Forest, Pooh 'N' You, Mouse Pad, Jungle Climber, Mickey's Circus, Applaudville Theater, Character Creations, Maddening Maze, and Now Playing. (The mix of play areas at other locations varies to offer slightly different experiences within the same Club Disney template.) The company designed each play area to fulfill the pledge posted near the entrance: "Our mission is to create a place in the community where children and their grown-ups have fun and bond with one another through enriching activities and imaginative play."

And it succeeds, in no small part because all four realms sweetly abound. Club Disney is still Disney, so entertainment naturally blends into the experience, with Disney's feature animated films shown periodically on projection screen TVs. But special kiosks also allow children and adults to inquire about the history of these Disney classics, combining the experiential realms of education and entertainment. One way that education is available more directly is through the arts and crafts classes offered each month. At announced times in the Applaudville Theatre, children don costumes and become characters in various Disney narratives. This gives the children a simple escapist experience while simultaneously entertaining the grown-ups in the audience.

Throughout the playsite, children across multiple age groups comfortably share the same space. Child and adult play together as well as separately; different events allow, even demand, various levels of adult-child interaction. Yet every element seems to touch on all four of the realms that constitute an engaging experience: Disney characters entertain, classes educate, play areas provide escape, and the textures, sights, and sounds of the place yield an unmistakable esthetic. As a result, Club Disney is packed with children and their grown-ups, at play together.

Consider how Club Disney stages individual birthday party experiences. Party Wonderland offers multiple birthday-party rooms, each with a specific theme, such as Pooh-rific Party, 101 Dalmatians Bow-wow Bash, Toy Story Search Party, Disney's Princess Tea, and Hercules Hero Hurrah. Within each party experience, the cast members leverage the four realms to engage participants. Groups sit on a pre-show bench, waiting for the party to begin with a growing sense of anticipation *(esthetic)*. Once in the party room, "celebration specialists" facilitate *educational* games using *entertaining* flannel-board characters, which of course correspond to the theme of the party. Then everybody eats pizza and afterward retreats to another room *(escapist)* to see Merlin, who draws the kids into simple magic acts and revisits the party room characters through his crystal ball. There's one activity notably absent from the event: the opening of presents by the birthday child. Why? The act of one child opening gifts before his playmates simply lacks experiential richness across the four realms (ask any five-year-old if he enjoys watching friends open gifts), and so Club Disney instead places all the presents in a take-home bag for opening back at the birthday family's house.

The price of the Club Disney birthday experience? Parties *start* at $250 for twelve children and twelve adults and include one hour of play followed by the one-hour party, plus one piece of pizza and a drink for everyone and one party favor per child, not to mention the cake. The richness of the experience translates down to the very words that cast members say to departing guests. Instead of saying "Have a nice day," which characterizes most unmemorable service interactions, they use an expression befitting a memorable event: "Did you have fun today?"

When all four realms abide within a single setting, then and only then does *plain space* become *a distinctive place* for staging an experience. Occurring over a period of time, staged experiences require a sense of place to entice guests to *spend more time* engaged in the offering. Today, time-conscious consumers and businesspeople want to spend less and less time with providers of goods and services, who seem all too willing to oblige. Think of fast-food chains and corporate call centers striving to minimize the *seconds* per service transaction. The obvious destination: not spending *any* time with customers, who learn to spend their time elsewhere.

But where? To places deserving of more time, where you can simply be and do and learn and want to stay. To understand the nature of such places, consider what turns a house into a home, and turns any space into place. In his *Home: A Short History of an Idea,* Witold Rybczynski, professor of architecture at McGill University in Montreal, examines five centuries of designed environments, from the Middle Ages to Ralph Lauren Home Furnishings. Among the multiple cultures that Rybczynski examines, he calls particular attention to the desire and ability of the Dutch during their "Golden Age" to successfully "define the home as a separate, special place."[31] For the Dutch, "'Home' meant the house, but also everything that was in it and around it, as well as the people, and the sense of satisfaction and contentment that all these conveyed. You could walk out of the house, but you always returned home."[32] To create such homes, furnishings in a

Dutch house strictly revolved around the use of each room, thereby defining the sense of place. Outside the home, gardens and other landscaping—however modest, given Holland's relatively small size—skillfully signalled the passage from the plain space outdoors to the distinctive place indoors. Such welcoming formed the basis for communing with family and friends.

Plain space **must become a** *distinctive place* **for staging an experience**

The sweet spot for any compelling experience—incorporating entertainment, educational, escapist, and esthetic elements into otherwise generic space—is similarly a mnemonic place, a tool aiding in the creation of memories, distinct from the normally uneventful world of goods and services. Its very design invites you to enter, and to return again and again. Its space is layered with amenities—props—that correspond with how the space is used and rid of any features that do not follow this function. Enter Club Disney. There, everything revolves around play. Anything detracting from that experience, such as the opening of birthday presents, is excluded. As a result, Disney has added yet another experience offering to its portfolio of businesses. Disney has no monopoly in the emerging Experience Economy, however; many other companies will certainly appear on stage. They may not out-Disney Disney, but they will offer experiences unknown to previous economic eras.

3 The Show Must Go On

● ●

FOR HIS OLDER BROTHER NICKY'S BIRTHDAY, Conrad
purchased a rather unusual gift. Feeling Nicky had become too stuffy and
set in his executive ways, Conrad contracted with Consumer Recreation
Services (CRS) to stage a rather elaborate experience. No present needed
unwrapping as Conrad simply handed his brother a CRS-furnished card,
inviting Nicholas Van Orton to participate in "The Game." Once he
accepted the offer, Nicky found himself involved in a world all its own,
with intriguing characters drawing him to seemingly life-threatening situations, curiously assimilated into his day-to-day routines. Every time he
thought he had it figured out, a new twist emerged until the events finally
spiralled into a fast-paced climax. To pull off "The Game," CRS had to put
on a well-orchestrated show. No company, not even Disney, has mastered
such intricate experience orchestration—staging rich, compelling, integrated, engaging, and memorable events—as well as CRS, the fictional
business depicted in the 1997 movie thriller *The Game,* starring Michael
Douglas as Nicholas and Sean Penn as Conrad. But the day approaches
when this type of staging will form the bulk of real commercial activity.

Far-fetched? To quote a line from the Broadway musical *Rent,* "real
life's getting more like fiction each day." Look around. Court TV broad-
casts actual litigation cases as entertainment; in other courtroom productions, litigants opt for celebrity judges in lieu of government magistrates.
Watch an old reel of game highlights from the National Basketball Association and compare its matter-of-fact action to today's sport, with its

colorfully decorated floors, lavish pregame light shows, and posterboy personalities. Today's NBA gives us Dennis Rodman, the personification of real-life fiction. Video feeds now make it possible to display everyday events at ordinary places—from repair shops to maternity wards—on the World Wide Web, where they can be viewed by anyone anywhere in the world. (Perhaps real life is less like *The Game* than *The Truman Show*—the 1998 film in which Jim Carrey plays a real person who unknowingly lives in a made-for-TV world.)

Eventually, experience orchestration will become as much a part of doing business as product and process design are today. The evidence of its beginnings is everywhere. In restaurants and retail stores, classrooms and parking garages, leading companies are setting the stage for what lies ahead. There are as yet no hard and fast rules to follow when it comes to staging experiences—it's still in its embryonic phase of development. Nonetheless, the practices and results obtained by the pioneering enterprises that are giving it their best efforts make a good starting point from which to explore the nature of successfully staged experiences. Clearly, it's show time!

THEME THE EXPERIENCE

Just hear the name of any theme restaurant—Hard Rock Cafe, House of Blues, Dive!, or the Medieval Times, to name a few—and you know what to expect when you enter the place. The proprietors have taken the first, crucial step toward staging an experience by envisioning a well-defined *theme.*[1] A poorly conceived theme, on the other hand, gives customers nothing around which to organize their impressions, and the experience yields no lasting memory. An incoherent theme is like Gertrude Stein's Oakland: "There is no there there."

Retailers often offend the principle. They talk of "the shopping experience" but fail to create a theme that ties disparate merchandising presentations together into a staged experience. Home-appliance and electronics retailers, for example, show little thematic imagination. Row upon row of washers and dryers and wall after wall of refrigerators merely highlight the sameness of different companies' stores. Shouldn't there be something distinctive about an establishment called Circuit City?

One retailer that does understand the experience of shopping is Leonard Riggio. When the Barnes & Noble CEO began to expand the chain of bookstores into superstores, he hit on the simple theme of "theatres." Riggio realized that people visited bookstores for the same reason they go to the theatre: for the *social* experience.[2] So he changed everything about the stores to express this theme: the architecture, the way salespeople acted, the decor and furnishings. And of course he added cafes as an "intermission" from mingling, browsing, and buying.

Or consider the Forum Shops in Las Vegas, a mall conceived by developer Sheldon Gordon (of Gordon Group Holdings) and developed along with Indianapolis-based real estate company Simon Property Group. It displays its distinctive theme—an ancient Roman marketplace—in every detail and fulfills this motif through a panoply of architectural effects. These include marble floors, stark white pillars, "outdoor" cafes, living trees, flowing fountains, and even a painted blue sky with fluffy white clouds that yield regularly to simulated storms, complete with lightning and thunder. Every mall entrance and

> **The first step is envisioning a well-defined theme**

every storefront is an elaborate Roman re-creation. Every hour, inside the main entrance, statues of Caesar and other Roman luminaries come to life and speak. "Hail, Caesar!" is a frequent cry, and Roman centurions periodically march on their way to Caesar's Palace casino. The Roman theme even extends into some of the shops. A jewelry store's interior, for instance, features scrolls, tablets, Roman numerals, and gold draperies. The theme implies opulence, and the mall's more than $1,000 per-square-foot sales in 1997 (versus less than $300 at a typical mall) suggests that the experience works.

Walt Disney's idea for Disneyland grew out of his dissatisfaction with amusement parks—un-themed collections of rides, games, and refreshments geared to the young. As he related to biographer Bob Thomas, "It all started when my daughters were very young, and I took them to amusement parks on Sunday. I sat on a bench eating peanuts and looking all around me. I said to myself, dammit, why can't there be a better place to take your children, where you can have fun together?"[3] And from these first thoughts Walt conceived the original idea of Disneyland—in Walt's words, "a cartoon that immerses the audience." It developed into a cohesive orchestration of *theme rides*—such as the King Arthur Carousel, Peter Pan's Flight, and the *Mark Twain* paddle boat (each "like nothing you've ever seen in an amusement park before"[4])—within *theme areas*—such as Fantasyland and Frontierland—within the very first *theme park* anywhere in the world, what its first brochure called "a new experience in entertainment."[5] What was the overarching theme of the Disneyland experience? Disney's 1953 proposal to potential financial backers begins with a very simple but engaging theme and then goes on to elaborate the meaning of this theme in very real, and soon realized, terms:

> The idea of Disneyland is a simple one. It will be a place for people to find happiness and knowledge.
>
> It will be a place for parents and children to share pleasant times in one another's company: a place for teachers and pupils to discover greater ways of understanding and education. Here the older generation can recapture the nostalgia of days gone by, and the younger generation can savor the challenge of the future.[6]

"A place for people to find happiness and knowledge" conjured up such a wonderful image that he quickly found financial backers. In less than two years the *themed* park opened to far more visitors than anyone had imagined.

As a model, consider the oft-used theme in novels and films: Crime doesn't pay. Three simple words say it all. Or consider the television tavern *Cheers,* "where everybody knows your name." Companies staging experiences must seek equally crisp thematic constructions. Of course, businesses wishing to impart very different experiences require very different themes. A mall might choose "a walk down memory lane" or "the downtown suburbia never had." A salon or spa specializing in high-end body care could use "a prestigious pause from the monotony of life" or "modern methods to pamper every sense." For a bank it might be "a bulwark never failing" or "a fountainhead for progressive businesses." Hospitals might be themed as "civilized care for better health" or "where the hopeless are cured, and their loved ones assured." "The Geek Squad" serves as a powerfully simple and appropriately nerdy theme for a computer repair firm. The two-word motto "Friendly Serve" suits Mobil Oil's latest "retro" rendition of the convenience store/gas pump combination. And "The Sargeant's Program" provides a perfect theme for the Washington, D.C.–based fitness program modeled after a boot camp.

Indeed, at its best, theming an experience means scripting a story that would seem incomplete without guests' participation.[7] Disney uses such stories for its rides, which are often based on movies or updated fairy tales. In establishing the theme "Step Inside the Great Outdoors!" the American Wilderness Experience places its guests in the narrative of a ten-year-old boy who desires more than anything else to become an architect of great buildings but then realizes he has left the animals out of the picture. Bamboola's theme of "The Island of Play, Adventure & Fun" lands each child in the middle of a fantasy tale in which two children lost at sea are rescued by giant turtles who bring them to the Island of Bamboola. There the children discover the island's natural

Theming an experience means scripting a participative story

beauty, as well as loads of debris washed ashore. Their task: Help clean up the island so the sea turtles can once again lay eggs there.[8]

Developing an appropriate theme for an experience is challenging. One place to start is with general categories of themes. In his insightful, albeit academic, book *The Theming of America,* sociology professor Mark Gott-diener identifies ten themes that often materialize in the "built environments" that he calls staged experiences.[9] These are:

1. status
2. tropical paradise
3. the Wild West
4. classical civilization
5 nostalgia
6. Arabian fantasy
7. urban motif
8. fortress architecture and surveillance
9. modernism and progress
10. representations of the unrepresentable (such as the Vietnam Veterans Memorial Wall)

Marketing professors Bernd Schmitt and Alex Simonson, in their instructive book *Marketing Aesthetics*, offer nine "domains" in which themes can be found:[10]

1. history
2. religion
3. fashion
4. politics
5. psychology
6. philosophy
7. the physical world
8. popular culture
9. the arts

But no matter what list prompts the discovery, the key to successfully theming an experience really lies in determining what will actually prove to be compelling and captivating. *Five principles are paramount in developing such a theme.*

First, an engaging theme must alter a guest's sense of reality. Gott-diener's themes each alter some dimension of the human experience, be it temporal age, geographic location, environmental condition (familiar/foreign, risky/safe), social affiliation, or self-image. Creating a reality other than everyday—for doing, learning, staying, and being—underlies any successful theme and is at the heart of establishing a sense of place.

Second, the richest venues possess themes that *fully* alter one's sense of reality by affecting the experience of space, time, and matter. Parking garages are a space we've all experienced. Typical parking lines occupy space in but one dimension, and only serve to **The richest** *identify* a stall—usually when a driver pulls in, more than **venues affect** when he returns. Signs provide a two-dimensional view, **the experience** helping one *see* where one has parked. The themed design of **of time, space,** the Standard Parking garage at Chicago's O'Hare airport, **and matter** however, offers a place to *experience* parking spots in full 3-D perspective. Indeed, the intent is to bring energy and motion into the process of locating one's car. As a result, returning guests do not waste time wandering around looking for their cars.

Time also feels different at the new ESPN experience at Baltimore's Inner Harbor. No ordinary sports bar, the ESPN Zone sports theme, "A place where the cheering never stops," alters the feasting fans' sense of the present. There's no longer just one game on the tube; rather, three hundred television sets serve up every contest televised anywhere in any sport. There's *always* something to cheer for. Similarly, Silicon Graphics' VISION-ARIUM, like Disneyland's revamped Tomorrowland, alters one's sense of the future, and the Hard Rock Cafe manipulates the past.

Likewise, matter can be neither slighted nor ignored in the formation of a compelling theme. Themes may suggest alternative sizes, shapes, and substances of things. FAO Schwarz's "Welcome to My World" theme welcomes guests to an altered state of toys; Cabela's and rival Bass Pro Shops' outdoor themes display the objects of a sportsman's desire, through taxidermy and other backdrops, and in the process bring the hunted closer to the hunter. The American Wilderness Experience combines real (animals), fake (artificial trees), and virtual (motion-based attraction) materials to help guests "Step Inside the Great Outdoors," its postmodern theme.

And space matters. Ogden's American Wilderness Experience theme required detailed study of the position, posture, and proximity of biome to biome, species to species, guest to guest to make the experience make sense. The upstart LAN Arena lacks a readily apparent theme; no wonder it sports bare walls and nondescript furnishings. Then again, billion-dollar airlines take similarly few steps to alter the sensation of crammed space experienced by the coach traveler on most airlines. Creativity expert and former dean of Disney University Mike Vance relates in speeches how he

travels with personal items in a bag he calls his "Kitchen of the Mind"—
family pictures, pieces of paper, and assorted knickknacks that he uses to
decorate his seatback, traytable, and window shade, especially on long
flights. Flight attendants look at Vance as if he, not the theme-less airline,
has a problem.[11]

Third, engaging themes integrate space, time, and matter into a cohesive,
realistic whole. To see how, consider a work of theology. In his apologetic
for the Christian faith, Dr. Henry M. Morris states, "It is not that the universe is a *triad* of three distinct entities [time, space, and matter] which,
when added together, comprise the whole. Rather each of the three is itself
the whole, and the universe is a true trinity, not a triad. Space is infinite and
time is endless, and everywhere throughout space and time events happen,
processes function, phenomena exist. The tri-universe is remarkably analo-
gous to the nature of its Creator."[12] Therein lies the power of storytelling
and other narratives as a vehicle to script themes. Great books and good
movies engage their audience when they create completely new realities,
altering every detail of the reading and cinematic experience. Lori's Diner,
a small chain of restaurants in San Francisco, creates an authentic 1950s
diner, complete with vintage jukeboxes, pinball machines, booths, waiter
and waitress uniforms—even a Fonz-like character outside beckoning
passersby to walk up the steps into this past world.[13] So why not bank
branches and car-rental shuttle buses, hotels, and airlines?

Fourth, themes are strengthened by creating multiple places within a
place. The five biomes of the American Wilderness Experience leverage
this principle. The change in scenery from Redwood to High Sierra to
Desert to Coast to Valley extends the story introduced by a video and simulated ride. It puts the guests in motion in the experience. This places-
within-the-place explains much of the difference between a
Club Disney and a Discovery Zone. Both employ a variation
of "play" as a theme, but Disney's masterful design of nine
distinct play areas within the same location allows child and
parent to construct their own play-time story. At Discovery
Zone, practically every corner of the place remains visible
from any other vantage point. See-through nets separate one

**Strong themes
create multiple
places within a
place**

section from another, with the so-called ball pit attraction often at the center of activity. Even if this setting helps parents keep track of their young-
ster's whereabouts, it calls to mind Gottdiener's fortress architecture and
surveillance theme more than a place for play.

Finally, a theme should fit the character of the enterprise staging the
experience. In 1947 Chicago developer Arthur Rubloff coined the term
"Magnificent Mile" to describe the famous stretch of commercial property

A theme should fit the character of the enterprise staging the experience

along greater North Michigan Avenue in downtown Chicago. It is a magnificently constructed theme, enduring for generations because it so befits the *walking* shoppers must do to shop and eat there. A crossover to politics supplies an example of a theme that misses the mark: the very moment then-Massachusetts governor Michael Dukakis donned a helmet and stepped into a tank for a photo-op, he lost the 1988 Presidential election. The theme "fighting man" did not fit who he was as a candidate—and voters knew it. If a theme is to succeed, it must be completely consistent with the character of the business that is promoting it. Anything less appears disingenuous and detracts from the experience rather than improve it.

An effective theme must be concise and compelling. Too much detail clutters its effectiveness in serving as an organizing principle for staging experiences. The theme is not a corporate mission statement or a marketing tag line. It needn't be publicly articulated—just as the term "Trinity" appears nowhere in the texts of Scripture—yet its presence is clearly felt. The theme must drive all the design elements and staged events of the experience toward a unified storyline that wholly captivates the customer. That is the essence of theme; all the rest simply lends support.

HARMONIZE IMPRESSIONS WITH POSITIVE CUES

While the theme forms the foundation of an experience, the experience must be rendered with indelible *impressions*. Impressions are the "takeaways" of the experience; the congruent integration of a number of impressions affect the individual and thereby fulfill the theme. Thinking about impressions begins with asking yourself how you would like guests to describe the experience: "It made me feel . . ." or "It was like . . . ." Professors Schmitt and Simonson again provide a useful list, this one delineating six "dimensions of overall impressions"[14]:

1. Time: Traditional, contemporary, or futuristic representations of the theme.
2. Space: City/country, East/West (to which we might add North/South), home/business, and indoor/outdoor representations.
3. Technology: Hand-made/machine-made and natural/artificial representations.
4. Authenticity: Original or imitative representations.
5. Sophistication: Yielding refined/unrefined or luxurious/cheap representations.
6. Scale: Representing the theme as grand or small.

Experience orchestrators can use these dimensions to think creatively about the enormous possibilities for rendering a theme with indelible impressions. The connection to space-matter-time is obvious.

Yet this list only begins to tap the relationship between impressions and the theme they support. For what may be the most comprehensive list of impressions imaginable, no source can exceed Peter Mark Roget's synopsis of categories. *Roget's International Thesaurus* (fourth edition), offers 1,042 categorized entries from "Existence" to "Religious Buildings" across eight classes, 176 subclasses, and, should you want the detail within the *Thesaurus* itself, 250,000 words and phrases.[15] It's the richest possible source for exploring the exact words to denote the specific impressions you want guests to take away from the experience.

Words alone are not enough, of course. To create the desired impressions, companies must introduce cues that together affirm the nature of the desired experience for the guest. Each cue must support the theme, and *none* should be inconsistent with it. In designing the British Airways experience, which is centered around a theme of almost lavish personal service, Sir Colin Marshall relates how the company arranged "all the elements of our service so that they collectively generate a particular experience. We try to think about what kind of impression or feeling each interaction between the company and a customer will generate."[16] Therefore, the flight attendants don't pile on food and drinks and then disappear into the back of the plane. Instead they oblige passengers only when asked, the purpose being to "create additional personal contacts with the customer."[17]

The experience must leave indelible impressions

In a similar vein, George Harrop, founder of Barista Brava, a chain of coffee bars based in Washington, D.C., advertises for franchisees with the trademarked slogan "Our Business Is Providing Customer Experiences. . . . Our Industry Is Coffee!" His underlying theme of "the marriage of Old-World Italian espresso bars with fast-paced American lifestyle" influences the entire design. The interior decor supports the Old World theme, and the carefully crafted pattern of floor tiles and the counter layout encourages customers to queue without the usual signage or ropes that would detract from that theme. Customers get the accurate impression of quick service in a soothing setting. Furthermore, Harrop motivates *baristas* to remember faces so they can presciently hand regular customers their "usual" order before being asked. At the time of this writing, Barista Christopher Mathis, who goes by the stage name "The Amazing Marceau," holds the record at sixty-two customers in a row!

In 1997 ARAMARK's Campus Services division unveiled a new cafeteria experience, dubbed *Pan Geos,* which marketing director Doug Martinedes calls "the next evolution in food service: a marketplace experience for virtually every taste profile." To fulfill its theme of "Fresh World Flavors," the development team decided on a set of impressions they call "The Five F's and a W." At seven modules, each featuring different foods from around the world with a *F*resh display of the seasonal ingredients that make up the day's specials, the costumed chefs cook each entree on the spot in a *F*ast and *F*orthright manner. Everything is laid out in front of the guests, with no backroom kitchens. Amidst the explosion of color and aroma, the chefs customize each meal to taste, just *F*or You, all the while keeping up an engaging banter that makes it *F*un for both the chefs and the guests, resulting in a decided *W*ow! as it all comes together.

Different kinds of experiences, of course, often rely on radically different kinds of impressions. At East Jefferson General Hospital in Metairie, Louisiana, just outside of New Orleans, CEO Peter Betts and his management team redesigned the hospital around the impressions of warmth, caring, and professionalism. They convey these three key impressions by means of having team members wear easily read nametags that list professional titles and degrees and knock before entering a patient's room, among other things. The hospital designates any area accessible to guests—which include not only patients but family members, clergy, and any other visitors—as on-stage and all others as off-stage. It then confines unpleasant activities (such as transporting blood) and "hall conversations" to off-stage areas, while carefully crafting all on-stage areas with appropriate cues that enhance the experience. Toward this end there are painted murals on the ceilings of rehabilitation rooms where patients frequently exercise on their backs, and different kinds of flooring to identify locations (lobbies are carpeted, paths to dining areas slate, to conference rooms terrazzo).[18]

Companies must introduce cues affirming the nature of the experience

Lewis Carbone, president of the Experience Engineering Co. in Bloomington, Minnesota, developed a useful construct for "engineering" preference-creating experiences. Carbone divides impressions, or "clues," as he calls them, into "mechanics" and "humanics," or what might be called the inanimate and animate. The former are "the sights, smells, tastes, sounds, and textures generated by *things,* for example, landscaping, graphics, scents, recorded music, handrail surfaces, and so on. In contrast, 'humanics' clues emanate from *people.* They are engineered by defining and choreographing the desired behavior of employees involved in the customer encounter."[19]

At Disney, for example, to avoid any possible association with rowdy local carnivals or run-down amusement parks, management set the impression of cleanliness as a cardinal principle. The designers translated this concern into such cues as: the mechanics of making sure a trash receptacle is always within sight of any guest and the humanics of assigning a large number of cast members whose sole role is to pick up any trash that does not make it into a receptacle. Well, not quite the sole role: they're also to make eye contact and smile whenever they're within ten feet of any guest to reinforce the "happiness" impression.

Different kinds of experiences rely on different kinds of impressions

The cues trigger impressions that fulfill the theme in the customer's mind. An experience can be unpleasant merely because some architectural feature has been overlooked, underappreciated, or uncoordinated. Unplanned or inconsistent visual and aural cues can leave a customer confused or lost. Have you ever been unsure of how to find your hotel room, even after the front-desk staff has provided detailed directions? Better, clearer cues along the way would have enhanced your experience.

ELIMINATE NEGATIVE CUES

Ensuring the integrity of the customer experience requires more than layering on positive cues. Experience stagers also must eliminate anything that diminishes, contradicts, or distracts attention from the theme. Guests to most constructed spaces—malls, offices, buildings, or airplanes—find them littered with meaningless or trivial messages. While customers sometimes do need instructions, too often service providers say it poorly or choose an inappropriate medium, such as the sign we encountered on a chair in a Wyndham Garden Hotel room: "For your comfort, this chair reclines." Cognitive psychologist and industrial design critic Donald Norman gives "a rule of thumb for spotting bad design: Look for posted instructions."[20] They can only serve to form poor impressions.

Seemingly minor cues can impair any experience. At most restaurants, for example, a host droning "Your table is ready" cues customers to expect a normal meal service. That phrase is now so familiar it forms no impression. At a Rainforest Cafe, however, the host sets the stage for what lies ahead by proclaiming for all to hear, "The Smith party, your adventure is about to begin!" Should the Smith party fail to appear at the third call, the host informs the other guests that the Smith's "safari has left without them."

Experience stagers eliminate anything that distracts from the theme

To avoid giving off cues at odds with its themes, Disney theme-park cast members always act their part, never stepping out of character while on-stage. Only when off-stage, in an area prohibited to customers, can cast members talk freely amongst themselves. Many historical villages, such as Old Sturbridge Village and Plimoth Plantation, both in Massachusetts, also require employees to stay in character (eighteenth-century farmers and the like at Sturbridge, Pilgrims and Indians at Plimoth). Others, such as Colonial Williamsburg and Jamestown in Virginia, significantly diminish the integrity of their experiences by allowing period-costumed employees to talk the talk of their present-day guests.

The idea of "role-appropriate" clothing and behavior can also apply to people with more workaday jobs. At East Jefferson General Hospital, all team members must personify "the EJ Look"—a set of dress standards that eliminates potentially negative cues. Not allowed, for example, are casual shirts without ties on men, extra-long fingernails and certain shades of polish on women, and strong colognes or perfumes on either. The "EJ Look" helps the staff create the hospital's desired impression of "professionalism" and has proved so effective that people they meet out and about in the community often immediately identify them as being from East Jefferson.

Too many cues, particularly when put together haphazardly—such as *over*servicing in the name of customer intimacy—can also ruin an experience. As a writer for *Fortune* put it in extolling the virtues of staying in chartered homes instead of hotels while traveling: "There

Too many haphazard cues can ruin an experience

are no check-ins, no checkouts, no bills to puzzle over, no inflated telephone charges (you dial direct and an itemized list of calls is sent to you later), and only a two- or three-night minimum. Even better, no *service-industry intrusions:* no bellman waiting to be acknowledged or tipped, no maids lurking in your room watching TV, no agents sneaking in at night to hide chocolates in the bed."[21] Lest they slowly lose their clientele to the better experience of an away-from-home home, hotel chains should work harder to eliminate negative cues: stop cluttering end-tables, dressers, and desktops with service communications; assign off-stage personnel to answer phones so front-desk staff won't have to interrupt conversations with paying guests to field telephone calls; make sure bellmen and maids perform their tasks unobtrusively; and so forth. Only then will their guests be made to truly feel at home.

MIX IN MEMORABILIA

People have always purchased certain goods primarily for the memories they convey. Vacationers buy postcards to evoke treasured sights, golfers purchase shirts or caps with embroidered logos to recall particular courses

or rounds, spouses select greeting cards to celebrate important occasions, and teenagers collect T-shirts to remember
rock concerts. They purchase such memorabilia as tangible
artifacts of the experiences they want to remember.

People purchase memorabilia as tangible artifacts of experiences

Such items are often among an individual's most cherished possessions, worth far more to them than the cost of
the physical artifact. Take something as simple as a ticket stub, a natural by-
product of many an experience. Perhaps you have some tucked away in the
bottom of a jewelry box (with other valuable items), or your children have
some carefully mounted and displayed in their bedrooms. Why do we keep
these torn fragments of paper? Because they represent a cherished experience. Your first Major League baseball game, a favorite musical, a meaningful date at the movies—all events that run the risk of fading away without that physical remembrance.

Of course, that's not the only—perhaps not even the primary—reason
we purchase memorabilia. Greater still may be our desire to show others
what we have experienced to generate conversation and, not a small factor
perhaps, envy.[22] This is more food for the thoughtful experience stager. As
Bruno Giussani, head of online strategy at the World Economic Forum in
Davos, Switzerland, related to us, "Memorabilia are a way to 'socialize' the
experience, to transmit parts of it to others—and for companies entering the
Experience Economy, they are means to entice new guests."

People already spend tens of billions of dollars every year on this class
of goods, which generally sell at price points far above those commanded
by similar items that don't commemorate an experienced locale or event. A
Rolling Stone concert goer will pay a large premium for an official T-shirt
emblazoned with the date and city of the concert he attended. That's
because the price point functions less as an indicator of the cost of goods
than of the value the buyer attaches to remembering the experience. In
addition to gaining a premium over run-of-the-mill T-shirts, the Hard Rock
Cafe induces guests to make multiple purchases simply by printing the
location of each particular cafe on its T-shirts (a practice the Rainforest
Cafe now emulates, with other themed establishments sure to follow). The
Ministry of Sound, a British nightclub and burgeoning media company, had
revenues of $40 million in 1997, but only $6 million actually came from
traffic at the nightclub. Most of the rest came from memorabilia.[23]

Selling memorabilia associated with an experience is one approach to
extending an experience; turning items inherently part of the experience
into personalized memorabilia is another. Sports-themed restaurants might
digitize a guest's credit card signature and transfer it to a baseball where it
would sit right below Ken Griffey Jr.'s autograph. At Planet Hollywood a

guest's signature could appear at the bottom of a digitally altered movie scene in which the guest stands next to a favorite movie star, Arnold Schwarzenegger or Demi Moore, perhaps, whose signature already appears on the photograph.

A third approach is to not sell memorabilia but to give it away. When the Ritz-Carlton in Naples, Florida, installed a new computerized safety system with key cards, management decided to give away the old doorknobs to past guests instead of selling them or tossing them out. Each of the 463 knobs was engraved with the classic Ritz-Carlton lion and crown insignia, converted into a distinctive paperweight, and given to those guests—among the more than six thousand who requested one—whose story of an experience at the Ritz most touched the hearts of the associates who read each appeal. The limited-supply doorknobs became a physical reminder of a memorable stay, and, Ritz-Carlton certainly hoped, a cue to relive that experience in the future. The sense of obligation created within guests was worth far more than the Ritz would have gotten by selling the doorknobs.

> **The price point is a function of the value of remembering the experience**

Finally, a fourth approach companies can employ is to develop a wholly new sort of memorabilia. For instance, Hillenbrand Industries of Batesville, Indiana, developed a new memorabilia capability for the funeral industry. The concept emerged from the practice in many funeral homes of craft producing "memory boards" for display at viewing and memorial services. Hillenbrand sought to bring greater efficiencies to the process but also to preserve the one-of-a-kind collages families now put together to commemorate the lives of lost loved ones. Hillenbrand did this by developing a proprietary system to digitize, merge, and print mass customized collages to both paper and video output media.

But these Lifescape collages serve merely as a prop for the experience Hillenbrand really offers. A self-guided kit that walks a family, group of friends, or coworkers through a series of steps to create their own memories. "What we sell," says Gary Bonnie, who headed the initiative, "is the *lifescaping* experience of gathering with others, rummaging through old photographs and other mementos, and recalling fond memories. The collage just happens to be the outcome; the true value is experienced in going through the process we've helped script." Accordingly, Hillenbrand charges for the kit experience, whether or not people actually buy the collage.

With the proper stage setting, any business can mix memorabilia into its offerings. If service businesses such as banks, grocery stores, and insurance companies find no demand for memorabilia, it's because they do not offer anything anyone wants to remember. Should these businesses offer themed experiences layered with positive cues and devoid of negative ones, their guests will want and pay for memorabilia to commemorate their experiences. (If guests don't want to do this, it probably means the experience wasn't all that great.) The special agents of the Geek Squad, for example, stage such a distinctive computer repair experience that guests buy T-shirts and lapel pins with the company's logo from its Web site. If airlines truly were in the experience-staging business, more passengers would actually shop in those seat-pocket catalogs for mementos. Likewise, mortgage loans would inspire household keepsakes; grocery checkout lanes would stock souvenirs in lieu of nickel-and-dime impulse items; and perhaps even insurance policy certificates would be suitable for framing.

ENGAGE THE FIVE SENSES

The sensory stimulants that accompany an experience should support and enhance its theme. The more effectively an experience engages the senses, the more memorable it will be. Smart shoeshine operators augment the smell of polish with crisp snaps of the cloth, scents and sounds that don't make the shoes any shinier but do make the experience more engaging. Savvy hair stylists shampoo and apply lotions not simply for styling reasons but because they add more tactile sensations to the customer experience. Similarly, better grocers pipe bakery smells into the aisles, and some use sight and sound to simulate thunderstorms when misting their produce, to create a more engaging experience. Indeed, in most any situation the easiest way to sensorialize a service: add taste sensations simply by serving food and drink. Barnes & Noble has found its cafes to be a wonderful addition to its superstores, encouraging people to spend more time there, thus increasing the likelihood they'll buy books, and more of them.

West Point Market in Akron, Ohio, founded by Russ Vernon, was one of the first to serve specialty foods in a grocery store. Retail guru Leonard Berry of Texas A&M University describes this upscale market as "a sea of colors, an adventure in discovery, a store of temptation with its killer brownies, walnut nasties, and peanut-butter krazies."[24] He quotes Kaye Lowe, director of public relations, as saying, "We don't hesitate to let customers taste a product. Some people come in on a Saturday and eat their way around the store. Russ's favorite saying is: 'Come see the sights, smell the delights, and taste the wonders of WPM.'"[25]

Services turn into engaging experiences when layered with sensory phenomena. This can be seen in the very earliest stages of life. Consider the task of feeding an infant.

The more sensory an experience, the more memorable it will be

One evening during dinner, then eleven-month-old Evan Gilmore pushed aside his mother's hand, refusing the food she offered. So daddy took over. In an act performed by countless parents before, the spoon no longer went directly from jar to mouth. Instead, it was taken two feet back and raised high in the air. With herky-jerky movements, the flying machine descended, accompanied by the sputtering motor-mouthed improvisations of Air Traffic Papa. Tightly clinched baby lips soon opened as wide as a hangar to receive a spoonful from each flight.

Believe it or not, this airplane game conveys the essence of what any eatertainment establishment does to turn an ordinary food service into a scintillating dining experience for paying adults: designing exactly the right *sensations* into cues that convey the theme for which the guests came. With Evan, everything fit the "Flying Food" theme and gave the impression that a safe landing was required. The experience stager eliminates negative cues (such as a sternly stated "Eat your food"), while tuning each positive cue (visually, aurally, tactilely, flavorfully, aromatically) to integrate the impressions into a believable and appealing theme.

To enhance its theme, the mist at the Rainforest Cafe appeals serially to all five senses. You first encounter it as a sound: Sss-sss-zzz. Then you see the mist rising from the rocks and feel it soft and cool against your skin. Finally, you smell its tropical essence and taste (or imagine that you do) its freshness. It's impossible to be unaffected by this one, simple sensory-filled cue.

Some cues heighten an experience through a single sense by means of striking simplicity. The Cleveland Bicentennial Commission spent $4 million to illuminate eight automobile and railroad bridges over the Cuyahoga River near a nightspot area called the Flats. No one pays a toll to view or even cross these illuminated bridges, but the dramatically lighted structures are a prop that city managers now use to attract tourist dollars by making a trip to downtown Cleveland a more memorable nighttime experience.

Similarly, a single, simple sensation can completely detract from an experience. Think of the recorded and/or mechanical voices now heard all over the place—fronting voicemail systems, beginning a telemarketing pitch, getting on and off shuttles, informing you of how to work a seatbelt on an airplane, even giving you a wake-up call at a hotel. People so quickly drown out these monotonous dronings because companies don't bother to explore alternative creative ways of yielding the same benefits without the negative sensory cues. Here, the four realms of an experience presented in Chapter 2 can be tapped to come up with schemes to enrich the senses. How could an automated voice entertain—by using humor? How might it not just inform but educate? How might it

A simple cue can heighten an experience through a single sense

induce action to create an escapist experience? And how might the sounds of—or behind—the voice be so esthetically pleasing that guests just want to listen to it?

Adding sensory phenomena obviously requires businesses to employ technicians who know how to affect our senses.[26] Experience-based enterprises will require architectural and musical skills not just to design buildings and select music but to fill the experience with senses that make sense. (In the future, hotels won't provide A/V technicians for meetings but "sensory specialists.") Not all sensations are good ones, and some combinations don't work. Barnes & Noble may have discovered that the aroma and taste of coffee go well with a freshly cracked book, but Duds n' Suds went bust attempting to combine a coin-operated laundromat and a bar—apparently, the smells of phosphates and hops aren't complementary.

COMPANIES THAT WANT TO STAGE COMPELLING EXPERIENCES should begin with the principles outlined above to explore the possibilities that await them. They must determine the theme of the experience as well as the impressions that will convey that theme to guests. Many times, experience stagers develop a list of impressions they wish guests to take away and then think creatively about different themes and storylines that will bring the impressions together in one cohesive narrative. Then they winnow the impressions down to a manageable number—only and exactly those which truly denote the cogent theme. Next, they focus on the animate and inanimate cues that could connote each impression, following the simple guidelines of accentuating the positive and eliminating the negative. They then must meticulously map out the effect each cue will have on the five senses—sight, sound, touch, taste, and smell—taking care not to overwhelm guests with too much sensory input. Finally, they add memorabilia to the total mix, extending the experience in the customer's mind over time.

> **Many experience stagers start with a list of impressions and then develop the theme**

Of course, embracing these principles remains, for now, an art form. But those companies which figure out how to design experiences that are compelling, engaging, memorable—and rich—will be the ones leading the way into the emerging Experience Economy.

YOU ARE WHAT YOU CHARGE FOR

The transition to an economy in which experiences fuel the engine of growth will undergo many of the same changes encountered in the earlier transition from the Industrial to the Service Economy. This transition begins when companies *give away* experiences in order to sell existing offerings better, just as IBM and others initially gave away services in order to sell their goods. Service providers, consciously or not, recognize the value clients place on the experience, but rather than charge separately for it, they just surround their core services with experiential effects. Theme-based restaurants, for example, still charge for the food when customers come in for the experience.

The transition begins when you *give away* experiences in order to sell existing offerings

Consider Chrysler's new showcase storefront, "Great Cars, Great Trucks" in the Mall of America outside of Minneapolis. Visitors learn about the history of Chrysler and the automobile, and among other activities get to see a tantalizing concept car, play a race car simulation, hear the sounds emanating from different engines, and sit for a picture in a Dodge Viper. The store manager told us that Chrysler designed the showcase "to get out the word to consumers—in a nonthreatening, nonsales environment—about what great cars and trucks Chrysler builds." When we suggested the company should charge admission to the showcase experience, he replied, "Oh no—if we did that, customers would feel they had a right to tell us what they wanted to do here." Exactly what it *should* want customers to do!

Ultimately, a business is defined by that for which it collects revenue, and it collects revenue only for that which it decides to charge. You're not truly selling a particular economic offering unless you explicitly ask your customers to pay for that exact offering. For experiences, that means *charging an admission fee*. Appealing to a buyer's five senses may create a greater preference for your offering versus its commoditized competitors, but unless you charge customers for *using* it—not for owning it—in a *place* you control, your experience is not an *economic* offering. You may design the most engaging experience around your service offering or within your retail establishment, but unless you charge people specifically for watching or participating in the activities performed—just for entering your place,[27] as do concert halls, theme parks, motion-based attractions, and other experience venues—you're not staging an economic experience.[28]

Even if you reject for now the idea of charging admission out of fear, uncertainty, or doubt, it should still be your design criteria. Ask yourself: *What would we do differently if we charged admission?* This exercise will force you to discover what experience will engage guests in a more powerful way. Bottom line: your experience will never be *worth* an admission fee until you explore how to stop giving it away for free.

Movie theatres, whose owners have always recognized they're in show business, already charge admission to see the movies—but what about the theatre itself? Jim Loeks, part owner of the Star movie complex in Southfield, Michigan, declares, "It should be worth the price of the movie just to go into the theatre." Today, the Star charges 3 million visitors a year 25 percent more than a local competitor for a movie thanks to its fun-house-themed experience, which, according to Loeks, "creates a sense of place people want to go to every week." With 65,000 square feet of restaurants and stores now being added to the complex in the future, the Star may charge admission to the theatre whether or not people also see a movie.[29]

You're not truly selling an experience unless you charge admission

Think about a pure retailer that already borders on the experiential. The next time you go to a Sharper Image or Brookstone—two retailers that provide a place where consumers can play with the latest high-tech devices—watch the customers as they meander around the store. Many wouldn't dream of actually using, let alone owning, most of these physical goods at home or in the office. But notice how many enjoy playing with the gee-whiz gadgets, listening to miniaturized hi-fi equipment, sitting and lying on massage chairs and tables, and then *leave without paying for what they valued*—namely, the experience.[30]

Could such an establishment charge admission? Today, only a few people would likely pay just to get into the store, though surely not enough people (not at least as the companies currently manage the stores) to sustain the enterprise on admission fees. But if the Sharper Image decided to charge an admission fee, that would *force* the company to stage a much better experience to attract guests, especially on a repeat basis. The merchandise mix would need to change more regularly, perhaps daily, even hourly. Demonstrations, showcases, contests, and a plethora of other experiential attractions would complete the sharpened experience of a visit to the Sharper Image. Indeed, it would no longer be mere image but an escape from the reality of shopping elsewhere in the mall. As a result, the retailer might very well sell more goods.

Or consider Niketown. It is steeped in such experiential elements as exhibits that chronicle past shoe models, displays of *Sports Illustrated* magazine covers featuring athletes wearing Nikes, a usable half-court basketball floor, and video clips of everyday athletes viewed in an intimate theatre. Indeed, according to a company press release for the opening of the first Niketown in Chicago, that store was "built as a theater, where our consumers are the audience participating in the production."[31] Through these flagship stores Nike aims to build its brand and stimulate buying at other non-Nike retail outlets. And despite selling shoes and apparel, which must cannibalize other retailers' volume to some degree, Nike nevertheless maintains that the locations are meant to be noncompetitive with other retail channels.

Your experience won't be *worth* an admission fee until you stop giving it away for free

If so, then why not explicitly charge people just to enter Niketown? An admission fee would force the company to stage compelling events inside. We might actually see guests use the basketball court, perhaps to go at it one-on-one with past NBA stars or to play a game of H-O-R-S-E against a WNBA player. Customized Nike T-shirts, commemorating the date and score of events—complete with an action photo of the winning hoop—could be purchased afterward. There might be interactive kiosks for educational and entertaining exploration of past athletic triumphs. Virtual reality machines could let visitors *be* Tiger Woods and then have themselves videotaped saying, "I *was* Tiger Woods." All of Nike's signed stars could talk about their favorite sports moment, teach clinics, and sign autographs.

We're convinced Nike could generate as much admission-based revenue per hour at Niketown as Disney does at its venues. Granted, an admission fee will make it more difficult to lure *first-time* guests ("You mean I have to pay to get in there to eat?"), but it will be easier to get them to come back. And there's another benefit to charging admission. For those experience stagers, like theme restaurants, struggling to attract guests for return visits, the admission fee alters the buyer's evaluation of the value of the total offering. For when restaurants try to recover all the costs of staging an experience from the food alone, people quickly get used to getting the experience for free and then begin to view the food as grossly overpriced. So why go back? With an admission fee, guests rightly perceive each offering they consume—goods, services, and experiences—as reasonably priced in its own right. The same principle applies to direct manufacturers, Web site operators, insurance agents, financial brokers, business-to-business marketers, and any other cue-less business that wraps free experiences around costly goods or services. Many retailers, in particular, would readily benefit from charging admission: Warner Bros., FAO Schwarz, the Imaginarium, Oshman's, Victoria's Secret, the Nature Company, and, of course, Disney itself.

Disney's foray into speciality retailing outside its primary properties disappoints. Other than the Disney videos playing in the background, its mall stores pretty much look and feel like everyone else's mall stores, and the blame lies squarely on Disney's failure to charge admission. Because no one pays to get in the door, Disney provides a pedestrian shopping trip rather than a magical adventure. Even when Disney puts real effort into the architecture and furnishings—such as at its flagship store in midtown Manhattan, where upon entering it seems for a moment that you have been transported to Disney World itself—it doesn't harmonize all the cues. The elevator at the midtown store, for example, appears both inside and out to be an entrance into Snow White's castle, but once on board blaring rock music confronts you that has nothing to do with the medieval surroundings. And everywhere you find costumed employees (here, they do not earn the term "cast members") totally out of character, talking amongst themselves. Perhaps this is not Disney's intention. Perhaps it is merely poor execution. But that execution stems directly from the lack of an admission fee—even one reimbursable later for merchandise—and it certainly diminishes the Disney brand by failing to live up to the company's high experiential expertise.

Perhaps the right way to start charging admission is to do so for only a *portion* of the store. At four fun-filled Jordan's Furniture locations across New England, the company stages myriad experiences (from audio-animatronic replicas of the co-owners, brothers Barry and Eliot Tatelman, to a Bourbon-Street-theme Mardi Gras atmosphere). Barry and Eliot still give these away, but at their Avon, Massachusetts, store they charge admission to the Motion Odyssey Machine, which takes audiences on a thrill ride simulating a roller coaster, a dune buggy, an out-of-control truck, and so forth, complete with wind and water effects. As Barry often says, "There's no business that's not show business."

In the full-fledged Experience Economy, we will see not only retail stores but entire shopping malls charge admission before a person is allowed to set foot in a store.[32] In fact, such shopping malls already exist. Disney's arch-rival Universal Studios, for example, charges admission (in the form of a parking fee) to City Walk, as does the Opryland Hotel complex in Nashville. But think also about the Minnesota Renaissance Festival, the Gilroy Garlic Festival in California, the Kitchener-Waterloo Oktoberfest in Ontario, Canada, and a host of other seasonal festivals that charge admission for what are really outdoor shopping malls. Consumers find these festivals to be worth the entrance fees because their owners explicitly script distinctive experiences around particularly enticing themes and then stage a wealth of activities that captivate guests before, after, and while they shop.

> **Not only retail stores but entire shopping malls will charge admission**

At the Minnesota Renaissance Festival, for example, handsome knights and fair maidens greet visitors to the twenty-two-acre domain of King Henry and Queen Katherine outside of Minneapolis, hand them a *News of the Realm* guide on simulated parchment, and invite them to enjoy the day's festivities. Throughout the day various merrymakers in Renaissance costume—magicians, jugglers, peddlers, singers, dance troupes, and even a pair of bumbling commoners known as Puke & Snot—frequently accost guests (many of them are clothed in period costume as well) with the express intent of ensuring that they, their companions, and everyone else within earshot have a wonderful time. Among the numerous categories of activities in which guests delight—and that could apply to any experience—are the following:

- Period *demonstrations* (armor making, glass blowing, bookbinding, and so forth)
- *Crafts* that guests perform themselves (brass rubbing, candle-making, calligraphy)
- *Games, contests,* and other *challenges* for which prizes are awarded (archery, giant maze, Jacob's ladder)
- Human- and animal-powered (never electric) *rides* (elephants, ponies, cabriolet)
- *Food* (turkey legs, apple dumplings, Florentine ice)
- *Drink* (beer and wine but also—in an admitted concession to modern concessions—soda and coffee)
- *Shows, ceremonies, parades* and various and sundry *revelry* (magicians, puppetry, jousts), some of which require an additional fee

Not to mention the hundreds of Renaissance-theme shops (make that shop*pes*) all selling hand-crafted goods appropriate to the period, such as jewelry, pottery, glass, candles, musical instruments, toys, apparel, plants, perfumes, wall hangings, and sculptures, or services such as face painting, astrology readings, portraits, and caricatures. With nearly every guest leaving with one or more bags of goodies, the Renaissance Festival experience clearly siphons off shopping dollars that otherwise would be spent at traditional malls and other retail outlets.

Fortunately for their conventional competitors, the proprietors of such festivals do not hold them year-round . . . yet. The Minnesota Renaissance Festival, for example, opens its gates weekends and Labor Day from mid-August to the end of September. Because of its intensity and unusual nature, most people do not repeat this kind of experience often enough to make staging it every day worthwhile. However, with appropriately malleable grounds and facilities, consumers could be enticed over and over again if different experiences were rotated through the same place. Mid-America Festivals, the company that runs the Minnesota Renaissance Festival as well as similar endeavors in other states, recently added Halloween-theme experiences (Trail of Terror, Gargoyle Manor, and BooBash) at the same locale, as well as a Christmas-theme gourmet dinner and entertainment called the Fezzwieg Feast. Shopping malls entering the Experience

Economy must learn how to stage revolving productions, just as theatres did long ago, that entice people to pay an admission fee again and again.

Do you think people would be crazy to pay for the experience of shopping at their local mall? Imagine the reaction if, decades ago—just after World War II, let's say, when the American economy was booming, flush with returning GIs buying houses in the suburbs and filling their garages with new cars and their kitchens with the latest in household gadgets—you had told people that in the near future the *typical* family would pay someone else to change the oil in their car, make their kids' birthday cakes, clean their shirts, mow their lawn, or deliver a host of other now-commonplace services. No doubt they would have said you were insane! Or imagine going back hundreds of years and telling rural farmers that in the centuries hence the vast majority of people would no longer farm their own land, build their own houses, kill animals for their own meals, chop their own wood, or even make their own clothes or furniture. Again, you would have been thought crazy.

The history of economic progress consists of charging a fee for what once was free

The history of economic progress consists of charging a fee for what once was free. In the full-fledged Experience Economy, instead of relying purely on our own wherewithal to experience the new and wondrous—as has been done for ages—we will increasingly pay companies to stage experiences for us, just as we now pay companies for services we once delivered ourselves, goods we once made ourselves, and commodities we once extracted ourselves.

Charging admission does not necessarily mean, however, that companies stop selling their goods and services. (Although some will indeed give away their lower-echelon offerings to better sell their high-margin experiences, just as telephone companies today give away cell phones to consumers that sign up for their wireless service.) The Walt Disney Company derives an awful lot of profit at its theme parks from parking, food, and other services, as well as from all the goods it sells as memorabilia. But without the staged experiences (not just of the theme parks but of the company's cartoons, movies, and TV shows) there would be nothing to remember—Disney would have no characters to exploit. While historically Disney started with the experience and then added lower-echelon offerings, the principle holds for those starting with goods and services that shift up to experiences. In the Experience Economy, experiences drive the economy and therefore generate much of the base demand for goods and services. So explore what experience *you* could stage that would be so engaging that your current customers would actually pay admission to experience it, and then pay extra for your services while they are so engaged, or pay more for your goods as memorabilia. In doing so, you would be following the lead of not only Disney but the Minnesota Renaissance Festival, the American Wilderness Experience, Bamboola, and a host of other companies that have already entered the Experience Economy.

The same principle applies to business-to-business companies: staging experiences for their customers will drive demand for their current goods and services. The business equivalent of a shopping mall is, after all, a trade show—a place to find, learn about, and, if a need is met, purchase offerings. Trade show operators *already* charge admission (and could charge even more, if they staged better experiences); individual companies can as well. If a company designs a worthwhile experience, customers will gladly pay the company to, essentially, sell to them.

In a business-to-business setting, Diamond Technology Partners of Chicago accomplishes this with an experience offering it calls the Diamond Exchange. This thrice yearly gathering of executives, "fellows" (top partners as well as outside authorities ranging from computer pioneer Alan Kay to University of Chicago economics and psychology professor Marvin Zonis),[33] and Diamond's own "knowledge leaders" explores "the digital future" to help determine its impact on guest companies.[34] Diamond Exchange director Chunka Mui describes it as "a long-term conversation between top executives and some of the world's leading experts in strategy, technology, operations, and learning. Its point of departure is how our members can compete in a world that is increasingly transformed by technology." Current and potential clients gladly pay tens of thousands of dollars a year to attend the Diamond Exchange for the simple reason that what they gain from the explicitly staged events—the fresh insights, revealing self-discovery, and engaging interactions—is *worth* it. And because it demonstrates its capabilities in a nonsales atmosphere (the company strictly forbids any solicitation of potential consulting engagements at the events) Diamond greatly increases its chances of gaining significant consulting work to help members further explore what they learn.

In business-to-business situations, stage experiences where customers pay you to sell to them

Will every company be able to charge admission? No, only those that, like Diamond or Club Disney, properly set the stage by designing rich experiences that cross into all four realms: the entertaining, the educational, the escapist, and the esthetic. And only those that use the principles outlined above to create engaging, memorable encounters. Charging admission is the final step; first you must design an experience *worth* paying for.

4 *Get Your Act Together*

● ●

REMEMBER THE LAST TIME you received particularly poor service, at a restaurant, automotive shop, or airline counter perhaps? For many, such ordeals create our most lasting recollections of a company—and often our best cocktail-hour stories. We forget consistently dependable service while remembering the occasional mishap. Companies that falter on the service front discover the hard way: The easiest way to turn a service into an experience is to provide poor service, thus creating a memorable encounter of the most unpleasant kind.

The surest way to provide poor service is to walk every client through the same rote, impersonal routine, never varying, no matter who the individual client is or what he really needs. Customers have been receiving such treatment ever since service providers embraced the same principles of Mass Production that manufacturers used to dramatically lower costs. And it's become even worse as the forces of commoditization that hit manufacturing now attack services as well. So service providers reengineer their call centers to reduce call time and downsize already harried front-line staff to save on fixed costs and overhead. The end result? Their employees spend less time with clients, and the time they do spend no longer delivers the same level of service. By focusing on costs at the expense of what clients want, these companies are commoditizing themselves. Why should customers pay a higher price for demonstrably poorer service?

To turn a service into an experience, provide poor service

But the inverse principle also holds true: Customizing a service can be a sure route to staging a positive experience. Certainly, customization is not the end all, be all; rather, companies should use it to create *customer-unique value,* the portal through which experiences reach individual customers. An economic offering confers customer-unique value, at its ideal, when it is:

- *specific* to individual customers—brought into being at a particular moment for this precise customer
- *particular* in its characteristics—designed to meet this customer's individual needs (although some other customer may have the same needs and may therefore purchase the same offering)
- *singular* in its purpose to benefit this customer—not trying to be any more or less than, but rather only and exactly, what the customer desires

When a company provides such customer-unique value, it takes an invaluable first step toward creating memorable interactions that stand apart from the routine transactions mass producers foist on their customers.

Progressive Insurance of Cleveland, for example, gives adjusters vans outfitted with a personal computer, satellite uplink, and everything else they may need for the *singular* purpose of efficiently resolving a claim from the site of the accident. While the other party may wait days or weeks for his insurance company's cost-conscious adjuster to fit him into the schedule, the Progressive claimant finds his *particular* needs handled right then and there. He receives not only a check but a cup of coffee as well and if need be, a few minutes to sit down and relax on the couch inside the van and to reassure his family (or arrange for a ride) over the adjuster's (free) cellular phone. Because Progressive customizes its claims service to the *specific* individual insured, its offering goes beyond the expected service to provide an experience appropriate to the physical and emotional needs of the claimant.

> Customizing a service can be a sure route to staging a positive experience

AUTOMATIC SHIFTING

The same effect works for goods: Customizing a good automatically turns it into a service. Look at the new General Nutrition Center format GNC Live Well, which aims to attract consumers that would otherwise be lost amidst the plethora of vitamins and extracts and the like at a normal GNC outlet. By customizing orders for vitamins, exercise programs, nutritional supplements, and other related merchandise, GNC has turned its line of goods into an opportunity to fulfill particular nutrition, relaxation, and exercise needs. When purchasing a Custom VitaPak, for example, a consumer is shown a brochure listing nine basic packages, each based on the needs represented by different lifestyles ("On the Road Again" for frequent travelers, "More Alive at 55" for older consumers, and so forth). The customer is then asked to choose the package that comes closest to matching his profile.

Customizing a good automatically turns it into a service

Next the associate describes the set of four to seven vitamins GNC suggests for that profile. Together, associate and consumer may change a selection or two, or even start over again from scratch, until the total package provides only and exactly what that particular consumer desires. The sales associate then enters the consumer's selection into a computer to verify that no nutritional supplement exceeds recommended levels. Within a short time, the consumer walks to a machine where he sees his daily supplements flowing down from bulk bins into a long plastic strip and hears the machine sealing and perforating them into a set of thirty daily packages, each printed with his name and selection information. GNC records every consumer's profile so that it can, if desired, automatically refill the VitaPak once a month via UPS.

Now consider GNC's Custom VitaPaks in light of the classic distinctions between goods and services. Goods are standardized for anonymous customers, while services are customized for a particular individual—check. Goods are inventoried, while services are delivered on demand—check again. Finally, goods are tangible, while services are intangible—and part and parcel of GNC's interaction with customers is the intangible service of helping each one determine exactly what combination of vitamins he or she needs. (Automatically refilling the VitaPaks wraps yet another service around the offering.) So even though at the core of the sale there lies the physical goods of vitamins, selling the Custom VitaPaks themselves means delivering a service. Since like all services this offering is inherently customizable, the Live Well format puts GNC in a better position to stage experiences for individual customers. Indeed, Richard Rakowski, head of New Paradigm Ventures of South Norwalk, Connecticut, which designed the original prototype store for GNC (called Alive!), told us that "Consumers today crave

To enter the Experience Economy, first customize your goods and services

experiences, and the surest route to give them that sensation is through individualization like they used to receive from the corner butcher or baker. That's central to everything we design."

BOTH GOODS AND SERVICES, then, automatically shift up the Progression of Economic Value when they are customized, as shown in Figure 4-1. (This shift does not occur for true commodities, however, which, being

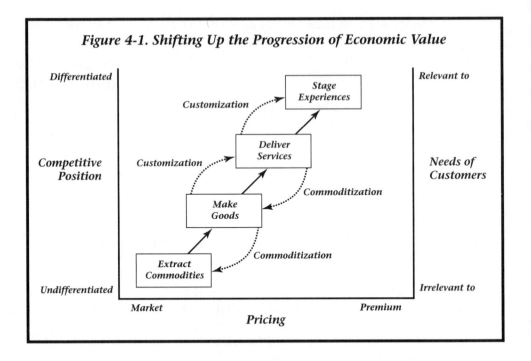

Figure 4-1. Shifting Up the Progression of Economic Value

fungible, cannot be materially changed, much less customized.) As a result, companies create offerings more relevant to the wants and needs of individual buyers, differentiate their goods and services from the sea of look-alike competitors, and thereby increase the value provided, and thus the price charged, to users and clients. Businesses that wish to forestall commoditization by entering the Experience Economy should first get their act together by customizing their goods and services.

MASS CUSTOMIZATION

Companies like GNC and Progressive mass customize their offerings. *Mass Customization* means efficiently serving customers uniquely, combining the coequal imperatives for both low cost and individual customization present in today's highly turbulent, competitive environment.[1] Of course, ad hoc customization, in which a company must determine what to do differently every time it changes operations, achieves the same benefits, but at a higher cost. Companies that hope to gain the best of both worlds—the "mass" and the "customization"—must modularize their goods and services. This lets companies efficiently produce standardized modules but combine them in different ways for different buyers, just as GNC does with the vitamins that go into its Custom VitaPaks.

To understand modularity, think of Lego building blocks. What can you build with Legos? The answer, of course, is anything you want. This is because of the many different sizes, shapes, and colors of blocks as well as the simple, elegant system of tabs and holes that enables them to be easily snapped together. These two basic elements—a *set of modules* and a *linkage system* that dynamically connects them—define the *modular architecture* that equips a company to mass customize.[2] This architecture determines what universe of benefits a company intends to provide for customers and, within that universe, what specific combinations of modules it will deliver at this time, to this particular customer. In the case of GNC's Custom VitaPaks, the modules are the standard vitamin pills and the linkage system is the way they flow from bulk storage into individual packets, the composition of which can differ greatly from consumer to consumer.

Mass customizers modularize their goods and services

Companies like Progressive Insurance that mass customize services build their modular architectures not out of tangible components but with process modules. Consider the Healthcare Support Services division of the managed services company ARAMARK. It created a program called INTERSERV that provides customized, integrated, nonclinical support services to hospitals. The company collaborates with its clients to design the specific process modules desired in the areas of food service (catering, menu distribution, etc.), distribution (patient transport, stocking of linen carts, etc.), maintenance (boiler room, carpentry, etc.), and environmental (discharge and cleaning, hose down, etc.). Together, company representative and client then redesign the overspecialized, functional-silo methods hospitals have traditionally used to create a customized, integrated, modular architecture that provides customer-unique value. Finally, Healthcare Support and the hospital develop a multiskilled, comprehensively trained workforce (which may include the hospital's personnel, ARAMARK's personnel, or, as often occurs, a combination) that operates as a team.

For each implementation, a local ARAMARK Resource Center maintains in a database descriptions of all team members, all process modules contracted by the hospital, and a list of which team members can execute which modules. It further classifies process modules as scheduled or unscheduled and interruptible or un-interruptible. This allows hospital personnel to schedule many tasks ahead of time yet still arrange for some tasks—such as "move this patient to X-Ray, stat"—to be requested and dispatched at any time. Whenever needed, the Resource Center software

(INTERSERV's linkage system) immediately determines which team member has the right skills, is performing an interruptible task, and is closest to the point of need. This person then receives a message via an on-premise pager system to perform the more pressing task.[3] In this way ARAMARK adjusts in real time to the facility's constantly changing needs, helping the hospital stage decidedly better patient experiences.

In addition to a modular architecture, Mass Customization requires an *environmental architecture*, again comprised of two elements: a *design tool* that matches buyer need with company capabilities, and a *designed interaction* within which the company stages a design experience that helps the customer decide exactly what he or she wants. Without this environmental architecture, companies often overwhelm potential buyers with so many combinations of modules that they can't figure out which one makes sense. Design tools such as ARAMARK's Resource Center software and GNC's Custom VitaPak brochure help to manage the complexity that, on the one hand, allows companies to tailor their products to individuals' needs but, on the other hand, gets in the way of customers determining exactly what they want.

In the early 1990s, window manufacturer Andersen Corp. of Bayport, Minnesota, developed a multimedia design tool called the Window of Knowledge to help its distributors collaborate with consumers. The computer software features an icon framework representing more than 50,000 possible window components that allow consumers and distributors to create and see exactly how potential designs will look. (The software also displays videos of beautiful, cloud-swept vistas in the background, making more than one customer respond, "Wow.")

Providing the design tool alone was not enough, however. Andersen found that success depended on training its distributors to use the tool itself and, just as important, to use it to interact with customers on a personal basis. Over several years, those distributors which were properly trained on the tool increased their sales of Andersen windows by more than 20 percent; those distributors which either did not accept the tool or did not accept the training that went with it actually decreased their sales of Andersen goods. The beauty of Andersen's approach lies in its ease of use: consumers can effortlessly sift through a seemingly limitless number of possibilities. Were it instead to present all of them, consumers certainly would find the interaction an unpleasant experience.

In situations with more limited possibilities, companies may *fully disclose* all possible combinations and let customers sort through them all. Such a "giant menu" approach need not be unpleasant. In fact, companies can make this interaction a unique experience by enriching the ways in which someone sorts through its menu or catalog, as when, for example, Land's End affixes Post-it Tape Flags in its catalogs to allow customers to easily mark pages before ordering.

Companies can disclose, reveal, or conceal all combinations of goods and services

A second approach to designed interaction *progressively reveals* the possibilities in segmented catalogs, fill-in-the-blank menus, selection matrices, configuration or design tools such as Andersen's, even the proverbial "blank sheet of paper." For its Custom VitaPaks, GNC uses a profiling method that depends on checklists, but then reveals all of the vitamin options only to those who want to go beyond the profile recommendations. For those who wish to delve even deeper, the Live Well stores also have a computer kiosk that lets customers ascertain the extent to which documented research supports the myriad beneficial claims made by the manufacturers of the products they are planning to buy. Design tools such as this give customers an opportunity to adjust selections until eventually determining exactly what each wants.

The third and final approach to designed interaction *deliberately conceals* the design tool from customers. Why would a mass customizer do such a thing? Because sometimes customers desire customer-unique value but do not want to be too involved in the decision-making process. Such is the case with the environmental architecture surrounding ARAMARK's Resource Center. The hospitals that turn over the activities have little interest in participating in moment-to-moment dispatching decisions. ARAMARK uses its design tool to respond with exactly the right combination of resources for each hospital need without intruding on patients or staff. Progressive also keeps to itself the proprietary Progressive Automated Claims Management System (dubbed PACMAN) that includes a design tool for claims adjusting. By not bothering their often agitated, dazed, or just plain embarrassed members with the details, the claims adjuster turns the normally loathsome interaction into an appreciated experience.

For these companies, Mass Customization presents a new stage on which to introduce experiential value to their customers. They identified the inadequacies of existing mass-produced goods and services, distinguished the individual characteristics of their customer bases, developed a modular architecture to efficiently serve their customers uniquely, and, finally, created an environmental architecture that used customization as the means to shift up the Progression of Economic Value. As a result, they now go beyond goods and services to offer what customers truly want.

WHAT *DO* CUSTOMERS WANT?

Most companies still resist mass customizing their offerings. Instead, they "manage the supply chain" by placing more and more variety into their distribution channels and leaving it to buyers to fend for themselves. Manufacturers maintain large inventories of finished goods, and service providers maintain excess personnel and provisions to meet an increasingly unwieldy number of potential demands. These practices offer a surefire way to add costs and complexity to operations.

Worse, customers must sort through numerous alternatives to find one that even approximates what they want. Increased variety may enable a few additional buyers to find a good or service that very closely matches their desires, but only at the expense of increased time sorting through alternatives—not an insignificant consideration given, for instance, the 35,000 stockkeeping units, or SKUs, in the typical supermarket. The vast majority of buyers, however, still fail to find an exact match. It all amounts to one bad experience after another.

Producing more and more variety in anticipation of potential, yet uncertain, demand often represents a last-ditch attempt to preserve the Mass Production mindset in the face of rapidly fragmenting markets. *But variety is not the same as customization.* Variety means producing and distributing product choices to outlets in the hope that some customer will come along and buy them. *Customization,* on the other hand, means producing in response to a particular customer's desires. So often businesses overwhelm customers with so much product proliferation that they throw up their hands and walk away rather than go through a lengthy decision-making process with little or no support. Fundamentally, customers do not want choice; they just want exactly what they want. A mass customizer's designed interaction with each individual provides the means for efficient, effective, and (as much as possible) effortless determination of customer needs. To shift up the Progression of Economic Value, whether from goods to services or services to experiences, companies must use such interactions to figure out exactly what their customers want.

Customers don't want choice; they just want exactly what they want

They must then bring that information about a customer's desires directly into operations for efficient, on-demand production or provisioning, effectively turning the old supply chain into a *demand chain.* Remember that mass customizing doesn't mean being everything to everybody; rather, it is doing *only and exactly* what each customer wants, when he wants it. Although a significant up-front investment may be required to develop the products, processes, people, and technologies required, mass-customized offerings may ultimately cost nearly the same as mass-produced ones, and sometimes less.

Take Hertz Corporation's #1 Club Gold Program as a case in point. The Gold customer, who is told the program costs $50 a year, with the first year free, receives the same basic vehicle as everyone else, but bypasses the line at the counter and need only give his name to the shuttle bus driver. He's then dropped off at the canopied Gold area, where he sees his name in lights on a large screen that directs him to the exact location of his car. When the customer arrives at his car, he finds the trunk open for luggage, his name noticeably printed on the personal agreement hanging from the mirror, and, when the weather demands it (and local laws permit it), the car's engine running with the heater or air conditioner turned on. By not doing anything until the customer steps on the bus and gives his name, and then doing only and exactly what each customer requires on demand, Hertz discovered that its Gold experience actually costs *less* to provide than its standard service. That's why it never asks for that $50-a-year membership fee, which in our view is a mistake. Companies should charge for the value they add, not the costs they incur. Moreover, that money could be used to make Hertz Gold a still richer rental car experience.

> **Companies should charge for the value they add, not the costs they incur**

Of course, determining what sort of customization would be worth a premium price is no easy task. Which features or benefits of the offering should be customized, and which left standard (such as the car, in Hertz's case)? Where in the value chain would buyers most prize customization? What key leverage points would provide the biggest bang for the buck? And what modular and environmental architectures would be most effective in creating memorable events?

To answer such questions, many companies turn to customer satisfaction, or "voice of the customer," surveys that use market research techniques to gather data. Such information provides a great foundation for understanding the *general* needs of one's customer base. However, these techniques do not go far enough to determine what and where a company should mass customize. After all, customer satisfaction really measures *market,* not individual customer, satisfaction. Few managers bother to scrutinize the individual results. They just view a few "CustSat" numbers that supposedly represent various market segments. They design surveys to ease tabulation, not to gain true insight into customer-specific wants and needs, and every customer who fills one out knows that he or she will gain no direct benefit.

Further, rarely do customer satisfaction surveys even ask for information about the particular needs and wants of whoever fills them out. Rather, they invariably ask buyers to rate how well the company or its personnel performed on a series of predefined categories. Managers gain precious little insight into what buyers truly want and need, as evidenced by what seems to be the most common theme of such surveys: How are *we* doing? What we are doing is inundating customers with incessant surveys that have little impact on what customers truly need. One airline questionnaire of this ilk even had a headline, incredibly, asking travelers to "Help Us Reinvent Our Airline"—an act that either overstates the impact of such generic customer input or underestimates the nature of corporate reinvention.

A MORE MEMORABLE MEASURE

As Dave Power III of J. D. Power & Associates says, "when we measure satisfaction what we're really measuring is the difference between what a customer *expects* and what the customer *perceives* he gets."[4] In other words,

$$\frac{\text{Customer}}{\text{satisfaction}} = \frac{\text{What customer}}{\text{expects to get}} - \frac{\text{What customer}}{\text{perceives he gets}}$$

Customer satisfaction measurements essentially focus on understanding and managing customer expectations of what companies already do rather than truly ascertaining what customers really want. While such measurements have their place, companies must do more than merely measure against perception to mass customize effectively. They must understand the nature of *customer sacrifice*—the gap between what a customer *settles for* and what he *wants exactly:*

$$\frac{\text{Customer}}{\text{sacrifice}} = \frac{\text{What customer}}{\text{wants exactly}} - \frac{\text{What customer}}{\text{settles for}}$$

When we understand customer sacrifice, we discern the difference between what a customer *accepts* and what he *really needs,* even if the customer doesn't know what that is or can't articulate it.

Waste occurs with activities or resources that some particular customer does not want

While companies employ total quality management (TQM) techniques to drive up customer satisfaction, they must employ Mass Customization techniques to drive down customer sacrifice. And while TQM programs help reduce the waste associated with mass-produced goods and services—by eliminating redundancies, bottlenecks, and other inefficiencies—focusing on customer sacrifice eliminates the waste that occurs anytime a business performs an activity or expends a resource that some particular customer does not want. Indeed, because TQM programs so often result in new features (of a good) or dimensions (of a service) geared to improving the satisfaction of the averred "average" customer, the solution for increased satisfaction becomes the source of additional sacrifice. No matter how many improvements are made, the offering remains uniform for all customers.

But individual customers differ in the exact combination of features or benefits they desire. They constantly face trade-offs, trying to decide if enough beneficial components exist to tolerate the marginal and offset the detrimental. Rarely do wants and needs match *exactly* the one bundle that comprises a company's product, so whenever a customer buys *any* mass-produced offering, he accepts the undesired components along with the desired, which means the company wasted resources in production or delivery. With products such as VCRs and video cameras, for example, manufacturers constantly add incremental features in the hope that some new one may prove desirably novel. The same dynamic occurs when a hotel furnishes every room with an iron and ironing board that go unused ninety-nine out of one hundred nights, or when most of those bags of pretzels and cans of soda an airline worker piles on a beverage cart end up right back in the galley.

Designing for the average is the root cause of customer sacrifice

Designing for the average is the root cause of customer sacrifice; every mass-produced product comprises a bundle of "take-it-or-leave-it" features or dimensions offered to all customers. The more features bundled, the greater the likelihood of introducing some element that disqualifies the product with a particular buyer (either because he flat out doesn't want the element or doesn't want to incur the perceived higher price for a marginal element). Similarly, talk about "designing for the customer" in many organizations really means designing for "the *average* customer"—who doesn't really exist. Unless people keep particular customers—real, specific, and known individuals—in view, such efforts only trigger initiatives to perform activities and expend resources without knowing the individual levels actually required.

Consider the airline industry. Customer sacrifice fills every flight across hundreds of service dimensions.[5] Let's examine, for simplicity's sake, a single dimension among many: the aforementioned beverage cart. Once a plane reaches a safe and comfortable cruising altitude, the beverage cart comes down the aisle, and the flight attendant asks, "Would you like something to drink?" A diehard Pepsi drinker would naturally request one, only to be asked (on most airlines), "Is Coke OK?" Backing off from his true desire, the customer generally accepts the Coke. He sacrifices. On the next two, three, or maybe four flights with the same airline, the same question, request, and answer arises. Finally catching on, the customer begins asking for—what?—Coca-Cola! Learning that the airline does not carry his favorite beverage, the airline finally trains him to *expect* an alternative.

Less customer sacrifice turns an ordinary service into a memorable event

Only then can the airline meet expectations. (And, of course, for those few airlines that offer Pepsi, the Coke drinkers sacrifice.)

To the airline, that individual represents another satisfied customer because he *always* receives what he expects. But underneath this faux satisfaction lies a source of innovation that can turn an ordinary airline service into a memorable event: the opportunity to help customers experience less sacrifice. Every time a provider of a good or service interacts with a customer, both parties have an opportunity to learn. Eventually, one party changes his behavior as a result of that learning. Unfortunately, all too often that's the customer. He starts asking for something other than what he really wants—or perhaps he simply goes away.

5 Experiencing Less Sacrifice

● ●

SOME BUSINESS COMMENTATORS say that conditioning customers (that is, coercing them to lower their expectations) to accept less than exactly what they want breeds good business practice, especially if a business reduces its costs without overly dissatisfying the customer. But herein lies another sure route to commoditization, for it unduly focuses the company on internal costs at the expense of customer needs. An attitude of "They won't mind" leads inevitably to operational practices replete with customer sacrifice. It also leads to *higher* costs if the company has sidestepped an opportunity to ascertain individual needs and eliminate wasteful practices.

The one airline that's working on tracking individual customer preferences not only for beverages but for meals, magazines, and other amenities is, not coincidentally, the one that focuses most on the guest experience: British Airways. Going online with a new software system from Industri-Matematik International in 1998, BA catering tracks the needs of more than 1,200 routes across 160 airports around the world to coordinate the right deliveries from more than 300 suppliers. The next step: downloading the individual preferences of the high-value customers it tracks to provide each with only and exactly the onboard services he desires. In the true spirit of Mass Customization, by doing only and exactly what each customer wants, BA not only turns its customized service into an individual experience, but *it lowers costs* to boot. How? Among other things, by eliminating the waste of both loading and especially carrying unused beverages, meals, and other items onto the airplane, where every pound of

81

weight adds to the cost of fuel burned. By linking its demand chain in this way, BA expects to save $5–8 million a year and to pay back its investment in the first year—and that's before it even begins to realize the individualized experience benefits.[1]

SEARCHING FOR UNIQUENESS

No longer should customers settle for standardized goods and services when companies can efficiently deliver, through mass customization techniques, only and exactly what each desires. If your company resists doing so, some competitor surely will soon, forever disrupting the dynamics of your industry. But early entrants often find that ascertaining customer needs that lie buried beneath the surface of countless "how did we do" surveys isn't easy. Indeed, customers have sacrificed for so long that they often have difficulty discussing their exact preferences. Even after the concept of sacrifice has been explained to them, most customers are unable to articulate the gaps between what they settle for and what it is, exactly, that they want.

Some skeptics cite this difficulty as evidence that customers cannot be counted on as sources for new ideas and innovation. The problem with customer input, however, doesn't derive from the inability of customers to identify and articulate their wants and needs; it stems from the context in which companies solicit that input. People tend to answer the questions posed to them. Often, their answers are as much a function of the Mass Production mindset that framed the questions as they are an accurate expression of customer needs. Harvard Business School professors Dorothy Leonard and Jeffrey F. Rayport, proponents of what they call "empathic design" (which is derived from watching customers in their *own* environments), say it this way: "Sometimes, customers are so accustomed to current conditions using company offerings that they don't think to ask for a new solution—even if they have real needs that could be addressed."[2]

Traditional research techniques—such as focus groups, "futures" scenarios, conjoint analysis, and yes, surveys—can still be leveraged to detect customer sacrifice. Just dust off your most recent research studies (which were likely searches for a *commonality* that would only point to shared— and preconditioned—expectations among customers), and examine them anew through a different lens: search for the *uniqueness* within the responses that suggests dimensions of sacrifice previously unnoticed or mistakenly thought insignificant. Even a single customer interaction can provide clues about an otherwise unarticulated sacrifice dimen-

Examine your research studies anew and search for uniqueness

sion across which all customers settle for less (or more) than what they want. Those thought to be "outliers" may in particular point to dimensions of sacrifice that "average" customers simply could not articulate.

Companies must also craft a new set of probes into customer behavior— "What do you really want?"—that displaces inquiries about satisfaction that ask merely, "How did we do?" For example, pneumatic valve producer Ross Controls of Troy, Michigan, asks its best customers (automakers, material-handling machine manufacturers, etc.) to work with its engineers (who are called "integrators" because they effectively combine the normally distinct functions of development, manufacturing, and marketing) to design the exact valve system that will create dramatic improvements in the customers' assembly-line performance. By focusing on the sacrifices customers currently face in their production lines, the integrator designs a prototype valve system starting from a library of modules. If the first prototype doesn't meet fully the customer's needs, he'll make adjustments and try another one, and often a third or fourth, until a customized valve system eliminates all the

> **Cyberspace provides a great new place for understanding sacrifice**

known sacrifice. Eventually, Ross wants to place this ROSS/FLEX service online to lower the costs of collaboration and to let customers participate in the design of their own valves.[3]

Cyberspace, in fact, because of its inherent interactivity, provides a great new place for understanding sacrifice. E-mail alone provides a wonderfully inexpensive means of interacting with customers to learn where they sacrifice. For example, every business morning NewsEDGE Corporation (formerly Individual, Inc.) of Burlington, Massachusetts, distributes to corporations purchasing its NewsPage service a customized database of online news, articles, and press releases covering more than 1200 topics. Individual users create custom profiles that sift through the 20,000 or so articles (across hundreds of original sources) to find the ten or twelve most relevant to their needs.

Inherent to this approach is the sacrifice of storing, viewing, and reading (or at least browsing) articles that turn out to be irrelevant to one's needs. To eliminate such sacrifice, for a fee, NewsEDGE will help users build individual profiles for filtering the corporate database, and then tweak the profiles every week or two based on which articles each user found relevant, which somewhat relevant, and which were not relevant at all. Instead of living with a once-and-done profile, as with most such services, corporate NewsPage subscribers watch the relevancy of the articles sent to them steadily increase until NewsEDGE finally achieves its goal of 80 to 90 percent relevancy, or just 10 to 20 percent sacrifice. If it tried to reach 100 percent, subscribers would experience a second form of sacrifice—they would not see a large number of relevant articles the company's software may have deemed too marginal to send along.[4] Helping customers experience less sacrifice in this way allows NewsEDGE to use its customized offering to build a stronger relationship with each customer.

CULTIVATING LEARNING RELATIONSHIPS

A rapidly expanding array of interactive technologies—including e-mail, pagers, electronic kiosks, online services, fax response, and the World Wide Web—is enabling companies to better learn the particular wants, needs, and preferences of thousands, and potentially millions, of individual customers. The combination of mass customization in operations with what marketing gurus Don Peppers and Martha Rogers call *one-to-one marketing* form the basis of a *learning relationship* that grows, deepens, and becomes smarter over time.[5] The more the customer teaches the company, the better it can provide exactly what he wants—and the more difficult it will be for competitors to lure him away. Even if a competitor were to build exactly the same capabilities, a customer already involved in a learning relationship with a firm would have to spend a considerable amount of time and energy teaching the competitor what the current firm already knows. That's why customers of Ross Controls remain so loyal to ROSS/FLEX. A $20 billion division of General Motors (the company that seems to have patented supplier squeezing) won't buy pneumatic valves from anyone else and won't let its suppliers go elsewhere either. James Zaguroli, Jr., president of Knight Industries, relates that when a competitor tried to win his business away from Ross, he told them, "Why would I switch to you? You're already five product generations behind where I am with Ross."

Mass customization and one-to-one marketing enable learning relationships

In effect, mass customizers that cultivate such learning relationships drive down a new learning curve, as seen in Figure 5-1. Everyone's familiar with the old learning curve in which costs come down with volume, the very basis of Mass Production. Here, customer sacrifice comes down

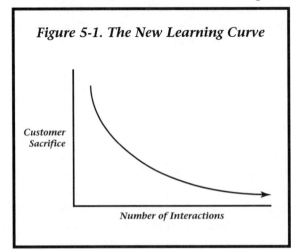

Figure 5-1. The New Learning Curve

Customer Sacrifice

Number of Interactions

over time as the company interacts with customers.[6] Think again about NewsEDGE. When a subscriber first starts receiving NewsPage, as few as 30 percent of the articles may be relevant, which means that as much as 70 percent of the articles are *irrelevant*—a measure of customer sacrifice at the beginning of this learning curve. As customers provide NewsEDGE with feedback, the relevancy goes up while the sacrifice comes down—until it reaches the flat part of the curve, where there's a sacrifice of only 10 to 20 percent (80 to 90 percent relevancy).

Sacrifice should decrease as a company interacts with customers

Now imagine that you are that NewsPage customer and a competitor comes along with *exactly the same capabilities* as NewsEDGE. It can search the same sources, deliver articles in the same way, even capture feedback and improve relevancy over time in the same way that NewsEDGE does. Would you switch? No way! It would take you *months* to teach this new company what NewsEDGE knows today. In the meantime, you would miss out on those relevant articles that the new company would neglect to send while still learning your needs.

In this way, firms can keep their customers forever—literally—with two provisos. One, the company doesn't excessively hike up its prices or cut back on service once in a learning relationship, and two, it doesn't miss the next technology wave. (A NewsPage-like service that relied solely on faxing articles, for example, would be dead in the water if it didn't move to the Internet as a delivery mechanism.) The advantages of this approach improve a company's fundamentals in some rather significant ways:

- *Premium prices.* Because your offerings are tailored precisely to customer needs, your customers receive greater value and, as a result, willingly pay a premium price.

- *Reduced discounts.* Every time you sell an offering at a discounted price, you in effect *pay* customers to experience greater sacrifice. The less they sacrifice, the less you must push the product at promotional prices or discard it outright.

- *Greater revenue per customer.* Because you know more about each customer than any competitor, they keep coming back to you every time they enter the market for what you offer.

- *Higher number of customers (at lower acquisition costs).* Because your customers find the experience so pleasing, they tell their friends and associates, many of whom will also want to do business with you. These new customers will tell others, and so on, and so on.

- *Increased customer retention.* The more each customer teaches you about his individual wants, needs, and preferences, the more difficult it will be for him to obtain an equivalent level of value from a competitor.

Most important, those companies which systematically reduce customer sacrifice—eliminating the negative cues of the relationship—heighten the experience their customers have when using their goods or partaking of their services, thus fulfilling needs left unaddressed by their mass-produced counterparts.

RESPONDING TO DIFFERENT KINDS OF SACRIFICES

Mass Customization bids return to an axiom frequently ignored in the homogenized world of Mass Production: *Each customer is unique,* and all deserve to have exactly what they want at a price they are willing to pay. Customers once were willing to subsume their uniqueness to benefit from the low prices of standardized offerings, but no longer. Companies must therefore efficiently and systematically reduce the customer sacrifice that occurs whenever a unique individual encounters standardized goods or services designed for some imaginary average. Surely no one-size-fits-all approach will serve to eliminate sacrifice—that would run contrary to the very notion of Mass Customization. Indeed, four different categories of sacrifice need attention. Each detracts from an individual's overall experience with a company's offering in a very specific way and this requires a different customization approach if it is to be eliminated.

All customers deserve to have exactly what they want at a price they are willing to pay

In response to individual customer sacrifice, mass customizers can change or not change the actual *product*—the functionalities of a good or the dimensions of a service. Similarly, they can change or not change the *representation* of the product—its description, packaging, marketing materials, placement, terms and conditions, name, stated use, or anything else outside of the good or service itself. (Whereas a company's modular architecture lies in the domain of the product itself, the environmental architecture lies in the domain of its representation.) As seen in Figure 5-2, these strategic choices yield four distinct approaches to customization: collaborative, adaptive, cosmetic, and transparent. Each is appropriate for reducing a different kind of sacrifice that, in turn, provides the basis for a particular type of experience.[7]

Collaborative Customization: The Exploring Experience

First, customers sacrifice when forced to make difficult and multidimensional *either-or* choices, such as length versus width, complexity versus functionality, or amount of information versus relevancy. The inability to resolve these trade-offs with mass-produced offerings propels many customers to work with mass customizers such as GNC Live Well, Andersen Windows, Ross Controls, and NewsEDGE, all of which employ *collaborative customization,* a process by which a company interacts directly with customers to determine what they need and then produces it for them. Collaborative customizers let customers explore ways to obtain what they desire in one dimension of the product without having to sacrifice in another dimension.

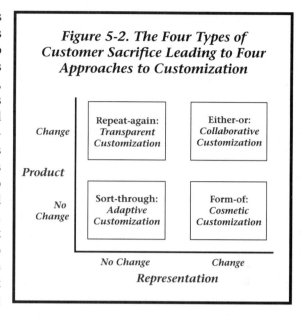

Figure 5-2. The Four Types of Customer Sacrifice Leading to Four Approaches to Customization

		No Change	Change
Product	Change	Repeat-again: *Transparent Customization*	Either-or: *Collaborative Customization*
	No Change	Sort-through: *Adaptive Customization*	Form-of: *Cosmetic Customization*
		No Change	Change
		Representation	

NewsEDGE's customers no longer must receive all articles to read one article; they read increasingly relevant news articles while reviewing fewer total pieces, and they may even experiment with the feedback they provide to see how it alters the selection of future articles. Ross Controls customers no longer must wait months for a new design specification. Instead, they explore with their ROSS/FLEX integrator potential improvements in their process lines through successive, rapidly manufactured prototypes. And Andersen Windows customers no longer have to wait for their homes to be built to see how the windows will look. Instead they get to see the final outcome on a computer screen after having explored myriad possibilities with an Andersen distributor. A host of celebrated companies—Dell in personal computers, The Hartford in insurance, Levi's with its Original Spin jeans, McGraw-Hill's Primis textbooks, to name but a few—embrace collaborative customization as a means of reducing the sacrifice so prevalent when customers face too much choice and unnecessary trade-offs. The end result: a new kind of design experience.

Consider choosing a pair of eyeglasses. Few people can walk into a store and easily figure out exactly what frames they want by wading through the row upon row of empty frames placed on shelf after shelf. Yet Japanese company Paris Miki draws exact eyewear specifications out of each interaction with consumers, thanks to collaborative customization.

The Tokyo-based company, one of the largest eyewear retailers in the world, spent five years developing the Mikissimes Design System. Called the Eye Tailor in the United States, this design tool both eliminates the customer's need to review myriad choices when selecting a pair of rimless eyeglasses and turns the design interaction into an *exploring experience.* The optician first takes a digital picture of the consumer's face, which the Eye Tailor analyzes for distinctive attributes. The system also takes into account a set of adjectives selected by the consumer about the kind of look he desires (formal, traditional, natural, sporty, elegant, etc.).

Collaborative customizers work with their customers to determine what they need and then produce it for them

The system then recommends a distinctive lens size and shape and displays the lenses on the digital image of the consumer's face. But this just begins the exploration. The consumer and optician next collaborate to adjust the shape and size of the lenses (by rotating, enlarging, or even using a mouse to create a new curve) until both like the look. In similar fashion, they together select from a number of options for the nose bridge, hinges, and arms until the customer discovers the pair of eyeglasses he desires—exactly. The final step: The optician presents a photo-quality picture of the customer wearing a pair of eyeglasses that have yet to be produced! (One more thing: The customer receives the actual glasses, mass customized, in as little as an hour.)

Collaborative customizers work with individual customers to change first the *representation* of the product and then, once the customer figures out his true needs, the product itself. Customer and customizer thus mutually determine the value to be created. The customizer relinquishes some control of the process, allowing the buyer to participate directly in decision making and even some of the set-up work. As Greg Horn, chief marketing officer at GNC, relates, "Our in-store experience involves customers with products that they designed, creating a level of individual commitment to 'their' product that far exceeds any other method." The seemingly necessary trade-offs found in selecting and using most mass-produced goods vanish when a customer more richly explores his unique needs in this way. Ideally, in addition to getting exactly what he wants, the customer uncovers aspects of his own wants and needs that he never knew existed.

Adaptive Customization: The Experimenting Experience

The second generic kind of customer sacrifice occurs when customers are presented with too many finished goods or too many component parts and must engage in an unwieldy *sort-through* process. Here, companies should adopt the approach of *adaptive customization.* In this case, neither the product itself nor the representation of the product is changed for the individual customer; rather, the customer customizes the good or service as desired using customizable functionality embedded into the offering.

If the universe of customer demand spans an enormous set of possibilities, it's imperative to use some form of adaptive customization. For example, Lutron Electronics Co., Inc. of Coopersburg, Pennsylvania, makes lighting controls (switches, dimmers, etc.) that allow for an immense degree of customer-unique variation. With the exception of cookie-cutter buildings, such as franchise restaurants, every customer's environment is unremittingly different.[8] The shape, decor, and window placement of each room vary. Additionally, weather conditions affecting external light change from day to day and hour to hour, as does the composition of people in the room and the way those people use it. So, while Lutron collaborates with customers on some issues (such as matching colors of switch plates), it makes use of adaptive customization by having customers experiment with the lighting system itself in their own office or home. The company's Grafik Eye System, for example, connects different lights in a room and lets users test and then program different effects for, say, lively parties, romantic moments, or quiet evenings of reading. Rather than having to adjust separate light switches for each use, customers spend time up front programming settings until they find the right combinations. They then achieve the desired effects merely by punching in the programmed settings each time they use the room.

Collaboration remains the right approach when each customer must choose from a vast number of elements or components to get the desired functionality or design. When alternative combinations can be built into the product, however, adaptive customization becomes a promising alternative for efficiently making many different options available to each customer. And the process of *experimenting* with the possibilities becomes an experience to itself. For example, Select Comfort of Minneapolis, Minnesota, designs and manufactures mattresses with air chamber systems that automatically adjust to the body contour of anyone who lies on them. Using a handheld remote control, people can play with various levels of firmness, and couples can even select different levels on each side of the bed. Similarly, Peapod, an on-line grocery-shopping and delivery service based in Evanston, Illinois, eliminates the "sort-through" sacrifice inherent in going to a grocery store filled with aisle after aisle of items. Its PC software and online service enable customers first to store only those items they want to peruse in one or more personal shopping lists. These lists can be

Adaptive customizers offer one product designed to let users alter it themselves

recalled at a moment's notice, while for less frequent purchases customers can search product information through various sorting methods (such as price, brand, or nutritional content).

With adaptive customization, the customer independently derives his or her own value. Adjustable controls, as represented in Lutron's programmable settings, Select Comfort's handheld device, and Peapod's software, allow customers to experiment time and again with different combinations and permutations. Once done, they no longer have to sort through all the alternatives each time they want to use the good or access the service. As Joel Spira, chairman of Lutron Electronics and the inventor to first put a microprocessor in a lighting control, says, "Creating adaptive controls differentiates us from the competition, and the way we do it lets customers easily and even enjoyably figure out the settings right for them." This approach to Mass Customization, fundamentally different from collaborative customization, also creates customer-unique value.[9] The adjustable nature of the designed interaction with the product itself promotes the experimentation required to find that value.

Cosmetic Customization: The Gratifying Experience

When customers sacrifice not on the basis of a product's functionality but its form—in terms of how it is packaged or presented, where or when it is delivered—then companies can exploit *cosmetic customization*. Based on what we call the *form-of* sacrifice, this third approach presents a standard good or service differently to different customers. The product is not customized (as with collaborative) or made customizable (as with adaptive); instead, a standard offering is *packaged* specially for each customer. By wrapping the good in a customized representation—perhaps through custom packaging, tailored marketing materials, personal placement on delivery, private labeling, or personalization of other stated terms and conditions—each customer obtains the ego-gratifying experience of seeing the item personalized "just for me."

Hertz does this with its #1 Club Gold Program. Each customized element alters only the representation of its rental cars, not the base product itself. Yet it is enjoyed by customers because each instance of customized packaging clearly shows that the company values the customer. Similarly, Austin-James of Menlo Park, California, created a simple but exceedingly effective design tool for customizing illustrations on T-shirts, caps, tote bags, and just about anything else on which anyone would want to place a logo, image, or other form of drawing. With the company's Hanes T-Shirt-maker software (developed in concert with Hanes, the famous T-shirt maker), a consumer can create personalized T-shirts at home. The PC software displays a picture of a T-shirt with the space available for an illustration. It then guides him through selection of one or more pictures (from a portfolio provided by the company or from pictures the consumer scans in) and accompanying text (including a choice of fonts, colors, and effects such as displaying the lettering across an arc). All the while, the consumer sees the changing digital representation of his work-in-progress until the design finally meets with his approval. The software then prints the illustration onto special paper through the customer's laser or inkjet printer, which is then ready to be ironed onto a provided T-shirt. Very quick, very simple, very "me."

Cosmetic customizers present a standard good or service differently to different customers

In the business-to-business arena, Whirlpool Corporation successfully wrapped its next-day delivery program, called Quality Express, around its standard Whirlpool, KitchenAid, and Roper appliance lines to create customer-unique value. Originally, dealers could order any quantity of appliances they wanted—as long as it was a full truckload. This meant that dealers couldn't always tell consumers when their appliances would arrive, as it depended on what and when others would order. Now the company schedules each distributor for five, four, three, two, or one delivery per week, based on annual volume, and efficiently delivers exactly the right set of appliances each dealer ordered (thanks to a sophisticated logistics system, that integrates manufacturing plants, regional warehouses, local distribution centers, and contract trucks via real-time information). Furthermore, because Quality Express can deliver every day, Whirlpool uses the service to accommodate customers that have an unusual need outside of their normal schedule, with a focus on making each dealer feel special. Quality Express also adds other tailored services to personalize each delivery. At home-builder sites, for instance, uniformed drivers de-crate boxes, rearrange door swings, and install ice makers immediately before mortgage closings. The drivers even call from cellular phones en route to make sure the dealers prepare for the delivery.

For many companies, cosmetic customization provides a starting point from which to offer customers a personalized experience. While the basic functionality of their product remains the same, cosmetic customizers signal an acknowledgment of the diverse "form-of" requirements found among their customers. They postpone many activities in order to perform them before the observant eye of the customer, who feels that the performance is being staged just for him. As Ralph Hake, senior executive vice president of operations at Whirlpool, says about Quality Express, "The value we provide to our distributors is visibly demonstrated whenever they see our truck coming down the road, and in every added service we perform for them, with them, or in front of them." Whether delivering appliances to distributors, graphics on T-shirts, or people to rental cars, this approach admittedly appeals to the desire for self-gratification inherent in each one of us. By customizing the representation of a standardized offering, the customizer gives its customers personalized attention.

Transparent Customization: The Elusive Experience

Finally, when customers must perform the same task or provide the same information repeatedly, they encounter *repeat-again* sacrifice. Such impositions only serve to bother customers and detract from their overall experience. In such cases, *transparent customization* does the trick, providing individual customers with a tailored offering *without* letting them know explicitly (through representational changes) that it is customized for them.

ChemStation, a manufacturer and distributor of industrial cleaning goods, transparently customizes the formulation of individual cleaning products for a wide variety of commercial uses—from car washes and truck depots to restaurant kitchens and paper mills. It doesn't bother sharing the details regarding the particular compounds used to address a customer's cleaning needs. Instead, it tacitly formulates exactly the right combination for each customer and then represents everyone's customized good as being the same "ChemStation Solution." Every customer even gets the same company logo emblazoned on the side of every storage tank. As a result, customers focus more on how nice and clean their facility is and less on the specific attributes of the supporting product, the exact nature of which remains elusive.

Transparent customizers fulfill the needs of individual customers in an indiscernible way. Instead of requiring customers to take the time to describe their needs, transparent customizers, including Barista Brava in coffee production and GNC Live Well in VitaPak delivery, observe behaviors over time to determine predictable preferences and then presciently fulfill those preferences. Of course, a business must have the luxury of time to deepen its knowledge of customers and to move progressively closer to meeting individual preferences. To become a transparent customizer, a business also must have a standard package—a Barista Brava coffee cup, UPS box, or ChemStation tank—into which it places the product's customized features or components. In this way, transparent customization is the exact opposite of cosmetic customization, which has standard content but a customized package.

Businesses ripe for transparent customization include those that have customers who don't want to be bothered with direct collaboration, often because the company asks them to repeat information they've already provided. For example, to avoid annoying customers by asking the same standard questions every time they check in to a Ritz-Carlton hotel ("King size or two doubles? Smoking or nonsmoking?"), the chain established a less intrusive means of learning about individual needs. Its associates *observe* the preferences that individual guests manifest or state during each stay, whether it be for hypoallergenic pillows, contemporary jazz radio stations, or Pepsi instead of Coke. The company then stores that information in a

> **Transparent customizers provide a tailored offering without customers knowing that it is customized for them**

database and uses it to form a learning relationship with individual guests, thus eliminating unnecessary service intrusions on subsequent visits. The more frequently someone stays in Ritz-Carlton hotels, the more the company learns, and the more customized goods and services it fits into the standard Ritz-Carlton room, thereby increasing the guest's preference for that hotel over others.

The Ritz chose transparent customization specifically because its management wants to create a "mystique" around the fulfilling of guests' individual preferences. How the hotel does it may elude them, but guests discover they've had a particularly pleasant experience when they stay at a Ritz-Carlton. Similarly, ChemStation founder George Homan hit upon this form of customization because he realized his potential customers all want to run their business, not manage their industrial soap: "We want them to discover the value we provide as they're using the soap, not think about what it is or how it gets there. We don't want our customers to ever think about how our product gets there, only that it always *is* there." Every order for soap, as with every request at a hotel, is a routine sacrifice. In any industry, those companies which practice transparent customization eliminate unwanted intrusions, simplifying interactions to let customers discover the offering's essential nature.

Choosing the Right Approach

Which approach should you choose? There's no simple answer to that question. As summarized in Table 5-1, not only does each of the four types of customization address a different kind of sacrifice, but each acts as the basis for a distinct kind of experience. Manufacturers and service providers must discern the uniqueness of their offerings, ascertain the sacrifices their customers currently experience, and then identify which form of customization will yield the best results. Often a combination of approaches is needed to address complex sacrifice issues.

Table 5-1. Customization Distinctions

	Customization Approach			
Characteristic	**Collaborative**	**Adaptive**	**Cosmetic**	**Transparent**
Sacrifice addressed	Either-or	Sort-through	Form-of	Repeat-again
Nature of offering	Customized	Customizable	Packaged	Packable
Nature of value	Mutually determined	Independently derived	Visibly demonstrated	Indiscernibly fulfilled
Process characteristics	Sharable	Adjustable	Postponable	Predictable
Nature of interaction	Direct	Indirect	Overt	Covert
Method of learning	Conversation	Solicitation	Recognition	Observation
Basis of experience	Exploring	Experimenting	Gratifying	Discovering

More important, why choose to customize at all? Very simple: Customizers stage fundamentally different experiences for customers. They *ing* the thing. Collaborative customizers NewsEDGE and Paris Miki create new newspaper-*reading* and eyeglass-*viewing* experiences. Adaptive customization yields unique Lutron *lighting,* Select Comfort *sleeping,* and Peapod grocery-*shopping* experiences. Hertz offers a distinctive car-*renting* experience through cosmetic customization, while Whirlpool uses this approach to stage a revolutionary new appliance-*delivering* experience for retail dealers and home builders. ChemStation, on the other hand, uses transparent customization to enhance the soap-*dispensing* experience, while Ritz-Carlton uses the same approach to turn a room into a truly memorable *lodging* experience.

All mass customizers create new value in the new Experience Economy. Rival mass producers, lacking any distinctive approach to eliminating customer sacrifice, will quickly find their offerings commoditized. We heard it best expressed some years ago by a Pennzoil Products Company executive who feared the day when people would say "Motor oil is motor oil is motor oil." Such a fate awaits any company that doesn't get its act together by helping customers experience less sacrifice.

A Refreshing Experience

● ●

WHEN SIR COLIN MARSHALL first realized that British Airways was really in the business of orchestrating experiences, he thought that the "wear-out factor" for the BA brand was "somewhere in the five-year range. Now I am pretty convinced that five years is about the maximum that you can go without refreshing the brand."[1] Actually, experience stagers must constantly refresh their experiences—change or add elements that keep the offering new, exciting, and worth paying money to experience all over again. Failing to do so denigrates the offering. Rather than an experience that remains the same between visits, people would rather try a new one where they don't know quite what to expect and are sure to be pleasantly surprised.

That's why the repeat business at some theme restaurants, the Rainforest Cafe and Planet Hollywood, in particular, is so poor; Guests know exactly what to expect each time, both in the restaurants and the retail stores. Restaurateur T. Scott Gross, who wrote a series of insightful books on what he calls "positively outrageous service," describes a strikingly simple way to surprise diners. He tells of Philip Romano, founder of Fuddrucker's and more recently the take-out food store eatZi's, opening an out-of-the-way Italian restaurant named Macaroni's.[2] Rather than issue discount coupons to encourage new patronage (a ubiquitous, expectation-setting practice among many restaurant chains these days), Romano gave away free meals to every diner in the restaurant once each month on a Monday or Tuesday. The random practice remained unannounced until a letter arrived at each table in place of the check, saying how awkward it seemed to charge guests for a meal, so this one was free. Whereas most restaurants might extend such generosity only when customers have experienced poor service or a bad meal (when some recompense is expected), Romano's restaurant did so only after guests had been very well served with very good food (and guests expected nothing more than to pay their check). The surprise of the free meal created both a desire and a sense of obligation in guests to return again . . . and again . . . and again. Gross figured that surprising customers in this way cost Romano perhaps 3.3 percent of his monthly gross, while it had a much greater impact on customers than an ad budget of that size or a 3.3 percent discount across the board. It turned an already good dinner service into a memorable experience.

STAGING CUSTOMER SURPRISE

Reducing customer sacrifice through Mass Customization requires an awareness of individual customer needs and the behavior they influence. This awareness lets companies deliberately and systematically take the next step toward more experiential offerings by instigating *customer surprise,* which is perhaps the single most important ingredient needed by any manufacturer or service provider to begin staging memorable experiences.

Contrasted with both customer satisfaction and sacrifice, when companies stage customer surprise they exploit the difference between what the customer *gets to perceive* and what the customer *expects to get.*

$$\text{Customer surprise} = \text{What customer gets to perceive} - \text{What customer expects to get}$$

Rather than merely meeting expectations (by providing satisfaction) or setting new ones (by reducing sacrifice), companies deliberately attempt to *transcend* expectations, to go off in new (and unexpected) directions entirely. This doesn't mean trying to "exceed" expectations, for that would suggest an improvement along a known axis of competition, nor does it mean uncovering new dimensions on which to compete; those are the domains of satisfaction and sacrifice, respectively. Rather, it means *staging the unexpected.*

Creating such events still requires a platform of satisfaction and sacrifice. As indicated in Figure I-1, without concerted and fruitful efforts to drive up customer satisfaction and drive down customer sacrifice, there will be no foundation on which to instigate customer surprise. Companies embracing the 3-S Model shown in this figure must go beyond "how we did" and even "what you want" to "what you *remember.*"

The most memorable flight experiences, for example, have nothing to do with the expectations of normal—good or bad—airline service but with events that occur outside the domain of expectations. These may include times you have read a particularly eye-opening book, met a celebrity, or become totally engaged in conversation with a seatmate.

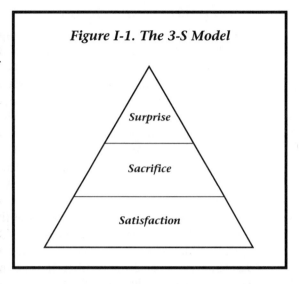

Figure I-1. The 3-S Model

Surprise

Sacrifice

Satisfaction

The Rev. Jim Ignatowski. Recognize the name? On one episode of the old TV show *Taxi,* this usually atrocious (but fun-loving) cabbie decided to become the best taxi driver in the world. He did it by surprising his patrons with totally unexpected events: He served sandwiches and drinks, engaged them in sparkling repartee, conducted tours of the city, and even sang Frank Sinatra tunes over a jury-rigged intercom. So engaging was Iggy's use of customer surprise that the experience of being *in* his cab yielded greater value to his customers than the service of being transported *by* the cab from point A to point B. And in the TV show, at least, Iggy's customers happily responded with bigger tips. By asking to go around the block again just to prolong his enjoyment, one patron even paid *more* for demonstrably *poorer* service—after all, it took longer to get to his destination. The service Iggy provided, taxi transportation, was simply the stage for the experience that he was really selling that week.

Real-world entrepreneurs also employ surprise to turn mundane services into truly memorable events. Consider one of the most basic of businesses, the shoeshine stand. Based in the airport of Kalamazoo, Michigan, Aaron Davis—not only a great shoeshine man but showman as well—uses customer surprise in many ways. In addition to his meticulous touch when applying polish and the syncopated snaps of his cloth, sensations rare but not unique to Davis, he introduces elements to the shoeshine experience that have little or nothing to do with polishing shoes. If he finds a loose thread on a stitch, Davis produces a pocket lighter to burn it off. And at the conclusion of the shine, he not only ties the guest's laces but then gently pulls up his socks. Davis also offers proverbs to guests in need of a pick-me-up. And should a

Managers must leverage some service dimension to stage memorable surprises

hurried traveler who regularly gets a shine fail to stop by one week, the very next shine is, as Davis says, "On me." From then on, such travelers make sure they leave enough time to take in a shine.

Unfortunately, larger enterprises often lack the surprise savvy of smaller businesses. But bigness begs no excuse. Managers must stop setting routine expectations and start thinking creatively about how to leverage some service dimension to stage memorable surprises. Why do airlines upgrade only their most frequent current flyers to first class? That well-dressed college kid flying to New York for an interview with a consulting firm, for whom he will fly every week in his imminent career, may be the best person to surprise with a seat in front of the curtain. A hotel could occasionally place a storage canister, the kind resembling a can of soda, in minibars so that a surprised guest may discover, say, a roll of fifty one-dollar bills inside with a note confirming that the guest may keep the money, compliments of the host. Wouldn't that create greater loyalty, repeat business, and guest referrals than issuing discount certificates via direct mail campaigns?

Companies should also rethink rebates. Automobile manufacturers, for instance, further commoditize their own products via constant rebate promotions—buy this or that model, get $1,000 back—setting expectations that focus prospects purely on price. Some 90 percent of car owners claim to be satisfied, according to an Arthur D. Little survey, yet car buyers defect by the millions each year. Only 40 percent buy their next car from the same manufacturer (let alone the same model) that supposedly "satisfied" them the last time. Surprise payments sent unexpectedly to car buyers—after the purchase—rewarding them for their selections would do more to generate repeat sales. Rebates assume a one-period model in a multiperiod world; surprise programs always help the company to influence the buyer's next decision.

Frequent purchase programs serve to commoditize offerings

Consider too the many "frequent purchase" programs sponsored across a wide spectrum of businesses, from airlines to parking garages, from credit card companies to coffee bars. Designed to foster customer loyalty, these programs in fact have a fatal flaw: they encourage customers to expect free goods and services. While some increased purchasing frequency may be stimulated by giving away merchandise (in what's essentially a retailing equivalent of the old manufacturing line, "What we lose on each customer we'll make up in volume"), many customers join multiple programs within a given product category, and they all know that other customers can participate in the same programs. Customers are simply not engaged on a personal level, and over time, they take the benefits for granted—after all, they "earned" their free stuff. Like rebates, this serves merely to commoditize a company's offerings.

Instead of leading customers to expect free goods, companies could use the same money to create a memorable experience. Like Romano, these companies could give away the same percentage of items at random on certain days. Every fifteenth or twentieth item could be free, for instance, or every fifteenth or twentieth customer could receive all their items for free. Alternatively, a store's register system could transparently inform the sales associate that this particular customer is highly valued and should be surprised with a purchase on the house.

WAIT UNTIL YOU HEAR THIS ONE. . . .

To truly differentiate themselves, businesses must focus first on increasing customer satisfaction, then on eliminating customer sacrifice, and finally on creating customer surprise. Taking these three steps will help shift any company up the Progression of Economic Value. But—surprise!—there's actually a fourth S in the 3-S Model. Once a company successfully stages customer surprise, customers start *expecting* to be surprised. There's nothing wrong with that, as long as the company then stages *customer suspense* as well. Built on a platform of surprise, customer suspense is the gap between what the customer *remembers* from past surprises and what he *does not yet know* about upcoming events:

$$\text{Customer suspense} = \text{What customer does not yet know} - \text{What customer remembers from past}$$

One example should suffice to demonstrate customer suspense. Gold Premier flyers with Continental Airlines (those who travel 50,000 miles or sixty segments per year) receive an elaborately packaged kit containing priority baggage check tags, upgrade coupons, a frequent flyer program guide, and other incidental reference material. The first year a customer receives this unadvertised package, he is indeed pleasantly surprised. In year two, Continental may manage to surprise a few customers (those who forgot last year's package). But for Continental's consistently high-traveling customers, after three, four, or five years of receiving the same old kit . . . well, they not only come to expect it, they consider it a ho-hum occasion. Now suppose that Continental cleverly changes the contents each year, one year adding a humorous letter from the chairman (à la Warren Buffet's annual stockholder letters), the next a gift gleaned from knowledge about the past year's travel (for instance, a subscription to *Elle* magazine, a free dinner at a restaurant in the frequent destination city, a fine cigar or bottle of wine), and the next maybe even a new piece of luggage to replace the one worn out by such frequent travel. Then Continental's very best customers would happily look forward to the next package rather than be bored by its inevitable arrival. This suspense, built on "how we did," "what you want," and "what you remember," creates a sense of anticipation that encourages customers to actively look forward to doing more business with Continental—"what will happen"—just to make darn sure they maintain that Gold status and get next year's package.[3]

When managed in unison, satisfaction, sacrifice, surprise, and suspense help companies encourage buyers to purchase goods and services for fundamentally new and different reasons. No longer do customers purchase goods merely for their functional use but also for the experiences created during purchase and use. Similarly, clients do not buy services merely for the sake of having a function delivered by another party but for the memorable events surrounding those services.

In the emerging Experience Economy, companies must realize that they make *memories*, not goods, and create the *stage* for generating greater economic value, not deliver services. It is time to get your act together, for goods and services are no longer enough. Customers now want experiences, and they're willing to pay admission for them. There's new work to do, and only those who perform that work so as to truly engage their guests will succeed in this new economy.

6 *Work Is Theatre*

● ●

BARBRA STREISAND HAD NOT YET gotten her act together as an aspiring actress and singer when she tried out for Harold Rowe's musical *I Can Get It for You Wholesale.* In his book *Audition,* casting director Michael Shurtleff relates how he thought the then-unknown actress was ideal for the role of Miss Marmelstein.[1] He was concerned, however, that Streisand's prominent nose would not get past producer David Merrick, who had told him, "I don't want any ugly girls in my show." Despite the admonition, or perhaps because of it, Shurtleff scheduled Streisand for the last audition slot.

Streisand, draped in a gaudy raccoon coat and wearing mismatched shoes, walked in late, chewing gum. (She found the "fabulous" shoes at a thrift shop on the way to the audition, Streisand explained to Shurtleff, Merrick, and director Arthur Laurents, but only one of each pair fit.) Curtly, she ordered a stool brought on stage. Once settled on the stool, she began to sing, but stopped unexpectedly after just a few notes. She started and stopped again, this time to remove her gum and stick it beneath the seat of the commandeered stool. Finally, she sang the full number and, as Shurtleff put it, "She mesmerized 'em." She then sang two more tunes and left. After a heated argument, Merrick succumbed to the wishes of Shurtleff and Laurents: Streisand got the part. As the three prepared to leave, Laurents, who had taken a seat on the stool, ran his hand underneath it, because he had noticed that Streisand had failed to retrieve her gum. To his surprise, there was no gum! Chomping so visibly—during the audition—was *an act of pure theatre.* She wasn't chewing gum in order to calm her nerves but to create a specific impression on the potential buyers of her theatre skills.

One can only speculate as to why Streisand chose this particular set of behaviors to portray her character on stage. Perhaps she wanted to make the impression "I can *sing* it for you wholesale," or "Appearances don't matter—it's the vocal cords that count," perhaps even "It ain't over 'til the ugly lady sings." Her tactics launched what became, by any measure, a remarkable career. Whatever her motivation, even during her humble beginnings, she understood the secret to her later success: recognizing that each and every action contributes to the total experience being staged, no matter what the venue. Businesses entering the Experience Economy must be no less deliberate.

Every action contributes to the total experience being staged

Consider the business of baseball. Perhaps no professional sport manages its business as poorly as Major League Baseball. Yet the remarkable turnaround of one its franchises, the Cleveland Indians, attests to the value of theatre in deliberately staging engaging experiences. On April 4, 1994, a new era of financial prosperity was ushered into the once-downtrodden enterprise. On that date, the Indians played the Seattle Mariners in their first official game in Jacobs Field, a new $175 million stadium built specifically to showcase professional baseball. Prior to 1994, fewer than 5,000 season ticket packages were purchased annually by Cleveland fans. Now, all 43,368 seats for each of eighty-one home games sell out each season by the preceding Christmas. Of course, the new stadium does not by itself account for the entire jump in sales; other teams have built new facilities and have not met with nearly the same success. The difference? The Cleveland Indians management, led by owner Dick Jacobs and general manager John Hart, recognized that Jacobs Field presented the business with a new stage for enacting deliberate performances of its own.

That crisp day in April 1994 was not, in fact, the first time the Indians played a game in the new ballpark. It happened two days earlier when the team contested the Pittsburgh Pirates in an exhibition game. A full house, made up of many of the same individuals who would later attend Opening Day, poured into Jacobs Field on a Saturday afternoon to get their first taste of the new Indians and their first view of the new ballpark. The event did not threaten to spoil the thrill of attending the first official game because this was a dress rehearsal, a chance for fans to preview the new Indians extravaganza.

Just outside the park, a uniformed man busied himself with a broom and dustpan-on-a-stick, sweeping the sidewalk immediately adjacent to the East Ninth Street entrance. His blue pants and red-and-white striped shirt stood out among the passing crowd, clearly demonstrating that this street sweeper worked as an employee of the ballpark. Many people witnessed the seemingly small act, but few paused to examine the extraordinary nature of his gestures: his whisks gathered no debris, for the place *already* sparkled! After all, the grounds couldn't very well get dirty when no one had yet visited. So why did the man perform this work? For the same reason Streisand chewed her nonexistent gum: his was *an act of pure theatre.* He did not sweep in order to clean the pavement but to create a specific impression on the passing parade of first-time customers. After playing for sixty-two years in Cleveland Municipal Stadium, the ball club had directed this individual to don his costume and sweep in order to support the Indians' new theme: "There Is No Place Like Home"—that is, to show ticketholders that the new ballpark was clean, safe, comfortable, and eager to come to life. No repeat of the Indian "product" fielded in bygone years, this was the dawn of a completely new offering, what the club calls, of course, "The Jacobs Field Experience."[2]

THE ACT OF ACTING

Political commentator and avid baseball fan George Will has helped many casual observers of baseball to see the game differently in his punctilious book *Men at Work.* His single-minded point: "Professional baseball is work,"[3] demanding mental as well as physical exertion of those who take the field. Will strove to encourage a greater appreciation of the game by persuading readers of one fact: The players are working. Major League Baseball, the business, furnishes the workplace. Players practice, analyze past performances, and constantly adjust the way they go about their duties. These star performers share the stage with extras, who, like the sweeper at Jacobs Field, labor in more minor roles.

All business, as well as the work that defines it, from executive suites to factory floors, demands the same kind of performance as that featured on Broadway and in ballparks. In the Experience Economy, performers of all sorts—executives, managers, and other laborers—must take a different view of their occupations. Work is theatre. Think about it. Pause. Reflect. And now say it aloud: Work *is* theatre.

In acknowledging this truth, we strive not to detail every nuance of theatre, nor to provide a comprehensive list of theatre how-to's. Neither can we resolve any number of alternative and/or conflicting views of how theatre is best conducted. Rather, we simply aim to share enough about theatre to persuade you to think differently about your work

Business performances must rival those featured on Broadway and in ballparks

and to embrace some principles of theatre as your model for work in the Experience Economy.[4]

Let us be very clear: We do not mean to present work *as* theatre. It is not a metaphor but a model. We do not apply the principles of theatre to work merely to force new comparisons. Too many metaphors already litter the contemporary business landscape. We have no interest in dancing with elephants, swimming with sharks, toppling the pyramids, jumping the curve, or pursuing any other kind of mismanagement-by-metaphor that all too often distracts executives and managers from the real issues they face.

Theatre is not a metaphor but a model

Rather, we seek to focus attention on the quintessentially dramatic nature of an enterprise. Thus, we literally mean: Work *is* theatre.

The word "drama" derives from the Greek *drao,* meaning simply "to do." In all companies, whether managers recognize it or not, the workers are playing, not in some game but in what should be a well-conceived, correctly cast, and convincingly portrayed real-life drama of *doing.* Indeed, understanding this crucial point brings whole new meaning to oft-used business terms borrowed from or shared with the performing arts, such as production, performance, method, role, scenario, and a host of others.

Studies of theatre often begin with Aristotle's profound *Poetics.*[5] It is the foundation of our Western understanding of theatre, even with its emphasis on literary forms. Aristotle's notion of plot—what he called "the arrangement of the incidents"—forms the basis of any staged experience and the sequencing of cues required to create a desired impression. And his components of plot—surprising reversals, progressive revelation of knowledge, unity and balance of events, and the emotional effect of tragedy—explain much about what makes an experience memorable. Likewise, his prerequisites for a compelling portrayal—good choices, befitting the role played, and consistency within character—delineate suitable job qualifications for anyone cast in the staging of an experience. Indeed, in defining theatre, Aristotle differentiated it from all other daily activities. Consider some of the theatre concepts advanced by Aristotle and their implications for work.[6]

First and foremost is the issue of *choice.* Acts of theatre demand that boundaries be drawn; actors must formulate and pose tough questions that no one else can ask or answer for them; and they must discern the significant from the insignificant elements in any play performed. Even those businesses which do not yet stage experiences must understand that whenever employees work in front of customers, an act of theatre occurs. What should occur on that stage, and what should be relegated to off-stage activities? One grocery clerk talking over a customer's head to the clerk in the next aisle about what they're going to do after work may seem to them insignificant, but for the customer it is an act of indifference. So what acts make for compelling theatre? The grocery clerk should ask himself how he might scan the canned goods with flair, what dramatic voice and entertaining words he might use when asking for a credit card, and especially how to perform the personal touches that come with exchanging cash, credit card, or receipt. The most important questions are often those for which no answer appears readily available, but you know an answer would prove invaluable to your performance.

Whenever employees work in front of customers, an act of theatre occurs

Second, consider the *sequence, progression,* and *duration* of events. How are work activities arranged? What continuums exist in the organization of events? Where does work begin, reach a dramatic climax, and have its denouement? Consider an office sales call. When does it begin? When the sales representative makes an appointment with a secretary, the moment he arrives on site, as he waits outside the door, or only upon making eye contact with the prospect? Different answers yield decidedly different performances. Once face-to-face with the prospect, how should the event proceed? With small talk? Or should the rep dispense with that and get right down to business? What sequence of discussion points—call them sales scenes—should be painted in the mind of the prospect over the course of the call? What's the best way to move toward the intended climax of the call, known as clinching the sale? The old saw in sales circles that you should stop talking once you make the sale should not be taken literally, but it does serve to signal that the culmination of the sales event has occurred and that now the task shifts to bringing about an effective denouement. Only after you thoughtfully answer questions such as these can any experience be captivatingly staged.

Where does work begin, climax, and have its denouement?

Finally, consider the *rhythm* and *tempo* of work, for these define the relationships between dramatic elements. What transitions present themselves and need to be managed? What building, diminution, contrast, and release enrich the scene's energy level? How many incidents of what intensity occur over specific periods of time? FedEx employees deliberately rush about to convey the impression of speed as the essence of the company, but so should the burger flippers in a fast-food joint, even when they aren't busy. Or think of a waitress in a fine restaurant, where every course presents a dramatic scene in the dining experience. How long should she make each last? How should the end of one course flow into the next? Should she unobtrusively remove the salad plates, while making a show of refilling the water glasses, or perhaps the reverse? And at what precise right moment should she deliver the check? Answers to questions such as these distinguish engaging performances from the monotonous on the one hand and the overly intrusive on the other.

Think back to your last encounter with a cab driver, sales rep, or checkout clerk and you will quickly come to the conclusion that these Aristotlean design elements, while known for thousands of years, remain regrettably absent from much work today.

Renowned stage director Peter Brook declared, "I can take any empty space and call it a bare stage. A man walks across this empty space whilst someone else is watching him, and this is all that is needed for an act of theatre to be engaged."[7] Business enterprises would gain an invaluable perspective by similarly declaring their work to be theatre. For when a business calls its workplace a bare stage, it opens up opportunities to distinguish itself from the myriad humdrum makers of goods and providers of services that perform work without recognizing the true nature of its acts. With theatre furnishing the operating model, even the most mundane of tasks can engage customers in a memorable way. Furthermore, new work elements, previously unimaginable within a goods and services mindset, can be introduced to this new stage solely to enhance the experience, such as sweeping clean sidewalks.

With theatre as the model, even mundane tasks engage customers in a memorable way

Technology-mediated interactions also present a bare stage for business theatre. Brenda Laurel provides a detailed application of Aristotle's philosophy to computer-based performances in her book *Computers as Theatre.* Laurel, believing human-computer interaction should be a "designed experience,"[8] defines principles and techniques using computers as a *medium* rather than an *interface.* Describing this technological stage she says, "Thinking about interfaces is thinking too small. Designing human-computer experience isn't about building a better desktop. It's about creating imaginary worlds that have a special relationship to reality—worlds in which we can extend, amplify, and enrich our own capabilities to think, feel, and act."[9] Exactly. It is clear from Laurel's book (despite her unfortunate use of the word "as" in its title) that she truly believes that working with computers is—or at least should be—theatre.

In the emerging Experience Economy, any work observed directly by a customer must be recognized as an act of theatre. Indeed, flight attendants and hotel staff routinely perform acts of theatre when they direct patrons to the nearest exit or rented room. The work of a retail store associate is theatre when he straightens merchandise on a shelf. Bank tellers, insurance agents, and real estate brokers engage in theatre when they explain terms and conditions. So do taxi cabbies when they converse. Your costumed UPS route driver performs an act of theatre with every package he delivers, and FedEx's overnighting is absolutely, positively theatre. Watch your food server the next time you dine out: the taking of orders, the placing of dishes, the bussing of tables—it's all theatre. Selling, whether pitching automobiles or bottles of perfume, is theatre. A presentation by an ad agency to a client's marketing manager, after all, is an act of theatre. Doctors that perform surgical operations in an amphitheater also perform theatrical operations by the side of every patient's bed. Even the trading of commodities in exchange pits is theatre of a particular attention-grabbing kind. But how differently (and more memorably) would all these activities be performed if those executing them understood that their work is theatre and acted accordingly?

Any work a customer observes directly is an act of theatre

We've all heard the phrase "Walk the talk." This platitude takes on more meaning when recognizing that work is theatre. That's because it not only means practicing in person what one espouses in public but also declares that *someone else is watching.* The very notion of aligning behavior with stated values presupposes an audience. While customers certainly are the primary audience for the on-stage work of business, sometimes the only audience is a vendor, a peer, or a supervisor. This internal viewing, without the presence of a customer, is no less theatre and no less important. Indeed, "off-stage" work affects the connections formed with customers because internal performance influences external relationships.

Thus a stevedore unloading cargo engages in theatre. Two guys tossing pizza dough back in the kitchen are performing. A floor full of claims adjusters shuffling papers for an insurance company is choreographed. A foreman overseeing workers on an assembly line observes the way they act. A proposal to the boss entails theatre; likewise, a presentation to the board of directors. All this work is theatre, even when the audience isn't paying customers, because internal acts make impressions on customers who do pay. In the Experience Economy, businesses must figure out how to make work, whether performed on stage or off, more engaging.

Sociologist Erving Goffman was perhaps the first to recognize that theatrical performances offer a model for work. In his *The Presentation of Self in Everyday Life,* published in 1959, Goffman examines the dramaturgical principles evident in a number of ordinary social and work situations. Studying personal expressions, he recognized that people exhibit differing degrees of awareness of how they appear to others from one moment to the next. Some are oblivious to everything, while others simply don't care what others think of them. Yet others, as a means to other ends, manipulate their expressions in order to create certain impressions in other people. Goffman called such people "cynical performers" who "are interested in deluding the

Internal performance influences external relationships

audience." But he called "sincere" those "individuals who believe in the impression fostered by their performance."[10]

For Goffman, all human activity is acted, whether rehearsed or not. "The incapability of the ordinary individual to formulate in advance the movements of his eyes and body," Goffman says, "does not mean that he will not express himself through these devices in a way that is dramatized and pre-formed in his repertoire of actions. In short, we all act better than we know how."[11] This point alone should encourage workers to gain a better understanding of the impact their behaviors have on customers and to exert what Goffman calls "expressive control" over actions in order to create sincere impressions. Calling one's work theatre, treating it accordingly, and developing the capability to influence perceptions through performance separates the magical from the mundane. It is the *act of acting* that, in the end, differentiates memorable experiences from ordinary human activity.[12]

STAGING BUSINESS PERFORMANCES

Richard Schechner, a prominent expert in the field of "performance theory," provides an invaluable perspective for thinking about the basic components of performance. Echoing Peter Brook, Schechner defines performance as "an activity done by an individual or group in the presence of and for another individual or group,"[13] which embraces not only the staging of plays but the bare stage of business as well. Within that construct, he developed a valuable framework for understanding different kinds of staged "enactments," as he calls them, centered around four key concepts: drama, script, theatre, and performance.

For Schechner, *drama* is central to the whole structure of performance. It consists of "a written text, score, scenario, instruction, plan, or map. The drama can be taken from place to place or time to time independent of the person or people who carry it."[14] Residing at the core of the performance, drama may be expressed in different media in different situations and cultures, business included. Drama depicts the theme of the experience for internal consumption, telling the actors what they should do. On the bare stage of business, *strategy is drama,* central to what an enterprise does but expressing itself through a wide variety of means, such as strategic visions, mission statements, business plans, competitive imperatives (such as Komatsu's single-minded focus to "Beat Caterpillar!"), or elaborate lists of programs (as in the objectives generated in a GE Workout session). No matter what form the strategy takes, the owners of the enterprise reveal the drama over a duration of time (the strategic horizon). Even as employees come and go, it remains the enduring crux of all commercial activity for those who play a part in the enterprise. Drama provides the substance of actions hoped for, regardless of the workplace in which the business stages its performance.

Similarly, *script* is "all that can be transmitted from time to time and place to place; the basic code of events"[15] that "pre-exists any given enactment."[16] The script, then, transmits the drama in ways that transcend specific moments, instances, or conventions. In business, *processes are script,* the (usually) codified approaches that an enterprise uses to enact its strategy. Employees must learn the script, identify its subtext (ideas not explicitly stated in the strategy), and refine it for production, modifying as required to ensure the best possible performance. The script must interpret the drama, remaining true to the drama's original meaning, surprisingly exploiting the expectations of the audience.

Within this context, *theatre* is "the event enacted by a specific group of performers; what the performers actually do during production . . . the manifestation or representation of the drama and/or script."[17] In other words, theatre embodies both the internal work of those who perform the production and the outward representation of that work to the audience—both the *function* and *form* that bring the drama and its script to life.[18] Theatre connects the drama and script to customers by staging a performance that engages them as an audience. Once again, we must recognize that in the Experience Economy *work is theatre.*

> The act of acting differentiates memorable experiences from ordinary activity

Last, according to Schechner, *performance* is "the whole constellation of events, most of them passing unnoticed, that take place in/among both performers and audience from the time the first spectator enters the field of performance—to the time the last spectator leaves."[19] It is the broadest category, the fullness of events enacted at a specific place and time. As seen in Figure 6-1, performance subsumes each of the other dimensions of enactment: theatre, script, and drama. Clearly, *the offering is the performance,* the economic value businesses create for customers. In equating theatrical performance with business performance, we then have the following result:

[drama = strategy]

[script = processes]

[theatre = work]

[performance = offering]

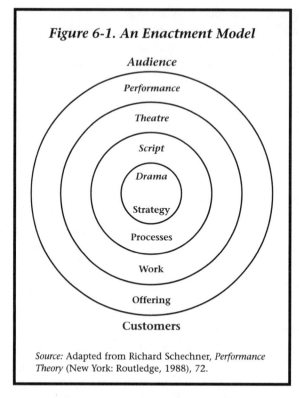

Figure 6-1. An Enactment Model

Audience

Performance

Theatre

Script

Drama

Strategy

Processes

Work

Offering

Customers

Source: Adapted from Richard Schechner, *Performance Theory* (New York: Routledge, 1988), 72.

All economic offerings—not just experiences but commodities, goods, and services—are the result of an enterprise's progression from drama through script to the theatre that stages performance. Returning to Schechner: "The drama is the domain of the author, the composer, scenarist, shaman [to which we add strategist and line executive]; the script is the domain of the teacher, guru, master [as well as the manager, supervisor, and team leader]; the theater is the domain of the performers [whether acting in plays or business]; the performance is the domain of the audience [which includes customers who now want experiences]."[20]

Whether or not your company fully enters the Experience Economy by charging for staged events, no matter what position you have in the company or what your coworkers do, *you are a performer.* Your work is theatre. Now you must act accordingly.

DID YOU SAY ACT?

Some people misunderstand acting. They regard movie celebrities as egotistical, flighty, or fake and Broadway stars as pretentious or worse. Outside the realm of show business, many associate acting with a showy realtor, an irritating infomercial emcee, or a conniving car salesman. Are we really suggesting, then, that you, too, should act? Absolutely. For such misconceptions confuse awful actors and bad acts with acting itself. Acting is the taking of deliberate steps to connect with an audience. To dismiss acting as dishonest or fake relegates oneself and one's employees to bland roles, with little prospect for engaging customers in new and exciting ways.

Aversions to acting may stem from a belief that only that which is completely revealed is completely genuine. But would Barbra Streisand have been more genuine if she had chewed real gum? No. In business terms, Streisand was simply "doing more with less," efficiently achieving the same output with fewer inputs. The decision to use or not use gum does not raise issues of authentic or inauthentic, fake or real. Rather, such decisions center on whether or not to use a particular prop to effect a particular impression. Nor was Streisand's act less genuine because it occurred before the audience expected her performance to begin. Drawing artificial (dare we say, fake?) boundaries around when work begins, or ends, often kills innovation. If servicing a car, for example, begins only when customers bring in their vehicles, Lexus never would have thought to send employees to customers' homes to retrieve them.

> You are a performer. Your work is theatre. Now act accordingly.

A reluctance to act may also arise from the view that acting means misrepresenting oneself. But acting does not mean pretending to be someone or something else. Rather, it entails making discoveries within, drawing from a personal reservoir of life experiences and using those experiences to create a new and believable character for the role one has accepted, whether in the performing arts or in business theatre. An actor must behave in a manner thoroughly consistent with that character or run the risk that the audience will disbelieve his act and lose interest in the offering.

The hallmark of bad acting is for the actor to constantly remind the audience that he, ahem, is acting. Only when a performer is poorly prepared to act do audiences perceive his behavior as pretending. The great Russian actor Michael Chekhov put it this way:

> The talented actor reads the play. The nonactor, or spoiled actor, reads the same play. What is the difference between the two kinds of reading? The nonactor reads the play absolutely objectively. The events, happenings, and characters in the play do not stir up his inner life. He understands the plot and follows it as an observer, an outsider. The actor reads the play subjectively. He reads through the play and by doing so he inevitably enjoys his own reaction to the happenings of the play, his own Will, Feelings, and Images. The play and the plot are only pretext for him to display, to experience the riches of his own talent, his own desire to act.[21]

Chekhov was renowned for his ability to transform himself so as to bring *any* role alive. He performed "character work" so well that people didn't realize he was acting.

The most thoroughly engaging people also have a sense of their role so keen, an ability to stay in character so perfected, and an effect so pronounced that observers seldom realize that they are constantly on-stage. We

Acting is taking deliberate steps to connect with an audience

see such actors in all walks of life: Jack Welch in industry, Warren Bennis in academia, Ronald Reagan in politics, General Schwarzkopf in battle, and the late Mother Teresa in charity, to name but a few. Everyone, even workers in business, should strive to engage others in this way. (Notably absent from those we named, of course, is William Jefferson Clinton. One could debate whether he's a consummate professional or one of Goffman's "cynical performers.") Too many workers fail to act, behaving no differently on stage from the way they do in their private lives. They execute their day-to-day responsibilities as mere happenings; their work is lifeless. To engage a customer in the Experience Economy, act as if your work depended on it!

Only with work explicitly staged for [audience = customers] will experiences flourish as the basis for new economic activity. You can begin this staging by examining the activities performed within your enterprise and then designating the workplace as a special place: the performance stage. Deliberately staging an engaging experience requires much more than simply designating such a place, but doing so is an indispensable (and not too difficult) step in that direction. So don't delay. Do it. And then proclaim: This is my stage.

GETTING INTO CHARACTER

Now that you have your stage, you are truly an actor. And how well you act will depend on how well you prepare to act. In fact, the vast majority of an actor's job is done before he or she ever goes on stage. Preparation takes on many forms, but perhaps the most important is the way you *characterize* your role, which determines the impressions people will form as a result of your work. Proper characterization makes any drama seem natural, believable, spontaneous, and real.

Eric Morris specializes in helping such actors as Jack Nicholson develop their characterizations. Listen to his advice: "For generations, the popular concept and the belief in the theater has been that 'the actor becomes the character.' This is taken to mean that the actor assumes or acquires the behavior, idiosyncrasies, thoughts, and impulses of a particular character in a play. But I believe that the reverse is true: *the character becomes you!*"[22] Exactly. Successful acting, as opposed to pretending, never creates a noticeable gap between the characterization of the role and the actual person playing the role. That is, the character conforms with self—who the worker really is—drawing on the emotional, physical, intellectual, and spiritual uniqueness of the individual playing the role. Morris further explains that "when you absorb the character into your person, all that you are in terms of your unique way of relating to the world, your impulses, thoughts, and responses, will be included in everything he does. It is thus that an actor makes a unique and personal statement through every part he plays."[23]

Building character into roles distinguishes the work of staging experiences from that of other business activity. In fact, the absence of such character explains why so many service workers seem to operate like automatons. How many times do hotel receptionists greet you in the same, monotonous manner? How many car salesmen use identical pitches? How many fast-food lines put customers through the same old drill? Proper characterization can turn these mundane service activities into memorable performances. Thus a bellman at a Ritz-Carlton warmly welcoming guests back by name—accomplished by reviewing a daily printout of expected new guests and their distinguishing traits (much like a soap opera actor learns new scripts on a daily basis)—makes a remarkable impression. Similarly, a visit to a Lexus or Saturn dealership offers a refreshingly different experience from the normal, in which customers are corralled into a cubicle to haggle over price. Even a soda-fountain jerk can create memorable events by characterizing his role. Consider the character at the refreshment stand at Cedar-Lee Cinema in Cleveland Heights, Ohio, who spins lines like, "Who's next to be refreshed?" His acting is better than that of some of the movie stars on the screen. Guests *want* to wait in his queue.

Too many workers behave no differently on stage than in their private lives

Actors may deploy a number of theatre techniques to develop ideas on how to fill an on-stage role with character. These include *journaling* (documenting daily events in a diary, and then decomposing each event into potential choices for future work), *charting* (creating a map of the actor's chosen behaviors that overlay the script, line by line, scene by scene), or *relationship mapping* (creating diagrams that assess the relationship between each on-stage character). In each instance, acting flows from role to character; the latter absorbs the former, becoming the basis on which the actor engages the audience.

Turning a role into a character requires careful management of the *subtext*—that is, everything not in the formal script. Agreed upon by the actors in collaboration with the director, who together translate the [script = processes] into real [theatre = work], subtext renders a fullness beyond the surface-level script. The on-stage actor completes the performance by using inflections, gestures, and appropriate items. This includes *body language*—such as posture, gestures, eye contacts, and other expressions (a sales representative's smile sends a powerfully positive message)—*props* (a pager conveys accessibility,

Proper characterization turns service activities into memorable performances

while a pager conspicuously turned off and thrown into a briefcase calls for attention), and *costumes*—clothing and accessories (a CEO's speech delivered in sandals and khakis conveys a dramatically different message from the same speech delivered in a three-piece suit, but either might be appropriate, depending on the characterization the CEO wants to convey).[24]

No element proves too small to contribute to the creation of character. Consider the lowly business card, one of the most basic props of workplace interactions with customers, yet so often treated in a pedestrian fashion, with little consideration as to how it contributes to the development of character. In most cases the only differences in the cards of different individuals working for the same organization are name, title, and telephone number. Certainly the basic design of a card can communicate a general message, but most cards present one standard look for every worker, as if all actors were merely extras in the performance. This approach reflects a Mass Production mindset, placing each person in one and only one box on an organizational chart.

> **No element is too small to contribute to the creation of character**

But people play multiple roles in today's changing productions, so they need multiple ways to characterize their performance. We know of a few individuals in large corporations who now carry multiple cards, each representing a different character they play. And we know entrepreneurs who use their PCs to desktop-publish unique cards for each business meeting they conduct. And they do this not to deceive others (like James Garner's title character in the old TV show *The Rockford Files*), but to represent the legitimately different roles they play in different situations. (We withhold their identity and that of their companies to preserve the transparent customization approach they use across customers and meetings.)

Names also characterize a role. Actors in most businesses today "play themselves" (not so in show business, where most actors take on the assumed name of their character). But here, too, change dawns. At the call centers for a major manufacturer of computing equipment, each representative *must* use a different name. Only the first "Susan" or "Bob" hired gets to keep that name. Anyone cast afterward takes on an assumed name. This characterization element allows callers, should they desire, to request the same representative when placing multiple calls into the call center, whether during a single series of ordering or servicing interactions, or across multiple, episodic interactions.

Customers value the policy in and of itself, which allows the same one-to-one relationship to become the basis of service. The most intriguing point, however, lies in how the policy could become a stage for further characterization of the role. No longer cast as interchangeable parts, the assumed names free these phone reps to express themselves as engaging performers through a unique style of personally selected expressions, routines, and other telephone mannerisms that shape and focus conversation in memorable ways. Great call center actors would find themselves in great demand, from customers and from the company.

Getting into character provides a sense of purpose

Getting into character gives each worker in an organization a sense of purpose, uniting them in the overall theme of the experience offered to guests. Without such character development, the work yields little opportunity to connect with customers. Perhaps no other company understands this as well as Disney. Each day, cast members—whether portraying a cartoon figure, ride attendant, or street sweeper—don their costumes, grab their props, and enter various staged experiences. Each contributes to the portrayal of the place as a haven for family, fun, and fantasy. Cast members keep off-stage work off stage and conduct on-stage work on stage. Period.

The Project on Disney, a group of observers that takes a dim view of working conditions at Walt Disney World (they title a chapter on the subject "Working at the Rat"), shares this insight: the paid employees, like the paying guests, "say they know it's not real, that it's not what it appears to be, and then proceed to talk about it *as though* it were."[25] This disposition goes to the very heart of characterizing a role. Konstantin Stanislavski labeled it the "Magic If."[26] Many acting teachers since have parlayed the notion into a formal acting technique called "As If." Says one such instructor, Michael Kearns, "Acting *as if* is a great technique to apply to real life. As obnoxious as it sounds, it's a bit like positive thinking. You're at a party, feeling glum and determined to have a lousy time. Sometimes an adjustment—acting as if you're having the time of your life—will actually alter your mood, allowing you to look at the occasion through a different filter."[27] On-stage service personnel who let it show when they're feeling blue, lacking any "as if" resources to characterize their role, only suggest realness in one sense—real rudeness. There is no room for such behavior in pleasant business experiences. When having a rough day (and we all have them), workers must act as if they are cheerful. When confronted with an ornery buyer (and some truly present difficult challenges), actors should act as if they don't mind. A funny thing then happens on the way to the performance: cheerful service presents the stage for memorable experiences, and insufferable customers often regret their behavior and lighten up.

Acting "as if" goes to the heart of characterizing a role

Trained actors—and any audience—know the difference between roles performed mechanically and those masterfully expressed through characterization. The former exemplifies most service positions today, with customers eager to end their transactions as quickly as possible. (As mentioned previously, managers in service industries know this and expend tremendous energy to reduce the time it takes to serve each customer, thereby promoting a world of poor-service, self-service, and no-service outlets.) But when workers choose appropriate roles and then characterize those roles well, they stage experiences with which guests willingly spend more time. And what induces this willingness? Simple: the way one acts.

ACTING WITH INTENTION

Konstantin Stanislavski constantly admonished actors to "Cut ninety-five per cent."[28] With this simple slogan, he addressed the frequent tendency among actors to do too much. Stanislavski not only meant that actors performed too many actions but also that they incorporated too much commotion into any given action. (For example, many workers, from doctors to auto mechanics, go through excess explanations and histrionics when customers want the simple facts.) He wanted to rid theatre of unnecessary gestures, movements, words, and other energies that detract from the main purpose of the activity. He reduced acting to its essential core, so that it clearly communicated the theme (what he called the "super-objective") of the play. Legend has it that Stanislavski once asked

Cut 95 percent

Sergei Rachmaninov the secret of his mastery of the piano, to which the great pianist and composer replied, "Not touching the neighboring key."[29] Stanislavski must have liked the answer, because he held it as a standard for theatre.

Thanks to the widespread influence of total quality management (TQM) and business process reengineering (BPR), most organizations now understand the idea of redesigning and improving work processes. These business improvement programs usually involve process mapping as a tool to redesign operational activity. In most instances, however, such exercises only delineate *what* activity organizations perform, not *how* the work should be performed. Simply put, the resulting work processes still lack a sense of *intention.* Merely completing an activity is not enough: some underlying motivation must invigorate the performance so that it ultimately affects the buyer of the final offering. Everyone can, for example, detect the difference between a receptionist who merely takes names and calls for parties and one who graciously greets each visitor and performs otherwise identical tasks with intentional style and color. The encounter in the lobby, however brief, affects the guest and sets a particular tone for the entire meeting that follows—and on occasion perhaps even alters the outcome.

Economic activity truly engages customers when each worker fills

activities consciously and thoroughly with intention. Every
movement becomes a meaningful action when richly
designed with intention in mind. Without it, work is dull,
monotonous, a cliché. (How many processes are as thor-

oughly unimpressive from start to finish as those which end with "Have a
nice day"?) Because so many people perform acts without deliberate intention, Stanislavski could comfortably and universally demand that actors cut
95 percent of what they do. The same admonition applies to business acts.
Process excellence—at least in the sense of truly engaging customers—surfaces only when a worker decides to enrich *how* he or she performs each
activity. As acting instructor Kearns relates: "Deciding what you want is
critical to your success. . . . If you haven't decided what it is you want,
you're likely to be un-focused . . . and the result will be a vague, meaningless encounter. When you've conscientiously spelled out your intent before-
hand, you are more likely to be specific and clear, and the result will be an
energized connection."[30] Any offering increases in value when every
worker on stage—in farmyards, on shop floors, at service counters, within
themed attractions—fills work with intention.

Kearns supplies a most useful tool for doing so. For every piece of work,
one must describe his intention using the phrase *in order to*.[31] Barbra
Streisand chewed gum *in order to* demonstrate that appearances don't matter—it's the vocal cords that count. The Jacobs Field performer swept the
street *in order to* show that the new ballpark was clean, safe, comfortable,
and eager to come to life. The inspired receptionist greets visitors *in order
to* welcome them to a place where great things happen.

Imagine that you're standing outside the closed door of your boss's
office. Your very next task is to knock on that door. How would you do it
differently if you were to knock *in order to* announce you had just arrived?
In order to apologize for being late? *In order to* let him know you were
there, but without disturbing his work? *In order to* state that the time for
meeting was at hand? Each intention calls for a decidedly different knock.

Or consider the very real world of doctor-patient relationships. Medical
research shows that women with breast cancer who choose lumpectomies
(simple tumor removals) live just as long as those who select mastectomies
(total breast removal). Despite laws requiring doctors to explain lumpec-
tomy as an option, the rates of breast-conserving surgery in some parts of
the United States remain unchanged. According to the *Wall Street Journal,*
"part of the reason for the lack of impact is that it's not just *what* the doctor
says, but *how* it's said."[32] Doctors must therefore provide patients with
options *in order to* ensure that each properly considers the alternatives.[33]

Lawyers addressing a court also must fill their work with intention. "You
want to plan every detail, the way you dress [and] the way your table

looks," says Fred Bartlit, who practices in Chicago.[34] Bartlit is one of a growing number of trial lawyers who closely scrutinize every single thing they do, from how they walk across the floor to where they stand to how and when they make eye contact to what gestures they make when handling files and using a laptop computer to how they deliver ad-libs and prepared quips.[35] Their intention in performing each activity determines how it will contribute to the overall performance. If no intention exists other than to be done with the work (that is, performing *in order to* be finished), then the work will lack the potential to engage.

It's not surprising that doctors and lawyers, whose decisions intimately affect the lives of their customers, must apply intention to work. Yet any activity proves more valuable, worthwhile, and meaningful when performed with intention. Consider this simple example. In the Hill House dormitory at the University of Pennsylvania, a woman everyone just calls Barb provides a daily demonstration of intention. Barb works in the dorm's cafeteria. For many, she remains the most memorable person encountered in their entire educational experience. Her job consists of only one activity. For three meals a day, Barb sits at a table at the entrance of the dining hall and swipes students' prepaid meal cards—one after another—through a machine that registers a green light if meals remain for the week and a red light if not. That's it. To the casual observer, this would surely constitute the most mind-numbing job imaginable. Yet Barb richly fills this one simple task with intention. First, she takes a student's card *in order to* learn his name. Then she takes the card *in order to* greet him back by name. If someone has missed a meal, she takes the card *in order to* inquire about his earlier absence. She will even take a card *in order to* inform its holder where a friend sits in the cafeteria. In every instance, by word or merely with gesture, her intentions fulfill her theme of warmly welcoming students to the school's dining experience. She may be one of the greatest welcomers ever to grace the globe. No wonder Barb's position has yet to be disintermediated, downsized, or automated by some self-serving turnstile.[36]

One meets such individuals in all lines of work. For every Barb the card-taker in Philadelphia, there's a Fred the lawyer in Chicago, an Aaron the shoeshine man in Kalamazoo, and a Christopher the barista in Washington, D.C. You remember them when you encounter them. Their intention-filled work spills over into passion for their character, caring for the company, and empathy for the customer. They are the world's true actors, and we all should follow their lead.

7
Performing to Form

• •

LINDA LEADS THE NEW OFFERING DEVELOPMENT team for a
U.S. automobile manufacturer.[1] She arrives at her office and reviews her
schedule for the day: "Let's see. There's my usual talk at the Executive
Briefing Center for a group of supply partners at 10 A.M., a 1:30 on the fall
strategy cycle, and then the 4 P.M. call at that local dealership. Not a bad
day, but I'm going to have to get right at finishing my prep. It'll take some
work. . . ."

Linda boots up her laptop and opens the EBC7.PPT file for her morning
presentation. Scanning through the slides, she realizes that the graph on one
slide is out of date. She accesses the company intranet, looks up the new
data, and revises the slide. She then goes over in her mind what she'll say to
reflect the latest information, jotting a few notes down on a pad. Soon,
another slide causes her to pause, as she remembers a snag in her performance the last time. Linda stands up, faces the closed door, and explores
what she will say—and do—at that point in the presentation. After a few
dry runs she figures out the problem: There's too much going on. The
slide's so busy that she has to keep looking back at the screen, she talks too
fast to get through it, and her mannerisms are all over the place.

To rectify the problem, Linda sits down and removes all unessential
information from the slide. She makes some more notes on what she'll say
to cover the streamlined points and then stands up again and talks from the
notes. Going over them again and again, she finally hits upon the cadence
and gestures that will bring home her crucial points. Satisfied with her performance, Linda takes one more run at it—this time without notes. Then

119

she opens up her CHAR7EBC.DOC file and updates her script, including descriptions of what mannerisms to use.

Just then she hears a knock on the door. It's Paul, one of her managers—again. Linda closes her notebook and flips down her laptop screen to show Paul that he has her undivided attention. She doesn't really want to hear about the latest problems with the market research data, but she acts as if she's hearing his woes for the very first time. The details of their discussion remain confidential, but suffice it to say that Linda thinks fast on her feet to diffuse the latest installment of the saga. As Paul and Linda shake hands to close their session, she briefly holds his right arm with her left in order to show that she appreciates him and his sincere desire to bring the problem to a resolution.

Linda then turns her attention back to the final preparations for her presentation to the group of suppliers, and finally heads down to the Executive Briefing Center. Shortly before arriving, she stops at the restroom to ensure that her outfit is neat, her hair just so, and nothing from breakfast remains in her teeth. Oh, and she remembers to take out that PartnershipPlus pin from her purse and puts it on her jacket. As she takes one last glance in the mirror, a look of reserved assurance comes over her face, whereupon she strides confidently out. "To the Briefing Center," she says to herself, as she begins reciting lines to an imaginary audience to help her get in the moment. In a few short minutes she's introduced by the host. Reaching the podium, just before launching into her speech, Linda pauses, eyeing the audience, beginning in the back, scanning down the middle, and finally making eye contact with a supplier sitting up in the first row. They both smile.[2] Then she delivers her four-word opening, "Partnerships demand learning relationships." A pause. And she's on. . . .

Linda performs flawlessly and finishes her thirty-minute talk with a spirited, "So no more guerilla warfare!" to great applause. She immediately exits with a last glance and a smile to that person in the front row. One of the purchasing managers in the back comments to the host's assistant, "Wow—I can't believe how spontaneous and informal she seemed, yet she just walked right through every pothole out there." "Yes," the assistant replies, "but I've seen her give this same presentation a half-dozen times before. Except for some minor changes here and there, virtually every word is identical each time." To which the manager could only respond again, "Wow."

Meanwhile, back at her office, Linda's already preparing for the 1:30 P.M. strategy meeting. This would not be like her morning performance: no PowerPoint slides, no prepared remarks, no applause. The key to success, in fact, would be ensuring that everyone across the line functions gets involved and provides input to the company's first-ever strategic exhibition, where the automaker's top management would experience what it's like to work in a business system where faultless development plans were flawlessly executed. No longer the Confident Executive, her role at this meeting event would be Inclusive Guide.

To that end, Linda reviews her notes from past meetings and interim telephone calls, a memo or two, and e-mails that various participants have sent back and forth commenting on how the desired results could be better achieved. She focuses her preparation primarily on ensuring that this meeting picks up on the outcomes from the last session, matches the tone of concerns expressed since, and moves toward delivering the set of impressions everyone has agreed the company should make on the exhibition participants. This will keep the meeting focused and on track, avoiding costly diversions (and as a side benefit, prevent her from being late for her 4 P.M. sales call). Linda takes out her list of "runplan" techniques, storyboards her plan for facilitating the session, and outlines the flip charts she'll use.

Once again her preparation pays off. While having to respond to a hiccup or two, as Inclusive Guide Linda not only keeps the meeting on track but pushes forward the greater agenda of planning the orchestration of the event. Now, she's off to the sales call, after first changing her clothes to a more casual look, befitting the culture of the company she's visiting, and meeting up with the vice president of leasing, Steve.

This won't be a "normal" sales call, like one she would make with a fleet manager. She and Steve are meeting with the owner of a large local dealership to enlist him in the automaker's prototype offering: the Pre-Lease Executive Automobile Sampling Experience (code-named PLEASE, which rhymes with "lease"). With PLEASE the company aims to stage an event at its test track in which potential high-end lease clients will pay more than $15,000 to test drive a number of high-end cars—from the luxurious to the exotic—under various exhilarating circumstances, whether racing others (including local celebrities) or sliding on rain-slicked surfaces. At the end of the day each guest takes home the car of his or her choice, receiving a year's free lease and a customized video of their driving experience. With the experience priced at two to three times the cost of an annual lease, Linda, Steve, and their cohorts know it will be very profitable. And now top management, finally warming to the fact that the company makes more profits from leasing than from manufacturing, has agreed to include cars from other manufacturers in the agreement.

As Linda and Steve drive to the dealership together, they map out their plan to sell the owner on participating in the pilot program for his area. From their past experience in selling the concept up the ladder, each has become quite adept at promoting certain aspects of the proposal, with Linda focusing on the nature of the PLEASE experience itself and Steve on the financial justification. Linda suggests she'll open with the panoramic "B" version of what they're going to accomplish. Steve will show what it could mean to the owner's bottom line, and then, after dragging out the formalities a bit to increase the anticipation, for the finale Linda will reveal the scripts and colored drawings their design firm created to demonstrate what a great experience PLEASE will be. Throughout, Steve will play the role of Straight Man to Linda's Affable Enthusiast. Just as they arrive, he reminds her of the line about the winter tires that works every time with the version "B" opening.

Once settled in the dealership owner's office, Linda and Steve masterfully play off each other, making their points in swift succession, even finishing each other's sentences on occasion. Everything goes perfectly, *except* for the twenty-minute late start, the constant interruptions by dealership personnel, and the frequent objections by the owner. But throughout, since Linda and Steve know each other's role and their own lines of explanation so well, they turn every interruption into a joke or an enjoyable respite, and turn every objection into a positive segue to the next point. To overcome the dealer's final objection—that **Understand how to turn every interaction into an experience** including other nameplates will cannibalize his own inventory of cars—Linda subtly motions to Steve, they rise in unison, go to the owner's bookshelf, and simultaneously point to the replica of a DeLorean sports car they had spotted earlier. Anticipating their question, the owner blurts out, "Well, that was my dream, my first sports car. . . ." to which Linda responds, ". . . and you loved the experience of driving it, didn't you? We're going to give your customers the experience of driving *their* dream cars, and you'll make more money off *that* than you would selling five of our average models. Who cares who makes the car? That's just a prop for the driving experience that'll line all of our pockets." Soon all three shake hands as they walk toward the door, with Linda slapping the owner on the back as they shake.

THE FOUR FORMS OF THEATRE

This vignette illustrates many of the elements of theatre discussed in Chapter 6—and a few new ones. Linda truly understands what it means to be an actor and how becoming one turns every interaction—no matter what the offering being produced, no matter where the workplace stage may be—into an experience. But notice how differently she approaches each of the four on-stage roles she filled this day. While preparing for her speech, she's confronted with a problem by her subordinate, Paul, and must extemporaneously handle the situation. Here, Linda performs *improv theatre*. As much on stage as when she's with people outside the company, Linda quickly decides how to respond to Paul by relying on the reservoir of managerial techniques she has stored up from past experience.

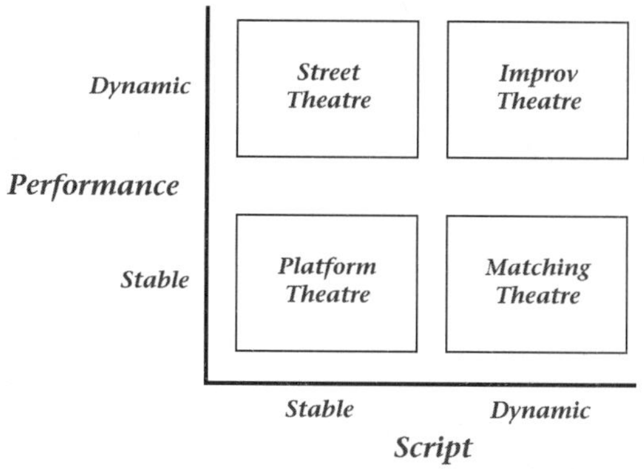

When speaking to the supply partners, Linda performs

Figure 7-1. The Four Forms of Theatre

platform theatre. She scripts in advance every line and every gesture, practicing each over and over again until she can confidently give a performance so accomplished that it comes off as fresh and spontaneous. In planning her performance for the afternoon strategy meeting, she is careful to review each and every prior interaction with those attending the meeting—telephone, E-mail, correspondence, and face-to-face meeting. She then engages in *matching theatre* by piecing all these disparate facts and events together in a unified whole, much like a film editor or director.

Finally, when working with Steve to sell the dealership owner on the preleasing experience, Linda finds herself in a setting that she cannot control. Rather than rely on improvisational techniques—too risky for this venue—the two of them perform *street theatre,* in which small, atomic units of activity are called on demand to construct a performance (and to handle whatever interruptions or objections arise). Although nearly every move they make is part of a practiced routine, the order of the routine isn't planned but occurs in the moment.

You must determine what form of theatre to perform

Now consider the various roles you must take on at work. Like Linda, before you can act, you must determine which form of theatre it makes sense to perform given a certain time, situation and audience. Figure 7-1 diagrams each of the four forms of theatre—improv, platform, matching, and street—drawing from the point made by Richard Schechner in his model of enactment (Figure 6-1) that theatre is bound on the inside by *script* and on the outside by *performance*.

The extent to which the performance and the script each change—whether they are dynamic (constantly changing) or stable (changing little)—for each audience—determines how the actor must act. Each of these four forms of theatre thus represents a different way of performing work, a different approach to plotting a sequence of events to generate economic output. It is the nature of the offering and the circumstances in which a company engages its customers—or any actor engages his fellow workers—that determines which of the four to use.

Improv Theatre

Improvisation involves imagination, creativity, and new-to-the-world performances. Improv theatre is a spontaneous, liberating, and unpredictable mode of work that is based on finding value from something new: creating, inventing, moving laterally or even impulsively from one idea to another, or simply ad-libbing. The dynamic movement of improv theatre, however, does not entail only simple acts of free association or aimless mental wandering, void of any structure or routine. Quite the opposite: Improv requires systematic and deliberate methods of originating creative ideas, fresh expressions, and new ways of addressing old problems. The script, while rarely written down (or codified) except in very broad terms, emerges from the improvisation.

Improv theatre involves new-to-the-world performances

In improv, the staging of performance anticipates mistakes, even going so far as to cause situations to "go wrong" just to see what happens. This occurs even in the course of performing other forms of work, by responding to mistakes—improvising—as errors surface unexpectedly. In any situation, improv involves a certain set of learned skills (meaning they can be taught), as well as various tools and techniques that take seemingly unrelated notions and combine them in unusual ways to make previously unarticulated discoveries. The methods of improv theatre fill courses and handbooks and include speaking in gibberish, gesturing in pantomime, interacting with random props, and wearing masks. Each technique relies on deliberate stimuli to force a changed perspective, a different set of possibilities, or an alternative approach, all aimed at facilitating the improvisational flow of new ideas for taking action.

These techniques date at least as far back as the sixteenth-century Italian *commedia dell'arte*. This outdoor theatre drew on stock characters who employed broad physical gestures and who always wore distinctive masks and simple but instantly recognizable costumes. The names of these over four-hundred-year-old characters remain familiar even today: Pantalone,

Columbina, Il Capitano, Scaramouche, Arlecchino (from which we get the English Harlequin), Pulcinella (which became the puppet Punch), Zanni (from which we derive the word "zany"), and so forth. Each play would be staged not from written dialog but from a *scenario,* which means, as John Rudin writes, "literally 'that which is on the scenery,' i.e. pinned up backstage. All it consists of is a plot summary, the bare bones of who does what when."[3] All of the dialog and much of the action would then be improvised, given the nature of each called-upon character, from this base scenario in the wings.

If you're "winging it," you're doing improv. And whenever anyone assumes the role of a particular stock character with no preparation or rehearsal, such as that of car salesman and sales manager taking on "good cop/bad cop" roles with a prospect, that person draws from the tradition of the commedia dell'arte. Performers may also draw upon such improvisational characters in more complex selling situations. Suppose a four-person, cross-functional team from a travel agency—we'll call them Bob, Carol, Ted, and Alice—gets together to sell a company on outsourcing its travel operations. With little time to prepare, they quickly settle on the three distinguishing characteristics of the offer they believe will win the business: cost containment, quality service, and improvement in employee morale. In addition to their functional roles of, say, sales, agency operations, finance, and human resources (respectively), each team member chooses a particular stock character to create an impromptu cast for the sales call and they quickly work out the proper scenario. Bob plays Glad-Hander, throwing smiles, filling coffee cups, and freely complimenting everyone's remarks. Ted unreservedly assumes the role of Penny-Pincher. He economizes his words, cuts off tangential conversations, and constantly pushes to keep the meeting on track. Meanwhile, Carol and Alice play Proposal Reviewers in a Siskel-and-Ebert-like routine in which they talk up various alternatives that will make the outsourcing proposal work. This improvisational selling performance will express the company's proposed economic value in an engaging manner.

Companies can also use improv theatre whenever they must create wholly new offerings for customers, as do research and development groups, architects, and graphic designers, or when they must handle the new, unforeseen situations that come up in all lines of work. This form of theatre applies not only to what people do but also to how they think. The techniques of creative-thinking guru Dr. Edward de Bono, for example, provide improvisational exercises for the mind to stimulate new ideas.[4] A definite structure lies behind de Bono's methods to focus,

If you're "winging it," you're doing improv

provoke, move to, shape, and harvest ideas. His techniques provoke active mental operations that structure one's cognitive improv work by setting up provocations and then stone-stepping from one notion to another. In one exercise, de Bono recommends the use of *random words* to stimulate new ideas about predefined areas in need of new thinking. Do you need new ideas for refreshing a marketing program? Then draw words at random from whatever source is handy: a dictionary, newspaper, even a children's book. Let's see: What principle can we extract from . . . a turtle? ("Well, a turtle's head pops out of its shell. Maybe our ad campaign is a shell—only in the final ad in a series does the message 'pop out.'") Or how can we compare it to a . . . tricycle? ("An adult riding a tricycle would look contorted. The sacrifices customers endure with our competition make them look similarly contorted, whereas our mass-customized product provides a 'perfect fit.' Now sell that!")

The emergence of the Experience Economy coincides with, albeit not coincidentally, heightened interest in creative thinking. It also introduces a real need for greater improvisational skills in the workplace, especially for work performed in new venues.[5] One example is the Home Shopping Network, where sales associates employ a host of techniques drawn from improv theatre. They make sharp, sure entrances and exits. They emphasize visual props. And they play off other members of the selling team (or, in improv terms, what might be better described as a retail selling *troupe*). Note, too, the important use of voice training: learning to select pitch, adjust volume, alternate tempo, change emphasis, and establish rhythm, all often taught in improv classes. Why is it that HSN sales reps give such good performances? Because they know there's an audience out there. Workers in all sorts of other situations demanding greater improv skills must come to the same realization.

Today these skills are often required from workers who interact over the phone. Here we can learn much from radio, which once played heavily in the theatrical landscape. Prior to the popularity of television in the years following World War II, countless audiences huddled around radio receivers only *heard* actors performing in their favorite shows, yet the performances captivated their imaginations. Even today, at the peak of television viewing, radio provides a stage for performing. Witness the popular shows hosted by Don Imus, Rush Limbaugh, Howard Stern, and the many local "zoo crews" who create and cast engrossing characters for their listening audience. In these radio performances, the performers must rely on improv skills to do their work, nowhere more so than when hosts field calls from listeners. One may question the politics or caliber of these performances, or simply dislike the shock jock mentality, but one cannot dispute the fact that these broadcasters perform acts of improv theatre. In fact, improv *is* their job!

So it is for those who use the telephone for a living: A phone line is empty space waiting to become a bare stage. How much more engaging might call center representatives be if they conducted their phone conversations as if they were performing improv? Take the worst type of live phone call, not the 900 numbers or even the psychic hot lines advertised on late night infomercials (these hired "psychics" surely understand that their work is theatre), but the telemarketing call. Does any other type of phone call come off more poorly? Could any other call benefit more from improv techniques? A telemarketer's script is intended to help the worker make more calls, but how often does a call truly engage the potential customer? Prospects tire of the telemarketer's prepared remarks and often hang up—an understandable response, since the prospect's answers have little or no impact on what question comes next. A telemarketing paradigm based on improv theatre would stand a real chance of drawing potential customers into stimulating conversations because the customer's remarks would prompt innovative responses to unique needs. Requests for repeat performances would replace abrupt hang-ups.

> A phone line is an empty space waiting to become a bare stage

Platform Theatre

The form of theatre that immediately comes to mind when most people think of the term is platform theatre. Its name harks back to the classical stage, where actors performed on a platform raised above the audience. The performance was further separated from the audience by a proscenium arch (a picture-frame opening, often covered by a drawn curtain between acts).[6] The actors in platform theatre work from a formal script of lines known as a playscript.[7] In business, the playscripts exist in the form of drafted speeches, lines of programming code, or standard procedural instructions—anything that codifies work to generate value from something done, including a factory's production processes. Platform work, linear and fixed, flows sequentially and so allows for little variation from the planned steps or prepared script. Platform performers seek to stabilize everything, through rehearsals, and then duplicate that one best way of working over and over again. No matter which performance one sees—be it a musical or product assembly—the lines delivered will be the same.

This stability is often a good thing, whether found in hard-coded routines set by cubicles of computer programmers or set talks to board members, investors, vendors, and employees meticulously developed and delivered by senior executives. For this reason, methodologies abound to help businesses develop information technology solutions and stabilize processes, and swarms of trainers (many with performing arts backgrounds) exist to coach presenters with their speeches. This assistance primarily addresses the delivery of lines. A mechanical reading of written words does not constitute good platform theatre—in fact, it can't even pass for bad acting! The *Wall Street Journal* reports that many chief financial officers are taking acting lessons to prepare for quarterly discussions with financial analysts, a situation in which improvising could land the company in financial hot water.[8]

In platform theatre, the actors must rehearse their lines, whether they intend to memorize them or read from cue cards or a TelePrompTer. They must internalize the lines until the script becomes second nature. When an actor knows his lines—really knows them—he doesn't merely recite them but brings them to life through intention.

There is a danger in relying too much on platform theatre. Too many companies, particularly mass producers, command their workers to follow standard scripts, having them do and say the same things repeatedly, in a vain attempt to gain efficiencies. (That's why telemarketers give the term "scripting" a bad name—they use platform scripts in an arena calling for improv or street theatre scripts.) The most bureaucratic organizations—think of the Department of Motor Vehicles or, to only a slightly lesser extent, airline service counters—create rules that workers must always follow, no matter what response the customer truly requires.

Platform theatre allows for little variation

But platform theatre can be the right form when workers perform standard activities in front of customers but do not directly interact with them. It may be the theatre of choice, for example, for the fast-food workers who supply those at the counter, for the technicians behind the glass at a one-hour eyeglass retailer, the maintenance workers fixing a bare stage, the flight attendants reciting FAA-scripted safety warnings, and anyone giving a keynote presentation.

Platform skills also befit people who follow a set script on audio or visual recordings, such as the pronouncements of every voice response unit or voice-mail system. Consider the billion-dollar audio book industry. While the audio book format as we know it is only about ten years old, major publishing houses and dozens of smaller firms now release hundreds of titles per year. Book publishers now call the William Morris Agency to schedule labor from a pool of trained voices! The industry often employs actors from Broadway and Hollywood to record audiotaped versions of best-sellers and specialty books. Rick Harris, the executive producer of Harper Audio, relates that "Musical comedy actors do well at this because they know how to inflect, to color, to phrase." The better reader, says Jenny Frost, president and publisher of Bantam Doubleday Dell's audio division, "really works hard on the scripts before going into the studio."[9] Other recordings in need of good speaking voices and great script reading include talking toys, hosted chat rooms on the Internet, CD-ROM games, and training materials.

Use platform theatre when workers do not directly interact with customers

Annual meetings, investor relations get-togethers, and trade shows provide other venues for platform theatre, which is often staged by outside companies such as Caribiner International, PGI, or dick clark productions. The latter, founded by Dick Clark of *American Bandstand* fame, charges $150,000 to $10 million to stage such platform events. "All these shows had the same format: a speech, a financial presentation with some graphics, then you'd end up with the chairman," Clark relates. "I figured I could use what I knew from television: Get the audience in, entertain them, then get the corporate message across."[10] The work involves adapting a standard script, then producing the platform event according to that set script.

Matching Theatre

Matching theatre, exemplified by film and television, requires the integration of work outcomes from one disconnected time frame to another. The end product results from piecing together distinct portions of work, performed at different times and often in different places, into a unified whole. The producers of matching theatre must concern themselves not only with the quantity of material lying "on the cutting room floor" but with the alignment of all those pieces, the way they should be linked together to complete the entire performance. People in show business rarely use the term *matching* to describe their work, generally referring to it simply as "film" or as "jump-cut" theatre, in recognition of the need to jump between various takes and scenes, then cut and splice them together.[11] As V. I. Pudovkin, the great Russian director of silent films in the 1920s and 1930s, put it, "the foundation of film art is editing."[12] Whenever companies integrate the outcomes of work across many disparate business performances, they, too, perform matching theatre.

Have you ever seen a movie or TV show in which (1) a character appears on screen, (2) the picture jump-cuts to another character, then (3) returns to the first character, whose position, pose, expression, temperament, or even outfit doesn't match that of the first shot? Then you've seen a poor perfor-

Matching theatre integrated portions of work into a unified whole

mance of matching theatre. Not only does this fail to engage an audience, it all to often disengages them by focusing on how (poorly) the work was performed. The same potential for mismatching exists in many business processes, particularly when mass producers partition work into functional silos, vertical slices of activities that often do not quite fit together. Companies that embrace Continuous Improvement (or Lean Production) business models solve this problem by focusing horizontally, via matching theatre, on linking together work activities into one seamless process.

While directors of matching theatre, as in platform theatre, generally start with a fully written script, it is the rare production in which the process of filming does not change the script, often significantly. Actually, such changes *always* occur. Why? Because the actual filming reveals the flaws in a script, just as the actual production of any economic offering—good, service, or experience—reveals flaws in the codified processes followed to create it. So scripts in matching theatre are always dynamic, sometimes via wholesale corrections and revisions and at other times *through real-time adjustments.* (Script changes occur in platform theatre as well, but only during the development process, before production begins. As in Mass Production, workers are not allowed to make script changes on the fly.) And as in Continuous Improvement, all parties involved focus on the highest quality outcome by getting better and better at their work activities, generating value from something improved.

Workers should thus employ matching theatre whenever they strive to improve the quality of the same basic outcomes. This includes marketing managers (as opposed to the advertising agencies they hire, who should use improv techniques to generate new campaigns), counter personnel at fast-food restaurants (as opposed to those in the kitchen, where platform theatre may be most appropriate), and retail shelf stockers (as opposed to sales associates, who should use street performance skills). Not to mention flight attendants greeting and sending off passengers and repeating the same salutations over and over, without conviction.

At a higher level, companies should embrace the techniques of matching theatre whenever the same customers interact with that company—often with the same workers—over and over again. Here, work must be *matched across time.* Consider a sales representative calling on the same customer on a periodic basis. What occurs during a visit should match the impressions left during the previous visit as well as match episodes to be performed in future visits. If, for example, the sales rep wants to give the prospect the impression that he is professional, qualified, knowledgeable, and helpful, then *every* visit must reinforce at least one—preferably all—each of these impressions, while *no* visit should contradict them.

And the communications between visits, whether via phone, fax, e-mail, or paper correspondence, must leave the customer with the impression of a harmonized and consistent performance. If a company wishes to achieve the desired effect, then it can perform no event without first considering all others in the sequence of visits and communications. As Arthur Shaw, senior vice president of electronic brokerage at Charles Schwab, told *Business Week,* "The challenge is to make the branch and the Web a seamless experience."[13] Exactly. Each episode with customers, across whatever media, should be scripted so as to progressively build toward a climax that accomplishes the particular objectives of the communications. Poor salespeople execute these tasks without regard to how they come off over time, while polished salespeople carefully match every detail. As a result, the work ultimately requires fewer takes and has a greater likelihood of creating the right impressions.

Matching multiple people from the same organization who must interact with the same customer over time must also been done with care. Situations requiring such matching include all retail operations, salespeople from different divisions or business units all calling on the same customer, and various order-processing, technical support, and customer service personnel who communicate directly with end users. Not only do such circumstances point to the need for someone to direct the overall performance, but each individual representative must be aware of how his or her work aligns with that of fellow actors. Employee uni-

Scripts in matching theatre are always dynamic

forms, whether the skimpy outfits at a Hooter's restaurant or the blue suits and white shirts of old-time IBM, represent management's desire to present a consistent appearance matched across all those who represent the company. The same attention should be given to sets, props, gestures, and a host of other details that together enhance the experience of interacting with the company.

The importance of matching people also exists in team selling, when everyone meets a customer at the same time and place. Even those people with no speaking part must match their performance with those in speaking roles. Their physical reactions must not only reinforce what a colleague (perhaps the "star") says and does, they must be chosen with a scrutiny equal to that with which they would select or emphasize a spoken word. One shouldn't just sit there behaving any which way, but act in a deliberate manner that enhances the credibility of the overall performance: a nodding head, an attentive look, a seemingly not-to-be-noticed gesture to be noticed by a key decision maker—all contribute to the performance. As in the closing scene of the classic movie *Casablanca,* in which a glance and a tear impart volumes, the final success of a sales call can be as much a function of what is seen but not heard as of the few spoken words that really matter.

Matching theatre isn't easy; it requires deliberation and thought. Yet the everyday pace of business often precludes spending much time rehearsing a performance scene by scene across the full spectrum of possible activity. In the performing arts, the amount of time devoted to rehearsing (and the tolerance for multiple takes) varies depending on the medium. Major motion pictures, indies, thirty-second commercials, television sit-coms, and soap operas all have different thresholds. In business as well, preparation time for meetings varies, and the need to succeed with just "one shot" often dominates the performance scene. Still, matching remains the key to success. Just as improv and platform techniques can be learned, so too can matching—even in such unfavorable circumstances. Thomas W. Babson instructs aspiring actors in the matching skills required within various film venues. His book, *The Actor's Choice: The Transition from Stage to Screen,* describes how to move from platform to matching theatre. Babson's "three-level system," which encompasses physical, motivational, and emotional behaviors across "six choices" (character, relationships, objective, opening emotion, transitions, and what he calls "speakout"—what the character thinks when he's not speaking), applies as much to any business venue as it does to any film set.[14]

Use matching theatre when the same customers and the same performers interact over and over

Street Theatre

The fourth and perhaps most engaging form of theatre is street theatre. Historically, it is the domain of jugglers, magicians, storytellers, puppeteers, acrobats, clowns, mimes—all those actors who must first draw people to their performance, then amaze this found audience with their skills and abilities, and, finally—often the most difficult part—ask them for money. While a doctoral student in performance studies at New York University, Sally Harrison-Pepper analyzed the street performers of Washington Square in lower Manhattan. She describes the essence of this form of theatre in her book *Drawing a Circle in the Square:*

> Foregoing the sanctity of a walled theater space, with darkened auditorium, fixed seating, prepaid audiences, and reassuring reviews, the street performer instead engages and manipulates the urban environment, using its

traffic, noise, and passersby as props for his shows. Buses rumble by; helicopters hover overhead; hecklers interrupt the rhythm of the performance; rain, cold, or police can defeat the performer entirely. The audience surrounds the street performer, restless, waiting, impatient. Yet the street performer succeeds in transforming urban *space* into a theater *place,* turning visitors resting on steps into an audience seated on bleachers.[15]

What a perfect description of successful selling. When going into a prospect's office, factory, or home, sales reps have no control over what they find there. They must instead "engage and manipulate" foreign space and thereby turn it into a stage on which to enact their selling performance. Rather than rely on the settings of a permanent stage, the best sales reps use whatever they find at hand as props by dynamically applying what worked in the past to the new situation. Neither bothered nor flustered by interruptions, they use the well-timed remark or expression to draw disruptions into the flow of the overall performance. Whether juggling, doing magic tricks, clowning around, or selling, street performers demonstrate a high degree of skill and ability.[16] How do they do it? Practice, practice, practice.

Seemingly improvisational, street performers in fact studiously rehearse—just as much as those in platform theatre, if not more so. In street theatre, though, every performance differs, depending on the composition and conduct of the audience as well as the specific "outside" elements that occur (an ambulance rushing by, for instance), not to mention the mood of the performer on that day. Street performers must gauge the audience, identify those who will go along with their gags and those unlikely to (sometimes even delaying or postponing performances when the audience doesn't seem "right"), and then turn every disruption into part of the act itself, lest they lose the audience completely and have to start all over again. While following a general outline based on past successes, every street performer determines on the fly which "bits" from his repertoire to include and which to forego. The end result: an audience-unique performance that creates value by re-using something known.

Street performers draw people in, amaze them, and then ask for money

In other words, rather than improvising their show, *street performers actually mass customize their performances.* Their bits—whether a clever remark, a particular routine, a sales trick, or a seemingly extemporaneous response to a naysayer—are standardized modules dynamically linked together on demand to create one seamless performance, or "gig." Each [bit = module] flows from a stable script, while the final street performance text "emerges" from the choices made along the way, as depicted in

Figure 7-2, just as mass customized offerings emerge from the choices made during the designed interaction.

The finale of all street performances remains the same, however. As Harrison-Pepper relates, "Often, the timing of the entire street performance is built around the crucial final phase—the pitch. . . . Street performers learn that the pitch must be precisely timed to transform [an] audience's greatest emotional energy into the greatest number of dollar bills." Consider again personal selling: whenever a sales rep draws from a portfolio of internalized selling routines, he performs street theatre. The timing of the entire performance flows into the final pitch, asking for the sale.[17] The sales rep determines in advance the basic script—just like the introductory segments, main points A, B, C, and finale of Figure 7-2—but adjusts it in real time based on the needs of the audience. He may lengthen one routine if a prospect gets excited, shorten another when the energy in the room declines, or throw in an unforeseen routine when he discovers a particular interest. All the while, he reacts to objections and interruptions (like heckles and disruptions on the street) as they occur by pulling the proper bit from his repertoire of practiced routines.

> **Seemingly improvisational, street performers in fact stabilize their scripts**

Interestingly, this aspect of street theatre, like improv, also draws on techniques first used in commedia dell'arte, which, after all, was first performed "in the market place where a crowd has to be attracted, interested, and then held if a living is to be made."[18] Over time, commedia players became adept at various standard bits and set gimmicks, called *lazzi*, many of which remain immediately recognizable even today: Arlecchino making a loud noise by sitting on a pig bladder; Zanni counting money in a "one for you, two for me" fashion; Pierrot pulling a chair out from under Il Capitano as he sits down; Arlecchino miming the catching of a fly buzzing around his head. And whenever a performance falters, a character might pull out a long stick and beat a fellow player (from which we get the term "slapstick").[19] These were not improvisations but dependable, repeatable routines, known to be effective from past performances, introduced at will whenever the situation seemed to warrant it.

Harrison-Pepper reports that fire-spitting Tony Vera, in the 1980s the acknowledged "King of Washington Square," always began his performances with the lazzo of drawing a large chalk circle on the sidewalk south of the square's prominent arch and then writing his name around its perimeter. Thus would he turn an empty space into a bare stage: "All I have to do is step into that circle and my crowd starts to develop," he said. "It happens by itself. It's magic."[20] To engage the growing audience, Vera would ignore

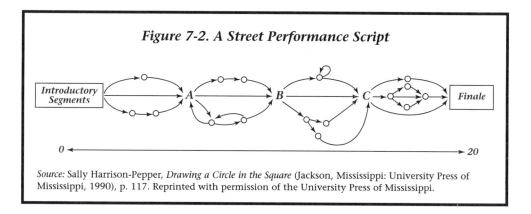

Figure 7-2. A Street Performance Script

Source: Sally Harrison-Pepper, *Drawing a Circle in the Square* (Jackson, Mississippi: University Press of Mississippi, 1990), p. 117. Reprinted with permission of the University Press of Mississippi.

them while focusing intently on the proper placement of his various props at strategic locations within the circle. (Again, a time-honored lazzo dating at least to the "medicine man" shows of the nineteenth-century Old West.) Finally, before beginning, he would "inspect" the area for debris and start whisking with a small broom (a lazzo shared with the Jacobs Field sweeper).

Each of Vera's shows emerged as he selected on-the-fly the routines he felt would yield the most money from a particular audience. He would always include the best of his bits and after first dragging out the finale to heighten its anticipation, not unlike Barbra Streisand and her gum-chewing routine, would conclude with his stock, yet utterly amazing routine of spitting ten-foot fireballs from his mouth. Throughout, he masterfully responded to the disruptions that inevitably occurred. Vera actually hoped a fire alarm would go off sometime during his performance, for it enabled him to employ one of his best bits, as related by a fellow street performer:

> One thing Tony did that I thought was one of the greatest things I'd ever seen was when he lit one of his fire torches and a fire alarm went off somewhere. He looked up, gave the torch to somebody in the audience, and left! Just stood in the audience, going "La dee da, I don't know what's going on." And it appeared to the audience that it was phenomenally spontaneous. I'm sure that it had happened before but, you know, it was just perfectly timed. It's a very flowing thing.[21]

Now *that's* how to handle what would otherwise be a very distracting disturbance. How much more should we be ready and able, no matter what our job responsibilities, to handle the questions, objections, disturbances, and interruptions that inevitably occur during any interaction with a customer?

While an executive's presentation to financial analysts must remain pure platform theatre, if he follows with a Q&A period, then he absolutely must *not* rely on improv skills. Rather, he should use street performance to anticipate possible lines of questioning, work out the perfect answers in advance, and then practice, practice, practice until they come off as great extemporaneous responses to each question that arises. Every performer, no matter what the circumstances, should be prepared with practiced bits to seize the spontaneous opportunities that arise in the course of doing business.

For example, customer service reps at inbound call center operations need exceptional street theatre skills to connect and empathize with customers seeking information, initiating orders, or simply asking for help with a problem. Some corporations retain coaches to help train their reps on how to handle calls. One of the best is the "Telephone Doctor," a stock character created by Nancy Friedman of St. Louis, Missouri. The good doctor appears in more than a hundred routines in a sixteen-tape video training library. Topic titles include "Determining Caller Needs," "How to Handle an Irate Caller," and "How to Treat Every Caller as a Welcome Guest." Each routine provides a bit that any rep can pick up, rehearse, and deliver on demand.

The Hartford uses street theatre in its Personal Lines Insurance Center, realizing that no one representative could adequately handle all possible calls from members.[22] Hugh Martin, the center's former head and now president of The Hartford's Affinity Personal Lines, modularized the organization into an ensemble of specific roles: generalists, who answer all calls and handle those they can, and a variety of specialists, who handle more difficult questions related to a particular issues, such as widowhood or the regulations of certain states. Each person keeps a stock set of routines that can be brought to bear at a moment's notice once the generalist realizes a caller's needs exceed his knowledge. In essence, the generalist has access to a raft of bits waiting to be called into action, even though they'll be performed by someone else. Martin says the center forms an "instant team" for every call, although "on-demand cast" would be just as accurate. He further relates, "No two phone calls are exactly alike because no two members placing them have the exact same needs. But we couldn't afford to look up answers all the time, so we designed a system where each response, while seemingly spontaneous, is really a preengineered routine performed by someone who knows the right answer."

Indeed, street theatre characterizes the work performed by all mass customizers, including Andersen Windows, ARAMARK, GNC Live Well,

Ross Controls, Paris Miki, and others introduced earlier in the book. Their work consists of bits made up of gigs or, if you prefer, modules made up of capabilities that stage a direct encounter between performer and audience. Mass customizers "profile" individual audience members to initiate the encounter's interaction, and in the process, amaze the audience by making the apparently complex seem simple, revealing only and exactly those elements which need to be made known. And then, before completing the performance in the finale, the audience first must wait so as to heighten the anticipation for the end of street performance work: the mass customized offering.

Every performer must have practiced bits to use as opportunities arise

Such [street theatre = mass customization] cannot be faked. The street performer must develop a high degree of expertise before even attempting to amaze an [audience = customers]. He must focus on the management of his repertoire of [bits = modules], how he will dynamically link them in new and exciting ways, and, most important, on his ability to sense and respond to the unique characteristics of individuals walking across his otherwise bare stage.[23]

ONE BIT AT A TIME

A street performer's bits cannot be picked fully formed out of a hat (even by a magician). Rather, they appear one bit at a time as the performer methodically advances his techniques—by determining which old bits don't work well anymore, responding spontaneously to new kinds of disruptions, or creating a new idea for a routine. Because just-invented routines have never before been performed, this first-time showing is no longer the province of street theatre; rather, it is improv theatre. All new bits must first be improvised, whether in front of an audience or in rehearsal. But rarely, if ever, does improvisation yield a perfectly formed bit. Perhaps a rejoinder falls short of the mark but provides the basis for developing a great routine. Or an idea for a new bit turns out wrong, though it leads down an unforeseen but fruitful path. However he arrives at the bit, once he's figured out its steps and nuances, the performer still isn't ready to use it in front of an audience. First, he must practice, practice, practice; the performer must repeat it over and over again until he has it down and can effectively replicate it at will, which means he's now performing platform theatre. He then must refine the bit via matching theatre, making sure that it gets the right reaction every time, tweaking it as necessary until it works consistently

A street performer's bits cannot be picked fully formed out of a hat

and, as a final step, ensuring that it fits in with whatever bits might precede or follow it. Only then can the performer recall the new bit on demand to provide the audience-unique value he deems appropriate. Only then can he renew his repertoire of street theatre routines, refreshing his performance with this new bit.[24]

This cycle of activities, from street theatre to improv to platform to matching and finally back to street theatre,[25] enables the accomplished street performer to work this new bit into his act on a moment's notice. This is exactly how the great Tony Vera creates bits for his seamless, on-demand performances, as he explained to Harrison-Pepper:

> "You work every day in the streets and find out what you're doing wrong, okay? And you're doing something wrong, you don't do that. Try something else. It works, keep it in the act. Keep doing it 'til your act is polished."
> What did he mean when he said something "works"? He replied: "People laugh, they have a good time, and mostly you can tell by what's in your hat at the end of the show. If it didn't work, that means not as much money— and vice versa."
>
> Essentially, then, the street performer constructs his performance text through a process of trial and error, adding, removing, or revising segments of his individual routines in a process of constant, often moment-to-moment revision. Each adjustment is prompted by ideas about what "works" in the show, that is, what entertains an audience and results in the greatest profits. But Vera is not selecting parts at random; rather he is dealing with the performance text as a whole, in which each choice affects the subsequent choices of his act.[26]

So it is for any street performer *cum* mass customizer, whether his bare stage be the literal street of a city or the figurative street of business theatre.

8
Now Act Your Part

• •

THE PROSPECT OF ACTING understandably may bring stage fright to many a worker: Improvise? Learn my lines? Match my peer? *Lazzi?* Oh my! You may feel like James Stockdale, Ross Perot's running mate in the 1992 elections, who was qualified to run, perhaps, but certainly unprepared for the vice-presidential debate against Al Gore and Dan Quayle, as he pondered "Who am I and why am I here?" Discomfort with the notion of acting, however, does not justify the dismissal of theatre as a useful operating model. This uneasiness just points to how individuals and groups must *learn to act differently* when staging experiences versus merely providing goods and services.

Sole practitioners—solo acts—know what it means to perform all the roles required in a business. Most enterprises, however, need a multitude of people to perform all the work necessary to generate output. The greater the number of people working for a business, the more likely some organizational model—that is, a set of assumptions, both explicit and implicit, about organizing people's work—influences the way things get done.[1] These sets of assumptions, varying with company culture, have existed for years, many evolving from a Mass Production mindset that seeks to classify all aspects of work into a single standard of behavior. Some examples that come to mind: Everyone has a title. Bosses conduct performance appraisals. Men wear ties to work. Many businesses today challenge these practices, seeking new means to attract, motivate, and retain a high-quality workforce. More and more we now see title-less organizations, 360-degree performance evaluations, and casual attire, all in an effort to rethink the most effective employment of human resources.

Theatre provides a new framework of particular value when seeking to stage experiences. Embracing the theatre model prevents the misappropriation of old economic paradigms, such as data "mining" and service "factories," which run the risk of perpetuating work practices out of sync with the competitive demands of the emerging Experience Economy.[2] Performing work as merely the delivery of services (or worse, as the manufacture of goods or the extractor of commodities) simply won't engage [audience = customers] in uniquely memorable ways. There are times when workers, from corporate executive to front-line rep, need a new vocabulary to see and respond to a changing world. Now is such a time.

TAKING STAGE IN THE WORKPLACE

Richard Schechner's Enactment Model (in Figure 6-1) can be amplified for use in our Performance Model shown in Figure 8-1, where people move to center stage in any performance of business theatre. They are the *cast.* Fully applying theatre principles to a business, therefore, begins with *casting,* the process of selecting actors to play specific roles. The success of any business obviously relies on picking the right people to play various parts. The notion that employee turnover stems from hiring under- or overqualified candidates for jobs often obscures a more fundamental source of employee dissatisfaction and defection: casting *mis*-qualified people in roles ill-suited to their capabilities in the name of getting the best and the brightest (arguably what Ross Perot did in selecting Mr. Stockdale as his running mate). To get the best talent for the role being cast, casting should match individual skills to appropriate roles. To effectively stage its [drama = strategy] a company must have the right [cast = people] to implement that strategy.

Your success relies on picking the right people to play the parts

Formally, a *role* is the part one or more workers play. It is divided into functional *responsibilities* to support the acting out of the [script = processes]. Contributing as much to the success of the enterprise's on-stage performance are many back-stage activities, some of which are completed before the performance (designers setting the stage) and some during the live performance (stage managers and crew getting the act together). Although usually associated only with those on stage, the terms *actor* and *role* apply equally to all workers and their responsibilities. For this reason, Disney refers to *all* employees as cast members. When a business views the responsibilities of all those individuals working in it as playing roles, those roles become the means to engage customers in more captivating ways. Without [defined roles = responsibilities], work becomes just another thankless job, done only for the sake of being done.

As discussed in Chapter 6, acting well requires thorough *characterization* of each role. A character represents all the choices made by each worker to depict the role in his [theatre = work]. People take on roles, but they act out characters. As Gillian Drake, part-time theatre director and coach of platform skills for lawyers, says, "In the theater, every sin-

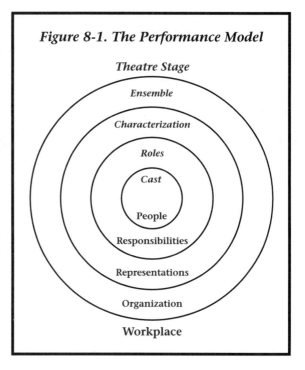

Figure 8-1. The Performance Model

gle thing that is viewed by the audience is a choice, down to the buttons on a character's costume, how they roll their hair, the props, the lighting; the same is very true in law."[3] The same choices inherent in [characterization = representations] engage audiences in accounting, banking, catering, dry cleaning, engineering—indeed, in any business.

When players perform their roles with character, the [performance = offering] transcends ordinary services. The individual characterizations, however, must fit within the entire *ensemble,* which according to the National Textbook Company's comprehensive *Dictionary of Theatre and Drama Terms,* is "the type of acting in which a cast works as a team to create a total effect rather than a group of individual performances."[4] The power of characterization lies in the integration of every worker's role into an organized whole. Whether a troupe, a

People take on roles, but they act out characters

more formal acting company, a production company, or a collection of street performers, this [ensemble = organization] gives individual performers freedom to create their own characters, with the proviso that their characterizations contribute positively to the total effect. In the performing arts, a "star turn" happens when a member of the cast promotes his or her own interests over those of the overall performance, upstaging a peer. In business, we call it playing politics. Great actors become true stars by gleaning diverse skills, bit by bit, from the many individuals they've worked with (not against) over the years. They observe, listen, and respect their fellow ensemble members and truly seek to promote the performances of each. In the process, they advance their own capabilities and reputation. Consider what everyone wants to know from those who have brushed with greatness, namely, "What's it like to work with Jack?"

The individual characterizations must fit within the entire ensemble

Great character work should exist in all industries, not just show business. As more and more Service Economy jobs become automated, the focus of human-to-human interaction in business is shifting to staging experiences.[5] Each role, therefore, must contribute to a unique audience-actor relationship represented in the company's experiential offerings. In the end, a company's

[cast = people]

must take on

[roles = responsibilities]

by each making choices to develop compelling

[characterization = representations]

that form(s) a cohesive

[ensemble = organization]

to engage guests in memorable ways.

This structure constitutes the essence of Experience Economy businesses, with profound implications for both the on- and off-stage actors within them. While the full effects of this economic shift on businesses and their workers cannot yet be fully known (the tremendous impact of the Industrial Revolution on people from all walks of life was not fully understood for more than a hundred years), we can discuss the nature of work in the new Experience Economy. In Chapter 6 we explained what it means to become an actor; here we describe what it means to be a producer, a director, or one of the various players who supports them (dramaturg, scriptwriter, technician, and stage manager and crews). We also discuss the role of the casting director, who helps producers and directors find the right people to fill all these roles, whether on stage or off.

A BIG ROLE TO FILL

In any business, the *producers* financially back the enterprise, whether it be closely held by private investors, financed by venture capitalists, or managed by executives representing millions of shareholders. They determine what the business will produce. Will it be extracted commodities? Commoditized goods and services? Or new experiences? No one else in the organization can answer these questions, for they point to the most basic consideration: *What productions do we want to stage?* There are no easy answers or cookie-cutter approaches to this question. Producers originate change, because crafting any strategy always entails desiring and envisioning the future. They choose which [audience = customers] they wish to serve and the nature of the [theatre stage = workplace] in which the drama will unfold before a buying public.

Producers inadequately fulfill their roles when they do not define what change their businesses seek to affect through their performance offerings. Unfortunately, we find today countless mission statements riddled with nebulous notions about just what this particular business seeks to accomplish. These are generic visions that could apply to any business; they make a poor substitute for rigorous thinking. Mission statements, strategic plans, and action steps must be grounded in the uniqueness of a business. This isn't a simple question of differentiating the business from its competitors but of discovering the *unexamined* dimensions of one's corporate self. This self-examination, like that conducted by any individual actor, supplies an organization with a source of renewal (just as examining the uniqueness of customers is the means to uncovering their unarticulated needs). A producer's vision is meaningful only if the actors called on to execute it understand—viscerally—how the company plans to alter the very nature of the world through its industry. Every activity of the [ensemble = organization] must be performed to advance external change.

What productions do you want to stage?

Too many companies seem to passively observe their futures, failing to understand that it is their behavior that may be the strongest influence on developments in their industries and the rise and fall of economic eddies that follow. The choices made by real people within a business, not some law of nature, determine its fate. Good producers make their own future by doing one thing: *exploring what leverage points in the economy they can exploit for their own strategic advantage.*

The emerging Experience Economy opens up possibilities for new strategies of moving beyond goods and services as the primary source of profits. In the face of rapidly commoditized goods and services, and an increasing number of customers who want experiences, producers must demand that their executives and managers be accountable for answering some key questions. These include:

- *Recognizing* how new experiential elements can be added to increase demand and/or charge higher prices for existing goods and services: How can you enhance your present offerings by appealing to the senses? What negative cues can be eliminated, and positive cues added, to better integrate customer impressions into an engaging theme? What could you mass customize and thereby shift up the Progression of Economic Value?

- *Identifying* which goods and services will command higher prices and therefore serve as critical resources for true experience stagers, repositioning one's goods as props and one's services as stages to support new experiential offerings of potential customers: How can the company help other businesses shift up the Progression of Economic Value? Can your things be *ing*ed to enhance a customer's experiential offering? Can services be restaged as platforms for customers' economic experiences?

- *Eradicating* current practices of providing experiential elements for free merely as a means to sell more goods and services, redefining these elements as explicit experiences that can command a distinct price: What would you have to do differently to charge admission? How would you move current experiences into the sweet spot of entertainment, educational, escapist, and esthetic realms?

- *Commoditizing* the competition by staging wholly new experience offerings: How would you set the stage by theming the experience, harmonizing impressions with positive cues, eliminating negative cues, mixing in memorabilia, and engaging all five senses? Which form(s) of theatre would best portray the experience you wish to create?

These strategic probes point to the mere beginnings of exploration. The bottom line: Good producers insist that these questions be convincingly answered before financially backing the full production. For the answers define the [drama = strategy] to be staged by the [ensemble = organization].

LEAVING A MARK

The role of *director* involves making the conceptual material of [drama = strategy] become operational reality.[6] Those people who fill this position face pressures unparalleled in other roles, because directors have accountability for everything, literally everything, that takes place on this new stage of business theatre. Directing requires coordination of all the players—

actors, dramaturgs, scriptwriters, technicians, and stage crews—while securing the producers' approval of decisions at key junctures leading up to the performance. And yet it involves so much more.

The directing role demands *organizational* skills: scheduling and conducting auditions (with the help of casting directors), ensuring that technicians meet timelines in the design and construction of sets, selecting appropriate costumes and props, and determining the day-to-day movements, or "blocking," of the cast. Directors must help actors prepare through formal rehearsals as well as coaching on the side. They must spend time alone with the [script = processes], developing their own point of view about how best to orchestrate all the activity. And time must be spent with the producers, keeping them apprised of the progress toward fulfillment of the [drama = strategy]. It falls to the director to create a harmonized whole.

To meet all these demands, the role of director has necessarily evolved into an authoritative position. At times, directors must tell people what to do. Enlightened directors, however, do not blindly impose their whims on the rest of the ensemble. Rather, they perfect a rare fusion of collaboration and command. This blend of collaborator and commander *is* directing. To successfully blend the two into one, directors require certain *motivational* skills. The resulting mix dictates to actors without having them lose their own sense of discovery in their roles. Characterization emerges through collaboration, while both director and actor maintain distinct, even dogmatic, points of view about the performance.

> **Directing is the fusion of collaboration and command**

The director must also exhibit *interpretive* skills.[7] What stage should be set? What actors should be cast? The answers to both questions require interpretation of the strategy into an appropriate set of actions. As the actual offering progresses from idea to implementation, this interpretation manifests itself in a constant stream of decision making during the preparations and rehearsals leading to performance: what to include and exclude from each performance, what to keep in and take out as the drama unfolds, and what work should be done off stage versus on stage. The basis for making these decisions, all along the way, resides in discerning which actions best fit the strategy. Such discernment necessarily puts the director in the world of concepts and principles, the stuff of interpretive action. To leave his mark, the director must learn to fly at 30,000 feet while managing the details of the performance transpiring on the ground.

Finally, directing requires *storytelling* skills. Indeed, every director ultimately aims to enact a performance that completely engages the audience in its story. Former Hollywood and now IBM scriptwriter Peter Orton makes the case to the IBM directors he teaches that "Stories enhance attention, create anticipation, increase retention. They provide a familiar set of 'hooks' that allow us to process the information that we hang on them."[8] As the title of the article in *Fast Company* quoting Orton puts it, "Every Leader Tells a Story."

TURNING DRAMA INTO PERFORMANCE, STRATEGY INTO OFFERING

To meet their primary obligations—turning drama into performance, strategy into offering—directors look primarily to four roles for support. Each corresponds to one of the four elements (as presented in Figure 6-1) that contributes to the staging of an experience for the [audience = customer]:

- *dramaturgs* assist in creating the [drama = strategy]
- *scriptwriters* help with developing the [script = processes]
- *technicians* aid the production of [theatre = work]
- *stage crews* coordinate the operational elements of the [performance = offering]

Each role, as discussed below, helps the director create a unified performance.

Dramaturgs

The *dramaturg* advises the director in matters of [drama = strategy]. Theatre arts professors David Kahn and Donna Breed explain: "The dramaturg may act as a sounding board for the director's analysis, pointing out patterns, issues, images, character functions, and other elements that contribute to the play's meaning. Dramaturgs should be skilled in the mechanics of dramatic structure and can be helpful in identifying how the play is constructed and what models might be useful for analysis."[9] In business theatre, internal *planning personnel* or external *strategic consultants* may play this role. In either case, the dramaturg researches and analyzes the economic and/or competitive environment in which the company plans to release its production and then synthesizes the findings for the director. Of critical importance to the dramaturg role is the ability to distinguish which customer phenomena should influence decision making, especially any industry discontinuities—such as the digitization and direct-connection potential of the Internet—that might be exploited to the company's advantage.

In the arts, dramaturgs help interpret previously written plays for ensembles performing them here and now. Similarly, previously existing strategies must be interpreted for front-line performance. Of course, all strategies are old the moment they're written. Dramaturgs must not alter the existing strategy to *fit* contemporary circumstances, but alter everything else to enact that strategy *given* contemporary circumstances. In fulfilling this role, dramaturgs must remember three important rules. One, the dramaturg must make the offering compelling for the audience of customers. Two, he must bring clarity of thought to parts difficult to interpret or characterize. And, finally, he must describe, not prescribe, scenarios and options for the director and cast. Whether inside or outside the organization, the dramaturg must not act like the producer or director—that's not his job.

The dramaturg must describe, not prescribe

Directors may differ in how participatory a style they wish the dramaturg to possess and will choose dramaturgs accordingly, but they should not tolerate any who usurp their directing powers. Any director who allows the dramaturg to migrate into his role, from providing input to dictating output, has weakened his authority to direct. And all the actors in the ensemble will know it. To help prevent this situation, dramaturgs should not try to have all the answers but to apply their expertise to crafting provocatively useful questions.

In the end, the director relies on the dramaturg to help tell the story he envisions. At 3M, for example, the company's internal dramaturgs—its planners and strategists—have pushed its directors—line management for each business unit—to completely overhaul their strategic dramas, moving from bulleted lists of stuff to what company executive Gordon Shaw calls *strategic narratives:* "Planning by narrative is a lot like traditional story-telling. Like a good storyteller, the strategic planner needs to *set the stage*—define the current situation in an insightful, coherent manner. . . . Next, the strategic planner must *introduce the dramatic conflict*. . . . Finally, the story must *reach resolution* in a satisfying, convincing manner."[10] It's imperative for company dramaturgs to tell the internal strategic stories that will help fulfill the director's vision of the external performance.

Scriptwriters

Directors ask *scriptwriters* to define what set of processes will generate the end performance.[11] They must therefore concern themselves with the four different forms of theatre and the unique combinations of [script = processes] and [performance = offering] highlighted in Figure 7-1. Improv requires systematic techniques to help the actor find imaginative responses to audience input and feedback. Platform theatre calls for formal lines. Matching benefits from highly refined and scrutinized schedules that define who does what when. Street theatre depends on a rich portfolio of bits dynamically used to create unique performances. In each form, the [script = processes] supplied by scriptwriters contributes a crucial component to the performance.

Scriptwriting in business has gained prominence as a result of the total quality management and business process reengineering movements. Much has been written about both TQM and BPR so only a few highlights need mentioning here. TQM sought to script processes through a series of small, continuous improvements, while BPR pursued dramatic, discontinuous improvements via large-scale redesign of processes. Reengineering proponents rightly pointed out that TQM efforts were susceptible to generating high-quality processes for work that was not really needed. "Don't automate, obliterate" such processes, urged Michael Hammer.[12] The message resonated with executive producers impatient with the results of TQM. And these BPR scriptwriters were right in one important aspect: for too many years companies used information technologies merely to automate existing business processes, when every new technology possesses characteristics with which companies could script entirely new means of performing work.[13] While powerfully articulated and clearly different, BPR mirrored TQM in assuming business strategy as a given. Reengineering proponents urged organizations to simultaneously rethink technology and processes, but the real need lies in simultaneously rethinking processes and strategy, as rightly pointed out by professors Gary Hamel and C. K. Prahalad, who urge the reinvention of entire industries through imaginative scriptwriting.[14]

Today, because of TQM and BPR, a plethora of process management techniques are available to business scriptwriters. And in no small thanks to Hamel and Prahalad, most businesses understand the importance of innovative processes not only in designing efficient production but also in crafting imaginative strategies. Too often directors (and meddling producers) look only to their dramaturg for advice in crafting their [dramas = strategies]— often to the point of relinquishing control of the drama altogether—when scriptwriters contribute equally, if not more so, to envisioning creative strategies.

Consider a few examples in which new processes enabled wholly new strategies, which in turn revolutionized entire industries. Prior to the 1980s, consumers looking for new eyeglasses went to a local optometrist working out of a small office, where after an eye exam they could choose from a few dozen frames. The office sent the order to a centralized factory, where it would sit for weeks before technicians finally produced a pair of glasses, which were then sent back to the optometrist for pick-up and fitting. The founders of LensCrafters—being entrepreneurs, they were producers, directors, and scriptwriters all—figured out how to bring the lens-manufacturing process to the very point of sale, refining it periodically over time. LensCrafters' new [script = processes] gave the company such a competitive advantage that the very nature of the industry changed. Today, retail stores employ or provide space for optometrists, who give exams, and then mass customize lenses in about an hour while consumers shop. Paris Miki (as mentioned in Chapter 5) now faces the opportunity of revolutionizing the industry again through the process innovation that enables it to "image" on a computer screen the best glasses for each individual and then mass customize not only the lenses but the frames as well. Time will tell if it succeeds.

One mass customizer that has succeeded spectacularly, via scriptwriting, is Dell Computer. Rather than move production to retail, Dell moved inventory *out of* retail and built personal computers to order, first out of Michael Dell's dorm room at college, and eventually in state-of-the-art factories in Austin, Texas, and around the world. In bypassing distributors to work directly with end-customers in the workplace and at home, Dell Computer eliminated *all* finished-goods inventory. By 1998 it had reduced component inventory on hand to just seven days. Further, this system enables Dell to integrate the latest technology into its machines months ahead of its competitors and to create a cash-conversion cycle (the time that elapses between the day Dell pays its suppliers and the day it gets paid by customers) of *negative* eight days.[15] No wonder nearly every other personal computer manufacturer has announced that it, too, will build personal computers to order.

Other companies where scriptwriting enabled new strategies include minimill steel producers like Nucor, Chaparral Steel, and Gallatin Steel, which now have dramatically lower costs and greater flexibility than the old-line mass producers; America Online, which helped people connect with others online; and U.K.-based Pilkington Brothers, which instituted a series of process innovations that enables large plate glass to be produced in one integrated process.[16] The scripting of processes is an inherently creative act that ought to be inexorably bound to strategy development. In the arts, who could imagine a drama without a script? Why, then, do so many businesses devise strategies without considering how processes affect what they want to offer?

The scripting of processes is inexorably bound to strategy development

Technicians

Various *technicians* also contribute to defining the nature of company offerings. The technical presentation of the performance defines the *context,* or operating environment, for the [theatre = work]. This presentation generally includes a designed set, supporting props, and costumes. The exact combination and presentation of these technical elements vary according to form of theatre and even to the offering employing each form. Sales representatives exert little design control over the set of the customers they call on. As a result, their improv or street performances become highly dependent on a collection of portable props and on their ability to take advantage of whatever props they find lying around (or happening by). Platform and matching theatre usually afford greater opportunities to design the desired set on which the ensemble stages the experience.

Set designers. In cases where the [theatre stage = workplace] remains under the company's control, as in platform theatre, set designers focus on the six areas that together comprise the set: backstage, stage, auditorium, proscenium, entrance, and exit. Only the backstage areas, unseen by the audience of customers, can be designed solely for functionality. All others must consider how the set design supports the [theatre = work]. Entrances and exits cannot be overlooked, for they introduce and reinforce the experience in the minds and memories of guests. Set designers must pay particular attention to the stage, of course, but also to the auditorium that guests occupy and the proscenium through which guests view the stage. Each store at Ontario Mills Mall, for example, extends into the mall aisles with a unique and very proscenium-like facade, inviting passing guests to enter its domain. One wide aisle that connects the north and south halves of the mall, called Off Rodeo Drive, actually resides inside a single store (Bernini's), which a clever set designer has made to look like an enticing passageway with ostensibly separate store entrances on the left and right.

Clearly, set design abides within the domain of architecture, and experience stagers must employ architectural expertise—for both internal and external purposes—to design new experiential settings. In this technical work, only three rules apply. First, traditional architectural considerations must be supplemented with explicit consideration of the impressions the set will make on paying customers. This extends to everything guests may encounter. One of the simple, but indispensable, cues Walt Disney used at Disneyland was trees; their utter normalness and everyday reality helped ground the fantasy he wanted to create. As explained by

Set designers ensure that *no thing* is out of character

biographer Bob Thomas: Disney "wanted trees to be part of the beauty and the drama of Disneyland, and to play their roles, they needed to be big. . . . Walt wanted each tree to fit its location—maples, sycamores and birches for the Rivers of America; pines and oaks for Frontierland, etc. He sometimes rejected a tree with the comment: 'It's out of character.'"[17] It falls to set designers to ensure that *no thing* is out of character—it would ruin the integrity of the performance.

Second, design around all five senses: sightlines, comfort level, acoustics, aromas, even food concessions. GNC, for example, found that customers wanted to see their own Custom VitaPaks being made—the tipping of the storage bins, the motion of the vitamins as they whooshed down the tube, the whirring of the printer, and the zapping of the perforator proved irresistible. So its set designers moved the machine from behind a counter to the front of the store, where it now also serves to attract new consumers. In other cases, set designers must design from scratch the proper sensory environment, like the Rainforest Cafe did with its five-sense water mist. The sensory design, like all other aspects of the design, must have integrity in the sum of its component elements.

Third, don't be bound by convention: for You make your own rules! As Francis Reid, for years head of the department of theatre design at London's Central School of Art and Design, declares, "Theatre has reached a development point where virtually anything goes. A point where a production's style is no longer expected to be either derivative of the past or based upon the logic of a new philosophy. The only requirement is internal consistency. . . . A production may take virtually any proposition as its starting point so long as the consequences of that starting point are followed through."[18] In business theatre, that starting point is the theme of the experience; everything flows from the manifestation of that theme in acting performances and, of course, in set design.

Prop managers. In addition to set designers, a director often needs technicians to recommend the appropriate mix of props to use during the [theatre = work]. Used wisely, props play a significant part in engaging customers in positive ways. Props may be introduced simply for esthetic purposes (to create specific impressions) or for functional purposes (to help an actor perform some task) but esthetic considerations actually come into play for functional props as well.

Consider again the legal profession. Jury consultant Robert Hirschhorn, of Galveston, Texas, advises law firms to consider every physical good that appears in their performances, not just on stage but in the entrance and exit areas of their sets. "You never know when a juror is going to see you getting in or out of your car in the parking lot,"[19] says Hirschhorn, who therefore counsels counselors to stay away from luxury cars in favor of minivans or no-frills utility vehicles. Is this trickery, or an indication of thoroughness that extends into the court room as well? Before answering too fast, bear in mind that the importance of automotive props extends beyond lawyering to other industries (you may use such a prop yourself). To this day, an international business machines company headquartered in Armonk, New York, directs sales representatives calling on the Big Three in Detroit to drive only American-made cars onto automakers' lots. More sweepingly, a consumer goods company headquartered in Cincinnati, Ohio, insists on U.S. vehicles for reps calling on *all* companies based in the fifty states. Clearly, the car model a company selects for its salesforce entails more than just what vehicle will best transport reps from point A to point B. Some of the largest corporations in the world use five-figure goods as mere props for their matching theatre.

Sometimes an on-stage actor serves as his or her own prop manager. Briefcases, pads of paper, even choice of writing instruments all contribute to one's act. But whoever selects the props, remember to eliminate negative cues. A prop that is misused or poorly selected can lose business. When in a meeting with a prospective client, don't stop your pitch midsentence to check your pager. If you must respond to it, improvise to turn the interruption into an opportunity to score points. (And if it works, add it to your repertoire of bits à la Tony Vera.) Above all, turn off the cell phones. Prospects may brand an entire selling team annoying because one person's phone proved bothersome.

Presentation materials offer another lesson: Never use a prop as a crutch. Overhead slides crowded with words all too often make a poor substitute for learning one's lines (as Linda demonstrated in Chapter 7 with her speech at the Executive Briefing Center). Lengthy presentations that exceed the boundaries of allotted meeting times are no replacement for meticulous scriptwriting. Don't expect props—even cleverly designed ones—to cover for failings elsewhere in the ensemble's act. Rather, prop managers should see to it that actors use props to enable and accentuate important features of an act that cannot be staged without their use. When in doubt, help them figure out how to do without, or at least with less.

Never use a prop as a crutch

Costume designers. Demand will also emerge for technicians skilled in the design and selection of wardrobes for the cast. The attire of workers has long been important in some businesses, especially those in certain service industries: airline pilots and crew, hotel staff, waiters and hostesses in restaurants, delivery company drivers, security guards, and so forth. In most instances, costuming these workers consists of fitting them with uniforms, standard costumes worn by all the actors on stage. Uniforms send visible cues to customers to help them identify members of a company's ensemble. Who doesn't immediately recognize a UPS driver because of his familiar brown garb (not to mention the brown prop he's driving)?

A few costuming principles can help in almost any line of work.[20] First, *segment costume assignments by role,* as did the cast of characters in commedia dell'arte, each of whom could be immediately recognized by a distinctive costume and mask. The airline industry is good at incorporating this element of theatre into its act. Folks at the check-in counter and gate wear one type of uniform, for example, pilots another, and ground crews yet another (and at British Airways, queue managers don red coats to play their parts). If a baggage handler ventures from backstage to the proscenium jetway, his knee pads and ear plugs make his role very clear.

Second, costume designers must *make sure each costume conveys a message consistent with the theme of the experience and characterization of the role* the director wants portrayed,[21] as is the case with the Geek Squad's nerdy attire. This explains why airlines such as Southwest abandoned traditional airline garb in favor of more casual attire. Conventional uniforms convey an aura of authority, especially if the costumes draw from military motifs in their design. And what do the polo-shirted and sneakered costumes of Southwest say? We're perky! And ready to jump up and down with you (in four connecting flights) to California, as if participating in an athletic *event.* Don't be misled by this example: the design of uniforms goes beyond assignment of formal versus casual costumes. British Airways' new no-frills airline, Go, outfits flight attendants in charcoal gray suits and, get this, lime green and purple T-shirts. Barbara Cassani, CEO of Go, calls the look "professional but not uptight."[22] The costumes combine informality and formality, brilliantly reinforcing BA's commitment to operate the new airline with both low fares and a high quality of experience.

The third costuming principle calls for directors and designers to *allow actors to personalize their costumes,* completing their characterizations, even if only in seemingly small details. For instance, restaurant chain T.G.I. Friday's, a business unit of the Carlson Companies, grants each food server license to supplement its standard-issue, red-and-white striped shirt with a hat of their choice and encourages them to adorn hat and shirt (and even suspenders, socks, and trousers) with buttons displaying slogans and symbols of the wildest variety imaginable (no profanity, though, thank God). The simple costuming feature contributes powerfully to the sights and sounds that connote a T.G.I. Friday's dining experience.

In many business roles, the only article of clothing traditionally available for males to personalize their costumes was the necktie. Over the past thirty years, however, this limitation has been lifting, and we now see a wide variety of colored shirts and styled collars, not to mention socks, shoes, and belts, in the workplace. Even the button-downed halls of IBM and Procter & Gamble have loosened their ties. But something's often amiss when companies relax attire standards: Who, then, coordinates the costuming, making sure the cast of characters matches from actor to actor and scene to scene? Without formal costuming roles, such as the team at East Jefferson General Hospital that put together its "EJ Look" book detailing the do's and don'ts of hospital costuming, these considerations usually go unattended.

Because costuming concerns more than formal/casual issues, the selection of clothing attire and accessories involves much more than a quick "dress-for-success" study. Costuming involves detailed wardrobe selection, quick costume changes, and the ability of the actor to use the costume to help assume his or her role. Consider a real-life version of Chapter 7's Linda: Rebecca Mark, head of energy giant Enron Corp.'s international business. Mark built Enron International's revenues from zero to $1.1 billion, with a backlog of $20 billion in projects, often while wearing three to four different outfits per day. She changes costumes for different meetings (performances) in different places (stages) with different staff (ensemble) for different customers and prospects (audiences). "It's a bit of theatre," Mark acknowledged to *Forbes* magazine.[23] More than a few bits, actually, if one calculates the permutations of choices residing in the assorted suits, tops, jackets, dresses, blouses, shirts, skirts, shoes, and jewelry from which she assembles her costumes. As a business celebrity, Mark literally has fans of foreign officials flocking to meet her at airports, a spectacle once confined to movie stars, but now coming to business theatres near you.

Consider, too, the Dogs-of-the-Dow investment advisors the Motley Fool, played by actor-directors David and Tom Gardner. Their costumes consist of just one article of unusual clothing added to the traditional attire of trusted financiers: a pair of jester's hats. Older brother David explains the significance of the hat: "There's a war for your money out there. And the more I study it, the more I realize that the guys wearing the pinstripe suits—with all their complicated graphs and their numbers that don't have any context you can understand—aren't on my side, and they aren't on your side either. Indeed, if those guys are Wise—and that's what they call themselves, on TV and in all the glossy financial magazines—then we want to be Fools."[24]

Image is everything in costuming

But they're wise to be fools, and wiser still to recognize the importance of costuming to the staging of an experience, which the Motley Fools direct on both the World Wide Web and America Online, with guests now visiting more than 17 million times per month. Traditional investment advisors may be reluctant to don crazy hats for fear of being associated with waiters at T.G.I. Friday's, but not the Fools. *Worth* magazine reported on the arrival of David Gardner to pitch investment advice at a convention in Marco Island, Florida. Gardner was dressed in a crisp blue shirt and stylish khakis, but no hat. The event's meeting planner immediately hurled an alarming cry, "Did you bring the hat?" Gardner calmed her nervous fears, "Of course, what do you think I am—a fake?"[25] Not at all, just a prudent businessman who knows how to act his part.

Image is everything, in costuming as with other technical facets of design. The trend toward casual attire in the workplace opens up opportunities to create unique [theatre stages = workplaces] for staging engaging experiences, such as an Enron sales campaign or Motley Fool investment advice. But relaxed standards of attire must be actively directed toward intentionally staged cues, lest relaxation itself become the new standard and roles become confused.

Stage Crews

Stage crews have one simple responsibility: to "ensure that everybody and everything is in its right place at the right time. They document every on-stage move by anybody or anything during the production. They must be calm in a crisis, patient with frayed tempers, and infinitely understanding of everyone's problems."[26] The crew must get the right sets, props, costumes, and even actors where and when they are needed so the [performance = offering] goes off without a hitch. Ultimately, the members of the crew are logisticians. Whether a warehouseman dispatching inventory to a distribution center or a housekeeper making a hotel bed, members of the crew must procure, maintain, transport, and shuttle the resources prescribed by the director, within a process outlined by the scriptwriter, using devices designed by the technicians.

The members of the crew are logisticians

In fulfilling this role, the stage crew must be both effective and efficient. They must richly attend to details with an intention all their own—*in order to* enhance the quality of the output. Without such precise care, a crew may turn a wonderfully conceived drama and a well-scripted strategy into an embarrassing performance. But the crew must also be careful not to drive up the cost of production by wasting money, people, or time. They must roll up their sleeves and perform the back-stage work that, more often than not, goes unnoticed and unappreciated.

The stage manager is responsible for ensuring that all goes according to plan. He must also track performance—from issuing periodic reports to monitoring and tracking moment-to-moment movements. For other than street theatre, the manager and his crew must document, document, document—institutionalizing *how* the ensemble runs the production so the performance is repeatable. They must measure, measure, measure, since, as we all now know, what you don't measure, you can't manage. And they must *stay out of the way* when on-stage actors prepare to enter, perform on, and finally exit the stage. Yet they must always be accessible, immediately on the scene when something goes awry.

Their tasks may seem thankless, but crew members should understand how significant these roles are to the overall offering. Stage crews, after all, run all the operational elements of production, the vehicles through which technical design adds value. Set design, props, and costuming exist to help bring the actors' unwritten subtext to life. The stage crew must make sure everything's in its place for on-stage actors to manifest such subtext.

Consider how stage crews enabled former President Ronald Reagan to capitalize masterfully on subtext for his White House news conference performances. Open doors to the East Room allowed cameras to see the Gipper emerge in the distance from a far-away room. He then purposefully made his way down the long, red-carpeted hallway to the platform where one last hop up brought him to the podium. Julius Fast, a leading expert on the use of body language, said of Reagan's performance, "The subtext was communicated before he spoke: vigor, authority, ease."[27] And when he spoke, Reagan's attitude and style provided a compelling context for his words. His appeal—like that of all good actors—manifested itself not in how he said his lines but what he meant when he said them. President Reagan's performances would have been impossible without a stage crew working behind the scenes to position cameras, place carpet, open doors, and signal Reagan on stage at the appropriate time. Front-line personnel—the on-stage actors of any performance—cannot by themselves make all the necessary preparations to act their part. No actor is an island.

A CASTING CALL FOR COMPANIES

To fully realize the Performance Model of Figure 8-1—providing an appropriate ensemble of actors, technicians, and stage crew members for each production created by directors, dramaturgs, and scriptwriters—the human resources department must become a *casting director.* Hiring candidates for jobs essentially becomes casting actors to fill [roles = responsibilities]. And this means significant change for the HR department. Any enterprise looking to stage experiences must discontinue its reliance on interviews as the dominant method of evaluation and must begin conducting auditions instead.

Words matter. Vocabulary affects behavior. Calling your offering an experience, your work theatre, and your interviews auditions will certainly bring about some movement in the right direction. But make no mistake: it will not be enough to sustain lasting improvement. HR departments, along with the producers and directors for whom they hire, must stage real auditions, for they present the principal means to gather information about how an actor will actually perform.

Most information gathered in traditional face-to-face interviews concerns the actor as individual; knowledge of his ability to perform (as well as his true desire to play this particular role) can only be garnered from auditions. Information gathering should be done, but only as a means to screen

> **HR departments must stage real auditions**

aspiring actors for participation in the auditioning process. Harvard Business School professor Leonard Schlesinger describes how the fast-food restaurant where he once worked as an executive effectively used auditions: "An integral part of the Au Bon Pain selection process is a paid two-day work experience in the stores prior to final selection interviews. This experience weeds out applicants both through self-selection and through management observation of behavior."[28]

Several principles then govern auditions.[29] First and foremost, companies must create places to conduct the simulations, role plays, or live tests that constitute real auditions. With candidates no longer paraded around interviewers' offices for a series of conversations, new venues need to be established—HR's internally staged experiences. Many consulting companies already put candidates in role-playing situations in real-world offices and team rooms; others should do the same. If you are staging auditions for a buyer role in the purchasing department, then have virtual vendors call on each prospective buyer, who is furnished with an office for the occasion. If auditioning for new bank tellers, set up a simulated counter or booth and have individuals process deposits, cut cashier's checks, and check balances. If in need of more call center representatives, set up a bank of phones to test how prospective reps field incoming calls. In every case, establish a place—perhaps even in the real customer place, as Au Bon Pain does— where you can observe the actor performing the intended role. The candidate need not act out the whole play before a full audience, just some important and revealing scenes for those doing the hiring.

Next, if you're creating a specific place for auditions, strip it down to its essentials. Minimize props, deliberately remove features normally present

Auditions are HR's internally staged experiences in the real setting for the everyday role, and position the auditors in prominent view of the applicant. Do this so the unaided performance reveals the raw approach with which each individual tackles the role. Don't let the prospective buyer bring a briefcase full of notes. Keep the teller's station clear of instructions, policy memos, and other "cheat sheets" that may typically surround the computer monitor. Furnish the call center with only a phone and one image fixed on a computer screen. After all, as Barbra Streisand demonstrated, it doesn't matter if the props are material or not, only if the acting genuinely fits the role. Observing the essence of how each person characterizes the role and fits into the ensemble of actors guarantees that the audition will help identify candidates well-suited for particular parts.

No less an experience stager than Disney uses such a place for auditions. In 1989, Robert A. M. Stern, a renowned postmodern architect who has designed many Disney facilities, including its new Celebration living experience, created the company's Casting Center for auditioning prospective cast members for parts. As the Project on Disney described the facility, "Stern's Casting Center tells a story about what it means to work at Disney, or, as [Stern] says, 'to clarify Disney's hiring process and give it an architectural dimension.' By channeling potential employees along a ramp between carefully spaced murals that tell a story, Stern alludes to the effects of rides at Disney World; the procession through the building's architecture is itself a kind of ride, in which one learns the story of the park's secret: that all is illusion."[30] It's also the place where Disney observes how well each actor fits into a microcosm of its larger-scale fantasies.

Regardless of the particular experience being cast, refrain from singling out any one characterization that *you* think fits the role. A vast universe of possibilities exists, and no preconceived notion of right and wrong should eliminate prospects so early in the selection process. Accept the fact that each person has not had an adequate opportunity to build a complete [characterization = representations] (there will be time for that after casting). Rather, consider how each individual might develop into the role.

Consider for a moment the world of baseball scouts, who enjoy the great luxury of auditioning players during actual performances. Yet even in these ideal circumstances, there are do's and don't's. Tony Lucadello, generally considered baseball's greatest scout, visited high school diamonds in Ohio, Indiana, and Michigan for fifty years in search of major league prospects, and in that tenure he signed more kids who eventually made it to "The Show" than any other scout—fifty in all, including Hall-of-Famer Mike Schmidt. Lucadello noted four basic approaches that various scouts used to evaluate talent, which he called the 4 P's.[31] The Poor scout, not a planner and never prepared, just reacts to whoever happens on the stage instead of rooting out potential stars. Most people evaluating talent know better or else quickly find themselves out of casting work. The next kind of scout, the Pickers, mistakenly single out a lone weakness in a player and eliminate him despite other notable strengths. Performance-based scouts, which account for an overwhelming majority, make their evaluations solely on the basis of the audition performance. This scouting approach has a significant flaw, which is that it places undo emphasis on the circumstances in which the player auditions, such as, perhaps, a high school star hitting or pitching against inferior talent. Finally, there is the Projector, which is where Lucadello counts himself and all other casting directors who understand that the audition performance doesn't matter. Does the actor have the skills required to act, and act exceptionally, once cast into the role? An audition takes place to answer that question alone, and to project such talent into the future of live performances.

> **Refrain from singling out any one characterization that *you* think fits the role**

How then does one select the right person to fill a role? Ironically, not by looking for the "ideal" person at all, at least not in terms of corresponding to some preconceived characterization. It's done by taking notice of who exhibits raw talent and an acuity for making compelling choices. Do that and you'll find someone ideal for the role—just as Michael Shurtleff found Barbra Streisand and Tony Lucadello found Mike Schmidt.

With interviews downplayed, the onus in casting switches to asking the right questions not of the candidate *but of oneself,* such as the following:

- How does the actor communicate? Pay particular attention to how he listens.
- How does the actor involve and play off others? Note how he relates to fellow actors in the audition, and in what circumstances he looks to seek, give, and avoid assistance.
- What does he want out of every interaction? Check for signals about what motivates the actor.
- How does the actor handle unfamiliar situations, disruptions, and interruptions? Look for demonstrations of self that emerge only when things move out of his control.
- Does his sense of rhythm and tempo make connections with the audience? Use the events in the audition to look for various sequences, progressions, and durations of activity that seem to go most smoothly.
- Does he have a sense of humor? What the actor finds funny and how he

improvises his own quips indicate volumes about both his level of intelligence and willingness to learn.

- Did the actor do something unusually creative? Look for unique combinations of choices made during the audition (not just the choices themselves).
- Were there any positive surprises? Consider how well the actor manages the audience's expectations.

Now design an audition that provides answers to questions such as these. Again, don't judge the particular choices made in the audition: auditioning remains, after all, an artificial environment. Instead, evaluate the actor's ability to make choices that create full [characterization = representations] for their [roles = responsibilities].

Final casting decisions should not be made immediately after auditioning all the prospective players. Instead, schedule callbacks for those under serious consideration, where now an interview provides valuable information. (HR departments today typically do this in reverse, interviewing all candidates while having only the one hired perform.) Probe for insights into each person's off-stage interests. Remember, individuals with the greatest reservoir of life experiences will make the most interesting choices once cast. And finally, when making these casting decisions, consider that, as one director advises, you are "casting relationships rather than individual roles."[32] Any new actor, however well qualified for the role, is really suitable only to the extent that his addition enhances the dynamic interplay between all cast members of the [ensemble = organization].

Again, the casting director shouldn't impose his own interpretation of the part as one of the criteria for hiring. That is not his role. Rather, the casting director must assist producers and directors in finding those who also know how to fill *their* respective roles.

RECOGNIZING THE DRAMATIS PERSONAE

Many people have seen the list of characters in a Broadway *Playbill* or the scrolling credits at the end of a movie but may not know its name: *dramatis personae,* described by *NTC's Dictionary of Theatre and Drama Terms* as "from the Latin, meaning the characters in a play; also, the list of them. Shown at the beginning of a play script or in the printed program for a performance, the list may merely give the names of the characters and the actors who play them or may include brief descriptions of the characters. The term is also used in a joking way for the participants in any event."[33]

The term deserves more serious consideration, and the practice more widespread use, in the Experience Economy.

On rare occasions, businesses acknowledge employees publicly in writing. Annual reports list senior officers. On-duty placards display the names of managers at some service establishments, ditto drivers of rental car shuttle buses. Slips of paper inform us our garment was inspected by #7, whoever that might be. Yet customers rarely see full acknowledgment of all the players involved in the production of a good or service. Why not? Because only staged experiences merit display of a dramatis personae—and all experience stagers should display one. Of course, guests may not care to read the names of every costume designer or supporting actor who helped stage the experience (just as few stay until the end of movie shows to read every last credit). No matter, because the dramatis personae exists not for the customers but the players, and not just for the stars but for those who never set foot on stage during a performance, the business equivalents of gaffers, key grips, and foley artists: the dramaturgs, scriptwriters, technicians, and stage crew (not to mention the casting director). The list recognizes their performances along with the on-stage actors, producers, and directors that so often they receive not only the credit but the fame as well. The dramatis personae sets the stage for the next production run by commemorating the last.

> **Only staged experiences merit display of a dramatis personae**

Just as business theatre can learn from the performing arts by means of such long-standing practices, so too can the arts learn from business. In *Standing Room Only: Strategies for Marketing the Performing Arts,* authors Philip Kotler, marketing professor at the Kellogg Graduate School of Management at Northwestern University, and his colleague Joanne Scheff encourage those managing the arts to embrace more business principles in order to keep the arts alive.[34] They recommend mixing both an "art-centered approach" that sees the arts in terms of unbridled expression and a "market-centered approach" that sees it as hard-nosed business. What concert pianist and educator David Owen Norris shared with Kotler and Scheff regarding musical performances—"We must make the experience relevant for the audience and either satisfy or surprise audience expectations"[35]— applies to *every* performance, no matter where or how performed, on the theatre stage or at the workplace.

The output generated by those who act on farms and in factories have long been the result of theatre performances, invented worlds distinctly different from other facets of everyday living. A two-hour performance of *King Lear* and the overnight performance of FedEx both compress time.

Both also help us see the world differently—arguably one more than the other. But which one? Today, successful businesses, like good art, must engage the audience. If one treats customers no differently from the balance of human affairs, one cannot shift up the Progression of Economic Value.

The Experience Economy liberates theatre from the area behind the arched proscenium. The staged performances of government-subsidized playhouses, community theatres, movie studios, and theme parks will continue to face rising competition from unexpected sources—not only from gaming arenas and wilderness experiences but from banks and insurance companies, airlines and hotels, and from every street corner and retooled mall. For every business is a stage.

9 The Customer Is the Product

- -

EVERY BUSINESS can indeed be a stage for offering economic experiences. Whether selling to consumers or companies, firms must recognize that goods and services are no longer enough; customers now want experiences. But to what end? Experiences can offer enjoyment, knowledge, diversion, and beauty, but more than the desire for such memorable qualities drives the Experience Economy. For not all experiences are fun, enlightening, distracting, or breathtaking.

Why, for example, do people pay good money to join fitness centers, where they expect to experience physical pain? Why do they pay $100 an hour to a psychiatrist, in whose office they may reexperience mental anguish? Why do tens of thousands of men pay admission to attend an event sponsored by the Christian organization Promise Keepers, whose goal it is to change men's behavior? And why do young managers leave well-paying jobs to spend tens of thousands of dollars on business school? There seems to be only one answer to all of these questions: to be affected by the experience.

The experiences we have affect who we are, what we can accomplish, and where we are going, and we will increasingly ask companies to stage experiences that change us. Human beings have always sought out new and exciting experiences to learn and grow, develop and improve, mend and reform. But as the world progresses further into the Experience Economy, much that was previously obtained through noneconomic activity will increasingly be found in the domain of commerce. That represents a significant change. It means that what we once sought for free, we now pay a fee.

This pattern can be seen in many spheres of our culture. We see people seeking spiritual growth outside the bounds of their local, traditional place of worship. Promise Keepers is one example. Another is the rise of spiritual directors, what one writer calls "personal trainers for the soul."[1] Troubled families no longer confine their search for help to other family members and friends in their religious or social community. They often seek advice from radio personalities like Dr. Laura Schlessinger or from the numerous books and tapes now available with recipes for self-improvement. In education, businesses increasingly establish their own institutions of learning, no longer able to rely on public schools to graduate educated students. Likewise, more families pay to send their children to private school for fear that public schools won't get the job done. The changing nature of labor also drives the demand for new kinds of economic experiences. Along with the decline of the Agrarian and Industrial Economies there has been a great decline in the number of people who support themselves by doing hard, physical labor. Many of us now pay to get and stay physically fit in venues outside the workplace. It is, after all, people with desk jobs who most often visit health clubs after work, not meatpackers and bricklayers.

But what are people really after as they enter into all these pursuits? Experiences, yes. But there is more than that: we want to transform ourselves, to become different. While experiences are less transient than services, the individual partaking in the experience often wants something more lasting than a memory, something beyond what any good, service, or experience alone can offer. The person who buys a membership in a fitness center is not paying for the pain but for an ongoing exercise regimen that will increase his or her physical well-being. Likewise, people return to psychiatrists as long as increases in their mental, or emotional, well-being are evidenced. People head for business school because they want to affect their professional and financial well-being. Many wives encourage their husbands to attend Promise Keeper events because they believe the experience will change their husbands' behavior, make them better husbands.

Welcome to the commoditization of experiences: "Been there, done that . . ."

Exercise routines, counseling sessions, learning courses, and religious excursions are actually a means of eliciting something that is more desirable, and more valued, than the experience itself.

In the healthcare industry, a sick patient wants more than pharmaceutical goods, medical services, or even a hospital experience; he wants to be well. The same goes for management consulting, where a struggling company wants something beyond informational goods, advisory services, or even educational experiences: it wants to grow. Companies clearly value an offering of economic growth more highly than they do the goods and services, or even isolated experiences, that still form the basis of much of the consulting industry. Even now, project methodologies (bound copies of physical goods), project team facilitators (on-site management services), and intervention programs (multidisciplinary experiences) command far lower fees than offerings such as systems outsourcing deals, which promise large-scale change.

As economic activity shifts further and further away from goods and services, those companies which stage experiences alone—without considering the effect these experiences will have on the participants and without designing the experiences in such a way as to create a desired change—will eventually see their experiences become commoditized. The second time you experience something, it will be marginally less enjoyable than the first time, the third time less enjoyable than that, and so on until you finally notice the experience doesn't engage you nearly as much as it once did. Welcome to the commoditization of experiences, best exemplified by the increasingly voiced phrase, "Been there, done that."[2]

THE PROGRESSION OF ECONOMIC VALUE REVISITED

Experiences are not the final economic offering. Companies can escape the commoditization trap by the same route as all other offerings can take: customization. When you customize an experience to make it just right for an individual—providing exactly what he or she needs right now—you cannot help *changing* that individual. When you customize an experience, you automatically turn it into a *transformation,* which companies create on top of experiences (you've heard the phrase "a life-transforming experience"), just as they create experiences on top of services, and so forth. As shown in Figure 9-1, transformations are a distinct economic offering, the fifth and final one in our Progression of Economic Value. A transformation is what the out-of-shape person, the emotionally troubled person, the young managers, the hospital patient, and the struggling company all really desired.

When you customize an experience you change the individual

By staging a series of experiences, companies are better able to achieve a lasting effect on the buyer than through an isolated event. It is the revisiting of a recurring theme, experienced through distinct and yet unified events, that transforms. As multiple experiences emerge and compete for guests, companies staging these events will begin to realize that any experience can become the basis for a new offering that elicits a transformation.

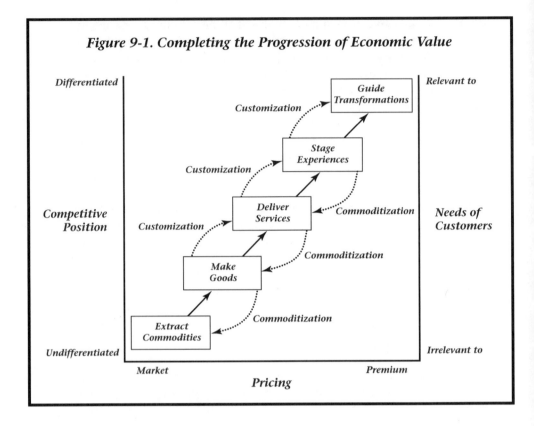

Figure 9-1. Completing the Progression of Economic Value

Let's return to one of our favorite experiences: the birthday celebration. As more and more companies compete with the staged birthday events offered by Club Disney, Gameworks, Chuck E. Cheese's, and the like—not to mention such locally produced experiences as New Pond Farm—this genre of experience will undergo commoditization, resulting in lower prices for single birthday events. Eventually, some experience stager will realize that shifting to birthday *transformations* would increase customer value and thereby forestall commoditization. What might such a company—a *transformation* elicitor— do? Well, rather than focusing simply on just this year's party, it might guide parents through multiple birthdays as the child grows, and it might concern itself not only with staging the party but also with selecting gifts, inviting guests, and encouraging post-party behaviors. Gifts, for example, could be aimed at a child's developmental needs. Guests might serve as professional role models, from spheres of life in which the child already shows interest—or in which the parents wish to encourage him. Thank-you notes, with preengineered templates and pre-stamped envelopes, might accompany the transformational birthday offering, to help birthday children become more conscious and appreciative.[3] And most important: Each year's birthday party would be treated as an incremental event in the overall management of childhood development. Such birthday guides may or may not emerge from the current birthday experience circuit, but they may just as well come from a toy manufacturer (leveraging its child development expertise), parenting magazine (which understands child rearing as a parenting issue), or sports management firm (with a portfolio of potential role models).

Perhaps martial arts teachers are the first experience stagers to realize the transformational power of their offerings. Many parents allow, encourage, or even force their children to join such programs as karate, kung fu, and tae kwon do. Many do it because they lack the skills or desire themselves to instill the proper respect and self-control in their offspring, others to complement and support what they see as their disciplinary responsibilities. Masters of martial arts promise not only to teach the skills of their ancient pursuits but to provide a set of rules by which students must live. As the business manager of one such establishment declares, when parents come for enrollment they're saying, "Fix my kid."[4] Many parents, however, want to limit the extent of this influence. In a *Forbes* story on the phenomenon, the writer reports that some parents seek out Christian or Jewish martial arts masters "to avoid schools they think may introduce their youngsters to Eastern mysticism."[5]

On a more material front, consider the food industry and the way dining experiences, such as those staged by theme restaurants, might progress into transformational offerings. Nutrition management may be the next shift, where themed establishments compete against Jenny Craig, Weight Watchers, Weigh Down, and others by making healthy food interesting and exciting to eat. Aiming all four realms of an experience at improving a guest's nutritional intake, the entertainment realm could make eating decisions fun, the educational realm might emphasize the personal effect of eating properly, the dining esthetics could encourage the proper pace and amount of eating, and the establishment might provide a place to escape when tempted to relapse into old behaviors. All foodstuffs, food services, and dining experiences would be managed by a single transformation elicitor, paid not on the basis of the food itself, the service surrounding the food, or even the experience enveloping both but for measurable improvements in cholesterol, fat, weight, and similar health-affirming measures. Other restaurants might elicit transformation by aiming to refine people's tastes or to enhance a couple's relationship. These are all viable strategic alternatives available to those who today consider themselves to be in the business of making or serving food.

Similarly, once all bookstores add coffee and espresso bars and perhaps even reading rooms—where one pays to read in places specifically designed to maximize the reading experience—companies will surface to offer reading transformations. People would pay these establishments to guide them through intellectual pursuits by identifying books and other materials worth reading, followed by observations and perhaps even examinations—not in a traditional schoolish sense, but as a new learning alternative to make sure people got the right ideas. Waldenbooks already offers corporations its W.I.S.E. Corporate Program to consolidate employee book purchases through a single source, yet competes via volume discounts. Why not make this offering transformational by charging a premium to ensure that employees read (via mass customized recommendations) what they need to absorb?

Another industry with the potential to get into the business of eliciting transformations is higher education. Consider the Harvard Business School. Its vast intellectual resources—professors, classes for both undergraduate and graduate degrees, executive education programs, the *Harvard Business Review* and Harvard Business School Press, and various and sundry newsletters, videotapes, CD-ROMs, Web sites, and other teaching resources—make it a perfect enterprise for transforming individuals into business executives prepared to face any strategic challenge. To do so, though, it would have to extend itself beyond selling book and magazine goods, information services, and educational experiences to viewing its business as *changing* customers. And for all those colleges and universities jostling to reach the top of the various rankings now promulgated in the press, this is the route to take.

Such transformation offerings will emerge across almost every industry that today views itself as part of the service sector. Healthcare providers will shift past performing fee-for-service procedures to charging fees based on making or keeping people well. Airlines and hotels may get into the business of transforming business travelers into well-rested road warriors equipped for the next day's battles. And, to complete just a short list of what's to come, computer service companies and system integrators will transform customers with well-running equipment into enterprises that use the equipment to run their businesses well.

Transformation offerings will emerge across almost every part of the service sector

And why not? Their competitors—management consultants and outsourcing firms—are already making the move to offer transformations. Many understand that customers no longer want tangible reports, intangible analyses, or memorable workshops that yield recommendations on what they should do. They're a start, but none by itself makes the customer a better company. One analyst notes that hiring a big consultant "is like going to your chiropractor. One hundred eighty-two visits later you still have to come back."[6] Rather, consulting customers aspire to become better businesses, and they want to engage consultants that yield sustained results. As Abbas Rizavi of EDS describes the company's practice of "co-sourcing"—becoming a partner in running businesses—"We think you should focus on outcomes. Outsourcing is done to you, co-sourcing is done with you. . . . We are really in the business of helping our customers evolve, align, regenerate, and restructure."[7] Exactly.

Like consultants, Lifeline Systems of Cambridge, Massachusetts (recently purchased by security firm Protection One), provides offerings that encompass aspects of goods, services, experiences, and transformations. At the core of its offerings for the "personal response industry" lies a variety of pager-like devices with a button in the middle. When the user presses the button, a signal goes through the telephone line to a twenty-four-hour monitoring center. There, trained monitors call back to assess the nature of the incident and, if necessary, dispatch an appropriate person—friend, relative, or public emergency personnel—to handle the situation. Fewer than 5 percent of the calls require emergency assistance, the ostensible reason for having the service. Rather, most people call because they feel isolated or lonely, and talking to someone at the center makes them feel better. But in the final analysis, most customers—that is, those who are paying Lifeline—are relatives of the person using the device. What they are really buying is peace of mind. That's Lifeline's true offering.

What's a prison's true offering? Corrections Corp. of America, based in Nashville, provides local, state, and federal governments with private detention and correction services. Bureaucratic wardens might simply consider it a service that keeps inmates off the street for the length of their sentences. But when asked by *Chief Executive* magazine to describe his company's "product," CEO Doctor Crants responded that CCA produced "quality corrections," which involve not just housing people but also creating

some positive impact on the chances that those inmates will have a better life after they leave our facility than they otherwise would. . . . For us, quality corrections means teaching our inmates to read and write. . . . About 50 percent don't have high school diplomas, so we have GED classes and educational courses. . . . For those who already have a high school diploma, we have various kinds of job training courses. We teach them a skill, such as diesel mechanics or automobile mechanics. . . . And we've devised what we

Table 9-1. Economic Distinctions

Economic Offering	Commodities	Goods	Services	Experiences	Transformations
Economy	Agrarian	Industrial	Service	Experience	Transformation
Economic function	Extract	Make	Deliver	Stage	Guide
Nature of offering	Fungible	Tangible	Intangible	Memorable	Effectual
Key attribute	Natural	Standardized	Customized	Personal	Individual
Method of supply	Stored in bulk	Inventoried after production	Delivered on demand	Revealed over a duration	Sustained through time
Seller	Trader	Manufacturer	Provider	Stager	Elicitor
Buyer	Market	Customer	Client	Guest	Aspirant
Factors of demand	Characteristics	Features	Benefits	Sensations	Traits

think is the finest drug treatment program in the world, superior to the Betty Ford Clinic. It takes seven months to get through.[8]

He acknowledged that CCA's methods do not work on about 20 percent of the prison population, the true psychopaths and sociopaths that could not, at least with known methods, become productive contributors to society.[9] Crants further explained that the government agencies that privatized their prisons to CCA save money, generally about 10 percent, because "what's cost effective is to give every inmate a sense of hope. He gets up in the morning and goes off to do something that, at the end of his sentence, may position him to have a chance for life outside of a prison setting."[10] It may only be a chance, but transforming a hardened criminal or even a first-time offender into someone who won't return to prison truly is a different kind of economic offering. As social entrepreneur Bill Strickland says of the culinary students at his Bidwell Training Center in Pittsburgh, "They're human beings who are now capable of participating in the environment in an effective way. . . . That's an outcome. That's a product."[11]

DISCOVERING THE DISTINCTIONS, PART TWO

As with experiences, some will surely argue that what we are calling transformations are really just a subclass of services. But there is just too much disparity between eating at a McDonalds and firming up at a fitness center, between providing information reports and partnering in business outcomes, and between cleaning a suit and cleansing a soul, to classify them all as a single economic offering. As delineated in Table 9-1, transformations are indeed a distinct economic offering, as distinct from experiences as experiences are from services. Identifying this new offering requires using words not normally associated with businesses and their economic output. But just as it took years for the now-familiar terms of the Service Economy— such as intangible products, clients, delivering on demand—to fall trippingly from the tongue, so, too, it will be a while before the new vocabulary of experiences and transformations will become second nature. But to fully discern the distinctions between all five economic offerings, consider the following:

Transformations are as distinct from experiences as experiences are from services

- While commodities are fungible, goods tangible, services intangible, and experiences memorable, transformations are *effectual*. All other economic offerings have no lasting consequence beyond their consumption. Even the memories of an experience fade over time. But buyers of transformations seek to be guided toward some specific aim or purpose, and transformations must elicit that intended effect. That's why we call such buyers *aspirants*—they aspire to be some one or some thing different. Without a change in attitude, performance, characteristics, or some other fundamental dimension, no transformation occurs. And this change should be not just in degree but in kind, not just in function but in structure. The transformation affects the very being of the buyer.

- While companies store commodities in bulk, inventory goods after production, deliver services on demand, and reveal experiences over a duration of time, they must *sustain* transformations *through time* if they are to take hold, to genuinely change the aspirant. If a change—losing weight, stopping a bad habit, or becoming financially secure, say, on the consumer side, or lowering fixed expenses, stopping wasteful practices, or becoming insulated from exchange rate fluctuations on the business side—is only temporary and not sustained, then it was not really transforming but merely a momentary uptick along the same old journey. Likewise, any relapses or digressions reduce the measure or intensity of the transformation attained.

- Finally, whereas commodities are natural, goods standardized, services customized, and experiences inherently personal, transformations are *individual.* The offering does not exist outside the changed traits each aspirant desires; it is that change itself. Experiences are events to which the individual reacts and thereby creates a memory, but transformations go much further, actually changing the *being* of the buyer, whether a consumer or business. Because an experience is inherently personal, no two people can have the same one. The effect differs based on past experiences and current state of mind. So, too, no individual can undergo the same transformation twice—the second time it's attempted, he would no longer be the same person. People value transformation above all other economic offerings because it addresses the ultimate source of all other needs: why the buyer desires the commodities, goods, services, and experiences he purchases.

Indeed, with transformations, the economic offering of a company is the individual person or company changed as a result of what the company does. With transformations, *the customer is the product!* The individual buyer of the transformation essentially says, "Change me." The company's economic offering is neither the materials it uses nor the physical things it makes. It's neither the processes it executes nor the encounters it orchestrates. When a company guides transformations, *the offering is the individual.*

This means that the exact form and content of any particular transformational offering has to be considered carefully. The transformation elicitor must understand customer aspirations before hoping to affect any change in the particular traits—whether they be along physical, emotional, intellectual, or spiritual dimensions. Aspirations of course relate to customer expectations; but here the expectations center not on some external good or service but on the customer himself, on what he wants to become.[12]

> **The individual buyer of the transformation essentially says, "Change me"**

Once the Experience Economy has run its course, the *Transformation Economy* will take over. Then the basis of success will be in understanding the aspirations of individual consumers and businesses and guiding them to fully realize those aspirations.

Let's examine how the insurance industry, as just one readily discernible example, will make the transition through successive economies. As we saw earlier, Progressive's claims adjustment process shifted the company into the Experience Economy by providing the customers with the time and means to settle their nerves. The on-the-spot check relieves them of all worry about how to handle the situation. Traditional policy carriers merely *insure* their policyholders, meaning, as shown in Figure 9-2, that clients merely secure a payment in the event of a loss. Something happens, they get money. That's it. The Progressive experience, on the other hand, *assures* its policyholders, meaning that guests secure confidence, encouragement, trust, or a feeling of satisfaction. When something happens, Progressive assures them that they will not only get their money but will also feel better about the whole unfortunate situation.

In the Transformation Economy, even that won't be enough. In addition, carriers will *ensure* policyholders, which means that aspirants will secure an actual event, situation, or outcome. For example, Skandia of Stockholm, Sweden, introduced an *en*-surance

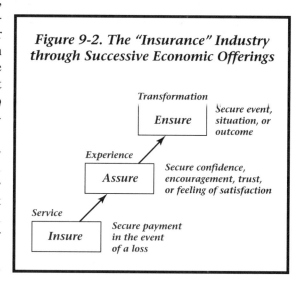

Figure 9-2. The "Insurance" Industry through Successive Economic Offerings

Transformation — *Ensure* — Secure event, situation, or outcome

Experience — *Assure* — Secure confidence, encouragement, trust, or feeling of satisfaction

Service — *Insure* — Secure payment in the event of a loss

concept called Competence Insurance. Flowing out of the company's focus on intellectual capital,[13] the program is designed to eliminate the problem of workers falling behind in the level of competence and knowledge required as their jobs change over time. As described in Skandia's proposal:

> It is the objective of the insurance to create security through competence. *Crisis-prevention* is the factor which characterizes the new insurance, when comparing it with today's standard social insurance protection. An individual's successive buildup of savings in a personal competence account serves to stimulate and encourage initiatives when the need for competence enhancement is felt—in good time prior to a crisis situation. A problem which is inherent in present-day social insurance is that measures are frequently not taken until the individual employee, workplace or profession has run into trouble, and *then it is already too late.*[14]

Awaiting regulatory approval before it can implement the program, Skandia hopefully will soon firmly put itself in the business of *ensuring* policyholders.

That's a transition that MMI Companies of Deerfield, Illinois, has to some degree already made. MMI insures hospitals and physician's practices against malpractice and other risks, but considers itself in the business of risk management. Rather than simply paying for lawyers and (when they lose) claims against policyholders, MMI works hard at ensuring its doctors don't get sued in the first place. Healthcare institutions cannot buy MMI insurance without simultaneously agreeing to participate in programs—encompassing data gathering and analysis, education courses, and hands-on consulting—that together help ensure that doctors, other healthcare professionals, and health administrators become less of a risk by focusing on a system of care delivery geared toward safety and quality. Every year MMI analyzes each institution's progress along this line and adjusts its programs to respond to changes in the industry, with the emphasis on improving clinical care as the means of reducing the chance of being sued.[15] As CEO Rick Becker related to us, "In today's litigious society no one can eliminate all possibilities of a lawsuit. But we're not interested in a business becoming a customer unless that business is interested in becoming less of a risk."

What are the equivalents to *insure, assure,* and *ensure* for your industry?

Now, if you're a service provider, think of your own business. What are the equivalents to *insure, assure,* and *ensure* for the industry in which your company now resides? It's unlikely you can find such simple words to describe the path from services to experiences to transformations (you may even have to invent a word or two), but thinking creatively about new economic offerings that surround the present ones will pay dividends as we move inexorably from the Experience to the Transformation Economy.

So what's a manufacturer to do? In the emerging Experience Economy, we already see them experientializing their goods—*ing*ing the thing by focusing on the experience customers have while *using* their goods. In the Transformation Economy manufacturers will of course *transformationalize* their goods—design and sell goods that help customers become something distinct. Here the focus moves from us*ing* to us*er:* how the individual *changes* while using the good. While offerings such as self-help books, "edutainment" software, and exercise videos and equipment begin to address this aim, they fall short of fully transformationalized offerings.[16] If exercise equipment were truly transformationalized, for instance, the manufacturers would stop thinking of their business as *selling physical goods* and start thinking of it as *developing good physiques*—and someone would show up occasionally to examine the results!

Some firms lead the way. In the greeting card business, Hallmark Card's fastest growing unit is Hallmark Business Expressions, which creates cards aimed at boosting employee morale and loyalty in the workplace. Hallmark's team of designers helps individual companies assess their needs, determines the appropriate series of messages to communicate to specific departments and individuals, and then creates customized cards for multiple occasions. Because the goal of the program is to change employee attitudes, Hallmark no longer sells the custom cards as ordinary goods but as tools for executives and HR departments to help improve employee retention and corporate culture.

Or consider the automobile industry. Just as a significant factor in automobile design today is the sensation of how the doors sound when they close, in the Transformation Economy people won't buy a car unless it makes them—or their kids—better drivers. Features such as H.E Micro wave's collision-avoidance radar system and General Motor's OnStar diagnostic system, which uses sensors, microprocessors, and global positioning satellite units to diagnose car emergencies and quickly recommend the proper course of action will become commonplace.[17] We can also expect to see a system that could prohibit teen-age drivers from exceeding the speed limit by more than 3 mph, unless they enter a special code (for emergencies) that would immediately trigger a call, fax, or e-mail to a parent to let them know exactly what their kid was doing.

Perhaps the greatest opportunities lie in biotechnology, particularly in the category of products known as "nutraceuticals," which promise to change our bodies as we ingest certain foods.[18] Elan Corp of Ireland offers chocolate shakes, instant soup, and other products that help Parkinson's disease sufferers better absorb their medicine.[19] And in Finland, Benecol margarine, specially made to reduce cholesterol, "is so popular . . . that stores can't keep shelves stocked even at prices six times more than regular margarine."[20]

Goods producers will make emblems to commemorate transformations

Just as many manufacturers now exploit the Experience Economy by making the memorabilia guests buy as physical reminders of their experience, in the nascent Transformation Economy goods producers can also make the *emblems* aspirants purchase to commemorate the transformations they underwent. Rings, crosses, flags, trophies, pennants, medals, badges, medallions, insignias, and other such emblems all tangibly signify that their bearers have transformed themselves in some way: from single to married, from team to champion, from civilian to soldier, from soldier to hero, and so forth. All of these emblems further enable people to identify those who have undergone the same transformations and thereby initiate conversations and form communities.

GUIDING TRANSFORMATIONS

Experts in grieving assert that everyone faced with a tremendous personal loss first must go through a series of experiences—such as shock, depression, confusion, guilt, anger—before recovery can occur. How much better we can handle these stages, and more quickly be transformed from grief to normal living, when someone—minister, counselor, friend—*guides* us than when we are left alone. In the same way, all transformation elicitors guide aspirants through a series of experiences.

The Progression of Economic Value forms an Economic Pyramid, viewed as successive offerings built on top of the ones below, as shown in Figure 9-3. Transformation elicitors must determine exactly the right set of life-transforming experiences required to guide aspirants in achieving their goals (commemorated with goods as emblems). Experience stagers must depict what services engage the guest and then stage them in such a way as to create a memorable event (preserved with goods as memorabilia). Service providers, in turn, must devise the proper configuration of goods (such as tables and condiment dispensers in a fast-food restaurant, or hangers, plastic bags, and cleaning equipment in a dry cleaner) that enable them to deliver the set of intangible activities desired by the client. Goods manufacturers, of course, must develop sources for the appropriate commodities

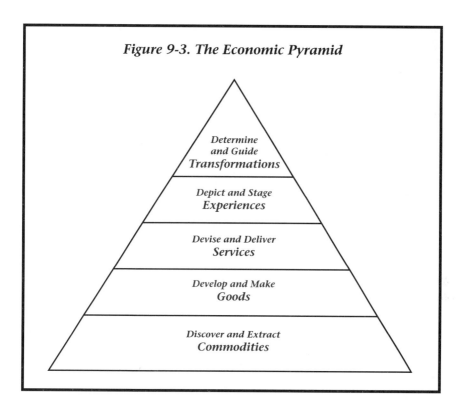

Figure 9-3. The Economic Pyramid

Determine
and Guide
Transformations

Depict and Stage
Experiences

Devise and Deliver
Services

Develop and Make
Goods

Discover and Extract
Commodities

used as raw materials for the tangible products they make for users. And commodity traders must discover where those materials lie and extract them for the markets they serve.

So transformations cannot be *extracted, made, delivered,* or even *staged;* they can only be *guided.* As the old saying goes, "You can lead a horse to water, but you can't make it drink." No one can force someone to change. All transformations occur within the very being of the customer and so must be made *by* the customer. Skandia President and CEO Björn Wolrath recognized this when he said that the "main pillar" of the company's competence ensurance proposal "is that it is not employers or society who are helping employees in an acute situation, *but the employees themselves who make sure they have the resources for a competence boost as soon as they feel it is needed.*"[21]

Transformation elicitors can, at best, bring about the right situation under which the proper change can occur, meaning staging the right experiences that involve the right services that . . . well, you get the idea. But that alone is not enough; there is more to guiding a transformation. As shown in

Figure 9-4, this economic offering requires three separate phases: diagnosing aspirations, staging transforming experience(s), and following through.

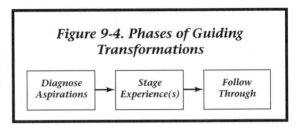

Figure 9-4. Phases of Guiding Transformations

| Diagnose Aspirations | → | Stage Experience(s) | → | Follow Through |

Diagnosing Aspirations

To what does the customer aspire? Where is he today relative to this aspiration? Along what dimensions can this transformation be achieved? Without a proper diagnosis, the customer cannot achieve it. And—as is the case with mass customizing mere goods and services, where customers so often do not know or cannot articulate what they want—aspirants often do not know or cannot articulate their hopes and dreams. Or they may even have the *wrong* aspirations—goals and desires deleterious to their own well-being. Just as financial service firms have a fiduciary responsibility to prevent clients from making terrible investment decisions and theme park operators have a custodial responsibility to prevent guests from acting in an unsafe manner, all transformation elicitors have an ethical responsibility to prevent aspirants from attaining inappropriate or immoral traits. Of course, what those may be necessarily depends on the conscience and world view of the particular elicitor.

Essential to every transformation, then, is understanding what the customer *truly needs to become* and how far away he is from fulfilling those needs within himself, even if the customer does not realize it or deludes himself about the direction or magnitude of the change required. Is he really capable of achieving the aspiration? If so, how can he be guided to the proper transformation? In some cases, where triage would be a better term than diagnosis, individual people or companies may not be capable of becoming that to which they aspire. There's no sense even starting down the *trans*formation path in these cases unless some other *pre*formation activities first fortify the aspirant in those areas in which he is too weak to proceed.

Without a proper diagnosis, customers cannot achieve their aspirations

During the diagnosis phase, a fitness center, for example, must learn the weight and/or muscle strength and/or body tone desired by each customer and assess his current state along each dimension before it can design a physical regimen aimed at fulfilling his particular desires. But it must also understand the aspirant's medical situation to guarantee that a recommended regimen first does no harm, and it must ascertain his mental and emotional disposition to determine the possible obstacles that may arise along the way. And in the healthcare field, doctors (including psychiatrists) presume all patients want to be physically (or mentally) well, but specific aspirations may vary greatly, from being "good as new" to returning to work with "good enough" function, from just wanting to get out of the hospital and go home as soon as possible to wanting to die in peace. Like other transformation elicitors, physicians may think some goals are set too low and reject others for being too optimistic, but they must in any case focus on the patient's best interests when designing the proper procedures (while always leaving room for the miraculous to occur). Similarly, management consultants must understand the strategic needs of a business as well as its current capabilities, taking into account the fact that both the company and the consultant are biased observers, before designing an implementable course of action.

Staging Transforming Experience(s)

What set of experiences will bring about the necessary transformation? How can the customer be changed from where he is today to where his aspiration lies, or should lie? Transformations, of course, build on experiences, specifically, the life-transforming experiences that will cause the customer to realize his aspirations, whether or not he can articulate what they are.

Psychiatrists, for example, hold a series of counseling sessions with patients, each one often with a different motive but all with the overarching intention of moving them, over time, from a state of relative mental illness to one of mental health (although many psychiatrists can be accused of viewing no one as mentally well and others of "treating" the perfectly healthy). Educational institutions, including business schools, provide a series of experiences within experiences, some major, some minor, but all with the intention of educating, grooming, and molding students into graduates who will have a certain store of knowledge and abilities. Golf pros and other sports instructors combine intellectual understanding and emotional encouragement with the physical activities necessary to improve their customers' skills. As is the case with many transformations, golf pros do not limit improvement experiences to the one small act of hitting a golf ball. Rather, to turn duffers into adept players, they offer guidance on mental preparation, address, and swing; woods, irons, chipping, sand shots, and putting; rules, course management, and scoring techniques; and so forth.

Elicitors may use any one of the four realms of experience as the basis

> Elicitors may use any one of the four realms of experience for a transformation

for a transformation. Entertainment experiences can alter our view of the world, while educational experiences can make us rethink how we fit into that world. Escapist experiences can boost our personal capabilities and characteristics to new levels, while esthetic experiences can imbue a sense of wonder, beauty, and appreciation. But again, the most engaging life-transforming experiences will center around the sweet spot, composed of multiple elements from all four realms—no matter the ultimate aim of the transformation—for it is in the sweet spot that an experience best engages us and focuses our attention on its transforming nature.

Following Through

Experiences thus set the stage for transformation. But once it has occurred, how can it be sustained? What must be done to ensure that the change does not degenerate? It's not truly a transformation unless it is sustained through time. To make a great shot, a golfer has to have a great follow-through as well as a great swing. The same goes for great golf instruction. No one can dramatically improve his stroke after one lesson or sustain any gained improvement without continued practice and playing. Alcoholics Anonymous and other self-help groups excel in the follow-through phase of transformation, acknowledging that while it's possible to forgo one drink at one time, it's hard as all get-out to forgo that drink time after time. Similarly, marriage counselors can get a couple talking again after an adulterous affair, and perhaps even bring them to the point of forgiveness, but rebuilding the shattered trust requires a lot of long, hard work from both parties.

It's not truly a transformation unless it is sustained

Transformation elicitors find follow-through the most difficult phase, and it is the one at which many fall short. Management consultants who deliver strategic analysis without guiding the client through implementation of the recommended changes remain in the service business; they are not in the transformation business. Educators that impart knowledge without ensuring that students can apply what they learn ascend to the experience business (at best). And doctors who treat physical diseases without considering their patient's emotional needs do only half the job, a realization that is slowly dawning on the healthcare community.

GETTING THE ACTS TOGETHER

In September 1994, the British medical journal *Lancet* created quite an angry furor in the healthcare community when it published an article applying the principle that work is theatre to the work of doctors. In "Acting in

Medical Practice," Drs. Hillel Finestone and David Conter of the University of Western Ontario asserted that physicians must be trained as actors and follow the three-phase approach outlined above to truly transform each patient. They show how doctors, and by extension all other transformation elicitors, should employ each phase:

> If a physician does not possess the necessary skills to assess a patient's emotional needs [diagnosis of whole person] and to display clear and effective responses to these needs [series of experiences] the job is not done. Consequently, we believe that medical training should include an acting curriculum, focused on the conveying of appropriate, beneficial responses to those emotional needs.
>
> In my practice . . . I frequently treat individuals who are in chronic pain. I find it essential to convey an encouraging, hopeful, often cajoling message to the patient [follow-through] to communicate concern and, more importantly, the need for the patient to work on self-improvement.[22]

We would simply add that, since work truly is theatre, physicians should *always* act to convey the proper responsiveness and concern, not just when it is more difficult to do so naturally.

Many physicians disagreed with, disparaged, or ridiculed the notion of doctors becoming actors. One humorous physician wrote that with drama "an official part of medical school curriculum" we would see scenes like this one: "*Problem:* Obesity. *Old way:* Doctor gives printed diet sheet. *New way:* Music swells as doctor stands in front of brilliant sunset, tears welling up, and makes the emotional, heart-rending promise, 'As God is my witness, you will always be hungry again.'"[23] But proper acting *does* help a patient tell more of what ails him during diagnosis, better understand treatment choices and determine the right set of experiences that will best treat him, and, finally, more readily handle the therapy and other actions required to follow through on treatment and sustain the transformation Further, medical research backs up the contention that doctors must be actors. Numerous studies demonstrate that those doctors who deal with their patients in a more caring, empathic manner—in short, those with better bedside manners—not only face fewer lawsuits but have better patient treatment outcomes.[24] The personal, caring doctor of yore is not an anachronism; it's a role that must be assumed by every physician—no, make that every transformation elicitor.

The three phases of transformation, diagnosis, staged experience(s), and follow-through, not only distinguish this economic offering from lesser experiences, but together represent a deeper sense of commitment to the well-being of

Transformation elicitors must *care*

each individual buyer than experience stagers alone may (or need to) demonstrate. Transformation elicitors must care enough to offer up-front diagnosis, to direct the staging of multiple events required for the buyer to change, and to follow through relentlessly. Noted philosopher Milton Mayeroff wrote perhaps the definitive book about this subject, called *On Caring.* It should be mandatory reading for anyone truly interested in the business of offering transformations. "Caring, as helping another grow and actualize himself," says Mayeroff, "is a process, a way of relating to someone that involves development, in the same way that friendships can only emerge in time through mutual trust and a deepening and qualitative transformation of the relationship."[25] By a "process," Mayeroff means a series of experiences that not only indicate but *develop* caring over time. (Aren't your best friends those with whom you've had the greatest, most intense experiences?)

Further, the ongoing relationships with individual aspirants needed to sustain a transformation are possible only if executives abandon "flavor-of-the-month" imperatives in favor of enduring—yes, even timeless—operating principles. Mayeroff uses terms such as knowing, patience, honesty, trust, humility, hope, rhythm, and courage to describe caring. Why don't we find more of these terms in the mission statements of businesses? After all, transformation elicitors must also focus on the *continuation* of care. "One-off" experiences seldom yield a transformation offering, if there is no care there. Ensuring the aspirant achieves his aim usually means providing a series of experiences, each guided by a constant set of principles.

The first requirement for workers in a transformation business is that they truly care. Transformation elicitors, therefore, must first transform their own employees into caring people enriched by the work they perform before those workers can act differently to transform customers. As C. William Pollard, chairman of The ServiceMaster Company, reminds us, "The spirits and souls of people can be enriched by what they do as they serve and work. And they can grow in the process of who they are becoming."[26] In his book *The Soul of the Firm,* Pollard relates how ServiceMaster trains and motivates employees not to deliver services but *to serve.* This requires a willingness among leaders to sacrifice their own needs in favor of the employees', and for employees to sacrifice their needs in order to eliminate the sacrifice of customers. Pollard relates that while Socrates said, "Know thyself" and Aristotle counseled "Control thyself," "another great thinker changed history—and the hearts of people—with His unique approach to a meaningful life. 'Give thyself' were the words spoken by Jesus."[27]

Now, gauge your own reaction to the mere mention of Jesus' name in a business book. How does it make you feel? In the forthcoming Transformation Economy, aspirants will entrust their futures only to those with whom they share a common worldview. The transformation elicitor must

All commerce involves moral choice

embrace a context for change—the values the business enterprise seeks to promote—leading eventually to companies that practice *worldview segmentation*. No longer can an enterprise take an agnostic attitude toward moral rightness and wrongness, hiding from such sensitive issues beneath the cloak of mere goods and services. Consciously—as with ServiceMaster—or not, all enterprises promote a worldview. Transformation issues cannot be avoided. Extracted commodities transform the earth into a subdued planet, with implications for all its inhabitants. Goods transform buyers into users of those goods, for ill or for gain. Services transform clients into recipients of those services, whether debasing or edifying. Experiences transform guests into participants in the encounter, whether the long-term effects are deleterious or therapeutic. And transformations turn aspirants into "a new you," with all the ethical, philosophical, and religious implications that phrase implies. All commerce involves moral choice.

10 *Finding Your Role in the World*

● ●

IN *THE END OF WORK,* a book decrying the loss of agricultural, manufacturing, and service jobs caused by technological innovation, author and professional pessimist Jeremy Rifkin rightly points out that "We are entering a new phase in world history—one in which fewer and fewer workers will be needed to produce the goods and services for the global population."[1] Rifkin acknowledges that a "fourth" economic sector exists, which he calls the knowledge sector, but doesn't believe it will "absorb more than a fraction of the hundreds of millions who[se jobs] will be eliminated in the next several decades,"[2] although he confesses "There is reason to be hopeful that a new vision based on transformation of consciousness and a new commitment to community will take hold."[3]

Indeed, there is great reason for hope: for it is the natural evolution of the economy away from goods and services that is bringing about the need for new and more work based on experiences and transformations. As shown in Figure 10-1 (an update of Figure 1-3), only the agricultural sector has actually lost jobs over the past forty years. Employment growth in both the experience industry and the transformation industry was double that in services, while nominal GDP for these newly identified economic offerings outpaced all others between 1959 and 1996—with transformations growing at an average of more than 10 percent every year.[4]

Similarly, Figure 10-2 updates the U.S. Consumer Price Index (CPI) statistics provided in Figure 1-2, using medical services as the sole transformation industry that can be

Transformation elicitors are increasing their share of the economic pie

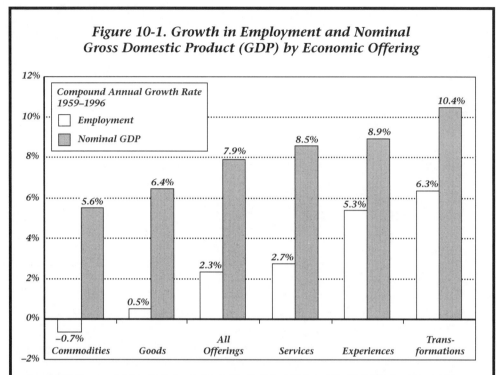

Figure 10-1. Growth in Employment and Nominal Gross Domestic Product (GDP) by Economic Offering

Source: U.S. Bureau of Labor Statistics, Labstat; *The Statistical History of the United States: Colonial Times to 1970,* United States Bureau of the Census; U.S. Census, Bureau of Economic Analysis, National Income and Product Accounts, unpublished detail; Strategic Horizons LLP and Diamond Technology Partners, analysis.

cleanly separated from the "service sector" statistics gathered by the federal government. Healthcare "inflation," as it's mislabeled, not only outpaces all services, it even (as expected) increases faster than experiences.[5] But healthcare isn't alone. Management consulting fees increased tremendously in the 1990s. Today it is not uncommon for junior staff at the top consulting firms to charge more than $3,000 a day, three to five times the per diem rates charged in the 1980s, on projects reaching eight or even nine figures in size. And the cost of total tuition, room, and board at colleges and universities grew more than two-and-a-half times from 1980 to 1996, almost three times the rate of inflation.[6]

In short, just like the experience stagers before them, transformation elicitors are greatly increasing their share of the total economic pie. Today, the only thing better than being in the business of staging experiences is being in the business of eliciting transformations. Both represent not only

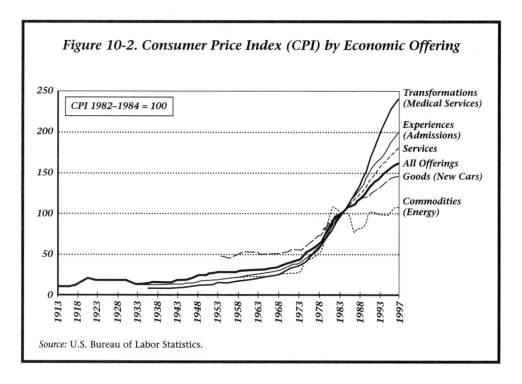

Figure 10-2. Consumer Price Index (CPI) by Economic Offering

CPI 1982–1984 = 100

Transformations (Medical Services)
Experiences (Admissions)
Services
All Offerings
Goods (New Cars)
Commodities (Energy)

Source: U.S. Bureau of Labor Statistics.

viable sectors of the economy but the very engines of growth that will create more than enough jobs and output to supplant slowdowns in the lower-echelon sectors. This fact will take some getting used to. As *Reason* editor Virginia Postrel so accurately comments, "We are, in fact, living more and more in an intangible economy, in which the greatest sources of wealth are not physical. We aren't yet used to an economy in which beauty, amusement, attention, learning, pleasure, even spiritual fulfillment are as real and economically valuable as steel or semiconductors."[7] Exactly. For the sources of wealth in these new economic sectors are not physical but intellectual.

PUTTING WISDOM INTO WORK

The very idea of transforming people (or companies) demands that we think about and apply a word little used in businesses today: Wisdom. As defined by the *Oxford English Dictionary, wisdom* is "the quality of being wise, esp. in relation to conduct and the choice of means and ends; the combination of experience and knowledge with the ability to apply them judiciously; sound judgement, prudence, practical sense."[8] Elicitors require such wisdom across all phases of a transformation. In diagnosis, they need wisdom to distinguish real aspirations from false hopes, lofty goals, and self-delusions. They especially need wisdom to judge whether the individual person or company is capable of the change desired.

In the staged experience(s) phase, transformation elicitors need wisdom to prudently determine the right "choice of means" to fulfill the "choice of ends" decided during diagnosis. And follow-through involves the same qualified judgments, choices of action, and applications of experience and knowledge required at the beginning of the journey. Without the benefit of wisdom, people will find aspirations very difficult to achieve.

Look again at the *OED*'s definition of wisdom above and see how it pairs "experience" and "knowledge." As shown in Figure 10-3, each echelon within the Progression of Economic Value corresponds with an echelon in what might be called the Progression of Valuable Intelligence.[9] At the bottom, commodities correspond with noise: the pure abundance of unorganized observations with little or no meaning, through which commodity extractors must wade to find, for example, the nuggets of gold or pockets of oil. When codified, or systematized into a code of symbols, these observations take on meaning and so become valuable data. The collection of physical and financial data is what made the Industrial Revolution possible. It was based on manufacturers' division of labor, standardized specifications, efficiency measures, and so forth. Indeed, the height of the revolution came with the creation of computers from what was once known as the data processing industry. Data became so abundant that it overwhelmed the ability of humans to process it.[10]

Without wisdom, people find aspirations difficult to achieve

The term *data processing* is now an anachronism, a throwback to the 1960s and 1970s, for what we now call the *information technology* industry. This exactly mirrors the shift from the Industrial to the Service Economy, for information is data communicated or delivered to others (a service) requiring a common context or frame of reference. Goods are manufactured in isolation and distributed to inventory; they are essentially instantiations of codified specifications. Services, on the other hand, cannot be proffered in isolation but require the common context of provider and customer together defining what particular activities the customer wants to execute. And the service of mass customizing goods, of course, substitutes information for inventory.

Now, as we shift to the Experience Economy, the term *information technology* sounds dated as well. People talk about "knowledge bases," "knowl-

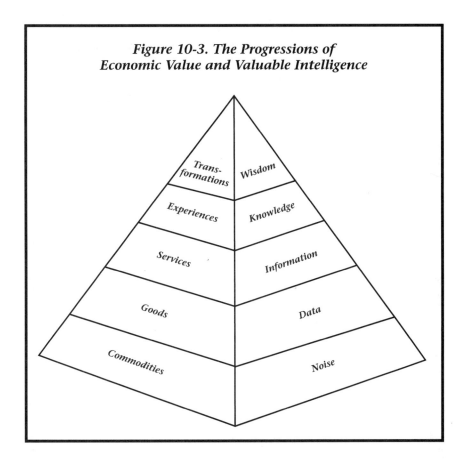

Figure 10-3. The Progressions of Economic Value and Valuable Intelligence

edge management," "knowledge infrastructure," and the like.[11] Knowledge is *experiential information,* intelligence gained from and applied through experiences.[12] None of the terms just mentioned applies to the embedding of intelligence within computer systems; rather, they refer to linking people with the right knowledge so that it can be immediately applied.[13] And, of course, staging experiences requires intimate knowledge of how human beings react to the cues they receive.

While we have yet to hear terms such as *wisdom technology* used, that is inevitably the next step. We do know of the first book to discuss moving beyond knowledge in companies: *Working Wisdom,* by John Dalla Costa. In it, Costa recognizes that wisdom is both *the result of* experiences—often painful ones (as with fitness centers, psychiatry, and grieving)—and *required for* transformations:

As a human construct with human foibles, it is inevitable that the practice of business will also include the experience of suffering. However, while other political, religious, and arts institutions see the need for suffering, valuing it as the price for the transformation to a new level of human experience, business organizations still regard suffering through that adolescent perspective of avoidance and presumed immunity.

One reason for this institutional immaturity is that the profits of business are often based on serving a need that eliminates pain, discomfort, or unhappiness. Suffering and sorrow are words that for fifty years have been squeezed out of our consumer culture by the endless stream of products [that is, goods] and services promising relief, convenience, self-fulfillment, and instant gratification. Business in many ways provides the antidote to suffering, so it naturally tends to devalue that which it seeks to profitably eliminate.[14]

Much greater profits will accrue to those businesses with the wisdom to shift beyond goods and services to the use of experiences, no matter how painful, to transform their customers.

Accomplishing this entails moving up the dual progressions shown in Figure 10-3. While the economic offering becomes more and more intangible with each step up to the next echelon, the *value* of that offering becomes more and more *tangible*. Economists often talk about the "line of intangibility" between goods and services—to which we would add the "line of memorability" before experiences and the "line of sustainability" before transformations—but economists refer to the offering itself, not the value it holds for the customer. As outlined in Chapter 1, goods and services remain outside of the individual, while experiences actually reach inside of the individual to affect him in an inherently personal way, greatly increasing the value of the offering. But, no matter how acute an experience, one's memory of it fades over time. Transformations, on the other hand, guide the individual toward realizing some aspiration and then help to sustain that change over time. There is no earthly value more concrete, more palpable, or more worthwhile than achieving an aspiration.

When the offering becomes more intangible the value becomes more tangible

Similarly, while the availability of intelligence diminishes as one ascends each echelon of the Progression of Valuable Intelligence (background noise is literally ubiquitous, wisdom all too scarce), the intelligence itself becomes more and more substantial. Nothing is more important, more abiding, or more wealth-creating than the wisdom required to transform customers. And nothing will command as high a price.

In his book *The Knowledge-Value Revolution,* Japanese author Taichi Sakaiya demonstrates how people in all societies "develop an empathetic impulse toward their environment that convinces them to hold off on things in short supply while making a point of using up whatever there is lots of."[15] For example, material and energy resources have always been abundant in the United States, so coal, oil, and other natural commodities have been wasted. The wealthy built enormous houses on huge plots of land and then always left the lights on simply to demonstrate their wealth. In Japan, material resources have always been scarce and therefore used sparingly. Human resources, on the other hand, existed in abundance, so the wealthy traditionally hired legions of people to tend their small houses, lawns, and gardens to demonstrate their wealth. With the economic boom of the latter half of the twentieth century, skilled labor became a scarce resource in both countries, yielding, at its zenith, disposable products that conserved labor through mass production techniques while simultaneously wasting materials, as they were thrown away after just one use.

Nothing is more important than the wisdom required to transform customers

In his own take on the same societal and economic shifts we identify, Sakaiya realizes that more and more companies, and the people within them, are moving up the Progression of Valuable Intelligence to supply what he calls *chika* in Japanese. Translating somewhat awkwardly into *knowledge-value,* this "means both 'the price of wisdom' and 'the value created by wisdom.'"[16] Eventually, he foresees wisdom itself becoming relatively abundant:

> It therefore follows that in the new society that is now forming, the life-style that will earn the most respect will be one in which the owner's conspicuous consumption of wisdom (in the broadest sense) is displayed, while the products that will sell best will be those that reveal their purchaser to be a person "in the know." Such products, which more than anything else manifest their owner's access to the best knowledge, information, and accumulated wisdom to be had, possess what I will hereafter refer to as "knowledge-value." It is my contention that we are entering a new phase of civilization in which the value attached to knowledge is the driving force.[17]

And it is our contention that the "products" that best display knowledge-value—the economic offerings that result from accumulated wisdom—are those which transform the customer. The offering is not, however, the wisdom itself; that is only a means. The offering is the changed individual. The customer is the product.

YOU ARE WHAT YOU CHARGE FOR:
ONCE MORE WITH CARING

Very few of the enterprises that work to change people or companies are truly in the transformation business. Far too many view their offerings as mere services, and, as a result, they far too often fail to elicit the transformation or to capture the full economic value delivered when it is elicited. More important, few charge for the transformation itself. Being in the transformation business means charging for the demonstrated outcome the aspirant achieves—the transformation itself—not for the particular activities the company performs.

If a fitness center were truly in the transformation business, for example, it wouldn't charge (solely) via membership fees or by the amount of time members spend on machines. Rather, it would charge for meeting the health and well-being aspirations of its members. If the aspirations were not met within a fixed period of time, the fitness center would not be paid— or it would be paid less, on some sliding scale commensurate with the progress achieved. In other words, it would charge not for the pain but for the gain.

Think about what such a business would do differently were it truly a transformation elicitor. First, it would spend much more time up-front, before it agreed to accept an individual as a member—on understanding the individual's true aspirations and, more important, his or her current capabilities, both physical and mental. Many people do not have the temperament to stick to a physical regimen and cannot sustain progress toward a defined goal. Indeed, we suspect that many fitness centers derive much of their revenue from people who pay their money but rarely encounter pain on the machines. Signing up such people may be profitable for one period, but surely it leads to the costly churn of constantly replacing expiring memberships. Meanwhile, fitness centers lose much greater profits by not charging for the full value gained by those who do have the mindset to follow through on their aspirations and by not first attempting to change the temperament of those initially incapable of follow-through. (And these diagnostic activities should themselves be treated and explicitly charged for as an experience and, for some, a transformation—yielding profits right up-front before someone even becomes a member!)

Once a fitness center determines that an individual can both physically and mentally achieve a specific aspiration, then and only then would it lay out the charge for a specific achievement, including reaching interim goals

> **Being in the transformation business means charging for the demonstrated outcome**

along the way. And the amount would be two or three or perhaps even ten times what such places charge today for mere machine usage. Who wouldn't pay more for a guarantee that he would lose those 30 pounds, gain those 5 extra inches of pure muscle around the chest, bench press 250 pounds, or (more subjectively) develop washboard abs or perfectly tight buns? And once it made such a commitment, the fitness center would be sure to design exactly the right set of experiences to make sure the aspirant achieved his goals—and therefore paid in full. Personal trainers earn so much more than fitness center instructors precisely because they *ensure* their patrons follow the proper regimen.

Workers need personal trainers, too, such as those supplied by Priority Management of Vancouver, Canada. Using the slogan "Helping People Turn Intentions Into Actions, Worldwide," Priority Management changes people's behavior—generally yielding at least a 20 percent improvement in business and personal productivity, among other clear benefits—while they work through a productivity challenge that diagnoses current levels of productivity, provides training workshops, and then provides personal follow-up by a certified trainer. Key to success: a guarantee that if the person does not meet his aspirations, he doesn't have to pay. As franchise owner Roger Wangen of Burnsville, Minnesota, told us, "With our training methods, most clients readily achieve their productivity goals. But if someone's in danger of falling behind the goals we've mapped out together or isn't taking to the new way of managing his priorities I've shown him, I redouble my efforts to make sure he gets the results he desires." It's no wonder that more than 95 percent of Priority Management's customers continue with the program. Even if it doesn't yet call its customers aspirants, this company truly is in the transformation business.

Consider also the business-to-business example of management consulting, another industry that typically charges for the service activities workers perform, rather than for the actual transformation of clients. If consultants truly viewed themselves as being in the business of transformation, they would, like fitness centers, spend much more time in the up-front diagnosis phase, identifying clients' strategic needs as well as their capacity for change. They would stop writing analytical documents (the tangible goods of the present-day, PowerPoint-driven consulting industry) and start staging memorable events that would enable the client first to experience what it would be like to live and work in a world where the strategy has been achieved and then to actually create that future world. (While, of course, providing appropriate memorabilia for each experience that would be very different from today's sterile binders.) Most important, they would follow through to ensure each client actually achieved its stated strategy, or else risk losing some or all of its fee.[18] Wholly successful engagements, perhaps commemorated with appropriate emblems, would result in even greater revenue than that received today for mere services.

We already see many consulting engagements paid for all or in part through stock options or as a percentage of the business results achieved. Boston-based Bain & Co. now does this as a matter of course, while competitors McKinsey & Co. and Boston Consulting Group view

You really are what you charge for

it with great suspicion, perhaps even as unethical. But as one Texas Pacific managing partner (and consulting client), Bill Price, notes: "I've often found it odd that some in consulting see a potential conflict. If anything, there is more potential conflict in traditional cash payment, since the consultant makes money producing reports, not results."[19] If it charges solely for the reports, then it's not in the transformation business.

You really are what you charge for. So let's be very clear about this as it applies to each echelon of customer value:

- If you charge for *stuff*, then you are in the *commodity* business.
- If you charge for *tangible things,* then you are in the *goods* business.
- If you charge for *the activities you execute,* then you are in the *service* business.
- If you charge for *the time customers spend with you,* then you are in the *experience* business.
- If you charge for *the demonstrated outcome the customer achieves,* then and only then are you in the *transformation* business.

It's not easy being in the business of transforming customers. Extracting commodities out of the ground may be the most physically demanding practice, but eliciting transformations out of customers is the most intellectually demanding, and it sometimes involves great physical (for example, fitness centers) and emotional (hospitals) demands as well.

WORK IS THEATRE: ACT 2, SCENE 1

Transformation elicitors still must stage experiences, extending them by orchestrating themes, impressions, cues, and even memorabilia in such a way as to move the buyer toward his aspiration, not just to present the experience itself. Work is therefore still theatre, but an important shift in roles occurs between buyer and seller with this new offering. With an experience, the employees of the staging company are actors performing parts, creating roles, and building characters to engage guests in entertaining, educational, escapist, and/or esthetic ways. With a transformation, all these experiential realms merely set the stage for helping *the customer* learn to act. Erving Goffman, the sociologist who first proclaimed theatre to be a model for work, points to boot camp as means of personal transformation from cynical to sincere performance for a "raw recruit who initially follows army etiquette in order to avoid physical punishment and eventually comes to follow the rules so that his organization will not be shamed and his officers and fellow soldiers will respect him."[20]

Consider again a birthday transformation offering. The selection of gifts, the invitation of guests, the postparty thank-you notes, and other aspects will aim to help a child learn to act; at first, acting "as if" he is thankful, for example, and later drawing on his emotional reservoir of thankful deeds past to make his own personal statements of appreciation whenever appropriate. Such an offering supplements the parent's most fundamental role, that of developing children into independent adults acting on their own. The entire ensemble of a transformation elicitor assumes a singular role itself, that of directing the aspiring actor to perform new parts. (And remember the metadrama involved: Directing is still work, and work is still theatre!)

Experiences set the stage for teaching the customer to act

Since Aristotle, philosophers, scholars, and artists alike have acknowledged the transformational power of theatre. Lift-Him Ministries Performing Arts, Company affirms it by offering instruction in drama, voice and piano, script writing, and the staging of full-scale productions. Like the American Wilderness Experience, the company is located in a retail mall, in this case outside of Cleveland. Its motif more reminiscent of the LAN Arena in its sparse decor and mom-and-pop feeling, Lift-Him Ministries may be a harbinger of other mall-based companies offering to help people learn how to act, or it may be an isolated case. It's clear, however, that for its founders learning to act is but a means to another end: a spiritual transformation. As the company brochure states, "Our mission is to provide performing arts classes and activities in a ministerial atmosphere, thereby contributing to the spiritual growth of our students as well as helping to develop their talents and gifts. We equip our students to perform with a sense of purpose that goes beyond entertaining. That purpose is to glorify God and to encourage others to do the same."

Director Harold Clurman says that theatre techniques "must be ultimately judged by their contribution to our human needs, our aspirations, moral concerns and philosophies. These questions lead to the role played by the audience in the theatre. . . . The audience is the theatre's wellspring, its leading actor. This is not a metaphor, it is a historical fact."[21] And the audience's role is to become part of the play itself, its members thereby becoming something different from what they were before the performance began. Unless customers act differently, there is no transformation. Transformation elicitors cannot change for the customer, they can only direct the change. And customers must be willing to put themselves in the hands of a guiding director. How does a company gain the confidence of customers to earn such responsibility?

For starters: *Customize.* No individual will entrust himself—or any part of himself—to an enterprise that has not established a one-to-one relationship with him. Mass-produced, mass-marketed, and mass-distributed offerings send one clear message to potential buyers: We don't care enough to know you individually. Buyers inevitably respond: You cannot help change me if you do not even care enough to know me. Getting your act together by mass customizing your offerings establishes connections with customers that signal you care.

Ever since Aristotle we have acknowledged the transformational power of theatre

Second: *Stage truly engaging experiences.* Make it the goal of each individual relationship to hear the customer say that when the two of you work together, he discovers things about himself he did not know before. Then go further: Make it your aspiration to hear him say that *only* when he interacts with you does he gain the deepest understanding of some part of himself. Make the customer's most memorable experiences his moments with you. These set the stage for creating a bond between you and the customer, a bond that fosters communication of his ultimate aspirations.

Third: *Furnish places for actors to rehearse new behaviors.* Use knowledge of each customer's individuality to orchestrate the appropriate set of experiences to elicit the desired transformation. Bring together buyers with similar aspirations into a community, eager to learn not only from you and the overall experience but from one another. Create *ensembles* of like-minded customers, not to lump them into detached and anonymous market segments but to form a close-knit cast of characters able to strengthen and confirm the rightness of the aspirations each seeks.

Take a cue from Dr. Robert Lucid, emeritus professor of English at the University of Pennsylvania, who, in his role as faculty master of Penn's Hill House dormitory, understood the aspirations of matriculating students. As Lucid explains, "When people come to a university, they're interested in it almost exclusively for certain utilitarian reasons—they're looking for a job or whatever it is—but they're also interested in it as a theater, in which they're going to act out a certain part. They've been thinking about it for quite a while, and they're ready to act it out now if *only* the other actors are there. And it's that almost desperate search for the other players—they've got the script pretty clear in mind; it's just that they want to be sure that they're in the right place."[22] Iron sharpens iron, and most performances—especially transformational ones—demand that the stage be shared with other people, so that each character is framed by the characters of others performing the same theatre. The interchange between actors is often the vital factor that drives transformational outcomes.

Everything else is just a prop supporting transformational guiding

Finally: *Direct the actors.* If aspirants could do it all themselves, they wouldn't purchase a transformational offering or entrust their aspirations to an outside party. They know that they need some guidance, but they don't wish to be told what to do. Handling this delicate balance between assistance and interference is the director's responsibility. Guiding is directing! And again, a skilled director embodies two seemingly contradictory roles: collaborator and commander. Directing certainly takes on the flavor of collaboration, with shared control of outputs and dialog with actors about how to best portray their roles. But there are moments within the transformation when the director must force decisions and dictate a particular course of action, helping the actors realize their aspirations. The director guides the moment-to-moment orchestration of themes, impressions, and cues.

Everything else is just a prop supporting this guiding activity. Any good (and the commodities it comprises) must be used only to help a customer learn to act, just as acting instructors use masks and other objects to facilitate the learning of new skills. Any service must be used only to accelerate this learning. Likewise, any experience must be staged only to promote the actor's progression of personal value.

The lower-echelon offerings able to retain the greatest value in the forthcoming Transformation Economy will be those filled with intention, those existing *in order to* help individual customers become all they seek to be. The issue of how one's economic offerings affect buyers will be unavoidable and inherent to any purchasing decision. In this world, businesses succeeding in the Experience Economy must confront the reality—always present, but previously veiled in economies dominated by commodities, goods, and services—that everything they do affects the character of those for whom the work is done. The intentions of every business will be scrutinized as never before, and the outcome of the assessment will determine which enterprises prosper and which become impoverished.

Figure 10-4. The New Competitive Landscape

	Commodities	Goods	Services	Experiences	Transformations
	The material is the offering →	The product is the offering →	The operation is the offering →	The event is the offering →	The individual is the offering ↑
Origination	New substances are discovered	New inventions are developed	New procedures are devised	New scripts are depicted	New aims are determined
Execution	Extracting is the core activity of the trader	Making is the core activity of the manufacturer	Delivering is the core activity of the provider	Staging is the core activity of the stager	Guiding is the core activity of the elictor
Correction	A poor site triggers further exploration	A problem triggers fixing of a mistake	A reaction triggers a response	Forgetting triggers preservation of memory	A relapse triggers stronger resolve
Application	A trade connects in markets	A transaction connects with users	An interaction connects with clients	An encounter connects with guests	Persevering connects with aspirants

AMPLE WAVES OF GAIN

To enrich an enterprise with greater intention, focus on the four universal elements that together constitute how businesses ultimately create value:

- *Origination:* work that generates value from something new
- *Execution:* work that generates value from something done
- *Correction:* work that generates value from something improved
- *Application:* work that generates value from something used[23]

Everything eventually offered for commerce must *originate* from somewhere and/or something. Commodities, preexisting to commercial enterprise, are extracted from animal, mineral, or vegetable substances. Since the beginning of economic activity these materials have been the wellspring from which a stream of new goods and services—and now experiences and transformations—flows.

All forms of economic output, however, require that the supplier *execute* some key activity to create the offering. And any activity, no matter of how well it is done, remains prone to error (we are, after all, only human). The company must then *correct* any flaws or failures that affect the offering. As Henry Petroski points out, "It is not that form follows function but, rather, that the form of one thing follows from the failure of another thing to function as we would like it."[24] The offering is improved—adding, subtracting, or modifying aspects of the offering—until it is *applied* to a specific person or enterprise. At that point, the offering is exchanged for monetary payment, and the act of putting an offering to use connects with the original request to fulfill an individual want or need.

Businesses need a strategy for managing these four dimensions of value creation

Every business needs a strategy to manage these four dimensions of value generation. As Figure 10-4 illustrates, companies must define their economic offerings (commodities, goods, services, experiences, and transformations) in terms of the type of work performed (originating, executing, correcting, and applying) for specific kinds of buyers (markets, users, clients, guests, or aspirants). Systematically examining this new competitive landscape and filling it with company-unique intention, each business must define its own offerings, core activities, corrective triggers, and buyer relationships to first explore and then exploit for strategic advantage.

The performance of commodity suppliers like Archer Daniels Midland and Cargill demonstrates that companies can compete successfully at the lower echelons and that sometimes focusing on the supply of commodities represents the right strategy for a business. Drawing from the four universal elements of work just discussed, any company doing so must excel at the primary value-generating work required of commodity-based companies:

- Discovering new substances
- Extracting materials efficiently
- Exploring alternative sites
- Trading in markets

Only a remnant of agricultural and mining companies has survived from the competitive attrition of previous eras. Most materials have traded for ages through firmly established markets, but whenever someone discovers a new substance, the processes of extracting, exploring, and trading form new markets. Access to these true marketplaces remains critical to success, and poor selection of both sourcing and destination market sites can spell disaster for these commodity extractors.

Location theory and practice, however, no longer play as vital a role in the success of goods-based businesses. Companies still make efforts to optimize plant, warehouse, and distribution sites, but these facilities do not provide the primary source of sustained strategic advantage. Instead, value must be generated from:

- Developing new inventions
- Making products efficiently
- Fixing mistakes
- Transacting with users

These elements of success differ significantly from the activities of commodity businesses. Research and development efforts must constantly invent new solutions to old problems as product life cycles continue to decrease. Efficiency—and quality—in manufacturing, whether based on craft production or more modern techniques, is critical to success. And transactions with customers must satisfactorily meet the needs of customers.

The increased importance of high-quality processes to create these goods led to wholly new economic enterprises supporting manufacturers and, eventually, to entirely new service industries. These service providers found ways to perform highly valued activities that manufacturers otherwise left for the customer to do. Their tasks involve:

- Devising new procedures
- Delivering operations efficiently
- Providing responses
- Interacting with clients

Innovation in services does not come via the isolation of the R&D lab but in face-to-face interactions with individual clients. Two-way communication—genuine dialog—becomes critical to ensure the routine delivery of outstanding service operations.

Similarly, mere service operations will not suffice in the staging of experiences. Work needs to be orchestrated, converting routine interactions into memorable performances by:

- Depicting new scripts
- Staging events efficiently
- Preserving memories
- Encountering guests

Any business, from repair firm to parking lot, can advance from delivering services to staging experiences if it declares that to be the business in which it competes, exploits the inherent sacrifice gaps of traditional service offerings in its industry, and designs an event enriching enough to charge admission.

Recognizing experiences as a distinct economic offering provides the key to future economic growth. Jeremy Rifkin is right to suggest fewer workers will be needed to deliver services in the future, just as past innovations have greatly reduced the need for factory workers to produce goods, and before that for farm workers to harvest agricultural commodities. But Rifkin, neo-Luddite Kirkpatrick Sales, political pundit Pat Buchanan, and others like them who bemoan the automation of jobs are wrong in believing the overall demand for labor will decrease. The future waves of economic growth will present ample opportunities to generate more wealth and create new jobs. Indeed, the masses will be employed by those businesses which recognize and create experiential output as a distinct economic offering— and learn to do it well.

Even higher-paying jobs will accompany experiences that richly understand, articulate, and ensure transformations (beginning perhaps with experts in transforming enterprises into experience stagers!). The processes required for transforming an aspirant are more exacting and elusive than those needed for the buyer of any other economic offering. They involve:

- Determining new aims
- Guiding the individual
- Strengthening resolve
- Persevering with the aspirant

Companies will certainly find transformations the most difficult offering to supply, for elicitors must be intentional about their own processes while also helping their customers learn to act with intention. Customers will value these offerings most highly, for they address the ultimate source of all other needs: *why* the buyer wants what he wants.

SO WHAT DO YOU INTEND TO DO?

The capabilities required to transform a customer are not unlike those needed to transform an entire industry: One must first aspire to bring about a desired change. Not change for the sake of change, which too often results in aimless wandering and constant doubting of one's direction, but something more. One must apply the principle of intention to strategy.

Premier strategists Gary Hamel and C. K. Prahalad popularized the notion of *strategic intent,* observing that "too many mission statements fail entirely to impart any sense of *mission.* For this reason we prefer goals that are focused on making a real difference in the lives of customers." Exactly. Hamel and Prahalad encourage organizations to embrace passion and pathos, and they point out that strategic intent is "as much about the creation of meaning for employees as it is about the establishment of direction." They even commend Jesus Christ's imperative, "Go into all the world and preach the gospel" as "perhaps one of the most ambitious, and emotionally compelling strategic intents ever articulated."[25]

The principle of intention must be applied to strategy

We believe Hamel and Prahalad assert something profound: Strategic intent is the foundation of any organization's energy and ambitions. It supplies meaning to otherwise humdrum activities. Recognizing the importance of strategic intent alone, however, is not sufficient to set the direction or establish the meaning of an enterprise. There remains the question of what one means by *intention.*

The intention of mission statements, strategic plans, and action steps must be grounded in one's uniqueness, not in a fixation on the activity of competitors. This is not striving to be differentiated but seeking to discover the unexamined dimensions of oneself, with competitive differentiation resulting as a natural by-product. This corporate self-examination provides the wellspring of renewal (just as examining the uniqueness of one's customers opens the wellspring of unarticulated needs so often pointed out by Hamel and Prahalad). The strategy of a business confers meaning only if those called on to execute it understand—ideally, viscerally—how the company plans to alter the very structure of the world through its industry. Every activity of the company must be performed *in order to* advance external change. The firm can then fulfill its specific strategic intention not by competing for the future but by actively attaining that future. And that can only be accomplished through rigorous thinking about what business the company truly is in.

Every activity of the company must be performed *in order to* advance external change

We do not wish to see executives use the frameworks presented here just to argue over whether they are today delivering services, staging experiences, or eliciting transformations. That is not our intent. Any such debates should serve only as a means to discover new ways of generating value. The Progression of Economic Value simply articulates a new competitive reality for the strategic options facing any enterprise today. The opportunities are vast, but so are the challenges. As the Experience Economy continues to unfold, manufacturers and service providers will increasingly see their offerings commoditized as more and more businesses charge explicitly for the memorable encounters they stage. And as the Experience Economy naturally progresses into the Transformation Economy, even experience stagers will find their offerings commoditized as more and more businesses charge explicitly for the demonstrated outcomes they elicit.

You must find your own role in the world. What business are *you* really in? Five economic offerings—commodities, goods, services, experiences, and transformations—yield five very distinct possibilities, with tremendous ramifications for your business, your employees, and your customers.

Exit, Stage Right

● ●

CUSTOMERS AND COLLEAGUES OFTEN ASK US, "What's next after transformations?" The question comes up particularly when people begin wondering whether transformations, like the other economic offerings before them, will be commoditized. Consider the following: The healthcare industry for much of the 1990s has focused on cutting costs via uniform coverage, resulting in lower prices and routine treatment. Internet learning programs might soon increase access to and slash costs of college education. Management consulting firms find themselves competing not only against business schools that hire out their MBAs at remarkably reduced billing rates,[1] but also against Web sites like Ernst & Young LLP's "Ernie" that offer Internet-based advice to small- and medium-sized enterprises—at a fraction of traditional consultancy costs. Are these signs of commoditized transformations? Perhaps.

Remember, in the nascent Transformation Economy, the customer is the product and the transformation is an aid in changing the traits of the individual who buys it. Transformations that effect this kind of change automatically ward off commoditization, because there can be no greater differentiation than a personally transformed individual. Certainly, competitors can duplicate specific diagnoses, experiences, and follow-through devices. But no one can commoditize the most important aspect of a transformation: the unique relationship formed between the guided and the guide. It is the tie that binds.

An offering of a higher order can supersede lower-echelon relationships. But the only offering that can displace a transformation is yet another transformation—one aimed at another dimension of self, or at the same

205

dimension but from a different worldview. By worldview, we mean a particular way—often religious or philosophical—of interpreting one's own existence. In the years ahead, we think that companies and their customers will increasingly acknowledge rival worldviews—ideologies, if you will—as the legitimate domain of business and as differentiators of competing offerings. The question, "What's next?" therefore becomes highly personal. To answer it truthfully requires our sharing our worldview with you. Consider the fundamental nature of each offering:

- Commodities are only raw materials for the goods they make
- Goods are only physical embodiments of the services they deliver
- Services are only intangible operations for the experiences they stage
- Experiences are only memorable events for the transformations they guide

Then reflect on our personal belief that:

- Transformations are only temporal states for the eternalities they glorify.[2]

All economic offerings do more than effect an exchange of value in the present; they also, implicitly or explicitly, promote a certain worldview. In the full-fledged Transformation Economy, we believe buyers will purchase transformations according to the set of eternal principles the seller seeks to embrace—what together they believe will last.[3]

Like every other economic offering, transformations will be scrutinized, lionized, and criticized—but not commoditized. Still, they must be customized to remain differentiated. Imagine the most highly customized transformation possible. What would be so right for a particular person, that it would transform him into someone who needs no additional change? What would the ultimate customer-as-product be? The utmost would be *perfection,* the perfect human being. According to our own worldview, there can be no sixth economic offering because perfecting people falls under the province of God, the Author and Perfecter of our faith rather than in the domain of human business. As the Apostle Paul said, "For by grace are ye saved through faith; and that not of yourselves."[4] We believe that no one can be in the business of extending this offer; it is a *free* gift. It cannot be fulfilled as an economic offering. And so, we contend, transformations are the fifth and final offering.

When transformations finally comprise the preponderance of economic commerce, many businesses and individuals will claim to provide the ultimate offering and charge for revealing its secrets. In doing so, they will glorify whatever they view as ultimate. Since all commerce is moral choice, every business is a stage for glorifying something. Who or what does your business glorify? Your answer may or may not help you accept what is next, but it will certainly help guide what you do today.

Notes

● ●

Chapter 1

1. For a backstage tour of the technology of Walt Disney World, see Scott Kirsner, "Hack the Magic: The Exclusive Underground Tour of Disney World," *Wired,* March 1998, 162–168, 186–189.

2. So pervasive have theme restaurants become that on 15 April 1998, online satirical magazine *The Onion* (www.theonion.com) posted a story with the title "Nation's Last Themeless Restaurant Closes," ostensibly about Pat's Place in Dubuque, Iowa, being replaced by the town's seventh "Paddy O'Touchdown's Irish Sports Bar & Good-Tyme Internet Grill."

3. Steven E. Prokesch, "Competing on Customer Service: An Interview with British Airways' Sir Colin Marshall," *Harvard Business Review* 73, no. 6, November–December 1995, 103. For a response to this interview that incorporated the first publishing of the concept of experiences as a distinct economic offering, see B. Joseph Pine II, "Customer Service on

British Airways," Letter to the Editor, *Harvard Business Review* 74, no. 1, January–February 1996, 162–164.

4. Howard Riell, "Upscale Grocer Chain Grows," *Stores,* March 1995, 26.

5. Russell Vernon, "Fighting Back—A Small Retailer Takes on the EEOC," *Retailing Issues Letter* 8, no.2, Center for Retailing Studies, Texas A&M University (November 1996): 2. See also Leonard L. Berry, *On Great Service: A Framework for Action* (New York: Free Press, 1995), 90–92 in particular.

6. See, for example, Louise Palmer, "There's No Meetings Like Business Meetings," *Fast Company,* April–May 1996, 36, 40.

7. Tibor Scitovsky, *The Joyless Economy: The Psychology of Human Satisfaction,* Revised Edition (New York: Oxford University Press, 1992), 67.

8. Julian L. Simon, *The Ultimate Resource 2* (Princeton, N.J.: Princeton University Press, 1996), 416 and 109, respectively. This book is a tremendous (and very possibly the ultimate) resource of data on how humans have fared with all the commodities discovered on earth.

9. For a summary background on the American System of Manufactures and the system of Mass Production, see B. Joseph Pine II, *Mass Customization: The New Frontier in Business Competition* (Boston: Harvard Business School Press, 1993), Chapters 1 and 2.

10. Deuteronomy 28:11 (King James Version): "The LORD shall make thee plenteous in goods, in the fruit of thy body, and in the fruit of thy cattle, and in the fruit of thy ground, in the land which the LORD sware unto thy fathers to give thee." Work (the fruit of thy body) here is clearly seen as extracting from animal (thy cattle), vegetable (thy ground), and mineral (the land) to make goods.

11. W. W. Rostow, *The World Economy: History and Prospect* (Austin: University of Texas Press, 1978), 52–53, cited in Alfred D. Chandler, *Scale and Scope: The Dynamics of Industrial Capitalism* (Cambridge, Mass.: Belknap Press of Harvard University Press, 1990), 4.

12. David A. Hounshell, *From the American System to Mass Production, 1800–1932: The Development of Manufacturing Technology in the United States* (Baltimore: Johns Hopkins University Press, 1984), 228.

13. Bureau of Labor Statistics, Labstat (a web-based database).

14. A great set of principles and frameworks for manufacturers to wrap services around their goods can be found in Christopher Lovelock, *Product Plus: How Product + Service = Competitive Advantage* (New York: McGraw-Hill, 1994).

15. See, for example, "Big MacCurrencies," *The Economist,* 12 April 1997, 71.

16. Suzanne Woolley, "Do I Hear Two Bits a Trade?" *Business Week,* 8 December 1997, 112. Patrick McGeehan and Anita Raghavan, in "On-Line Trading Battle Is Heating Up as Giant Firms Plan to Enter Arena," *The Wall Street Journal,* 22 May 1998, said that online commission slashing "threatened to lapse into absurdity" when Rickets said this.

17. Stan Davis and Christopher Meyer, in the book *Blur: The Speed of Change in the Connected Economy* (Reading, Mass.: Addison-Wesley, 1998), demonstrate that the markets for goods and services increasingly act like financial markets; i.e., they're commoditizing. The authors then provide compelling strategies for how to live in such a "blurred" world. See especially pp. 96–110.

18. The dual forces of service commoditization and manufacturers wrapping services around their goods has led to a blurring of the lines between the two, as in Davis and Meyer, *Blur,* and Michael Schrage, "Provices and Serducts," *Fast Company,* August–September 1996, 48–49.

19. Adam Smith, *An Inquiry into the Nature and Causes of The Wealth of Nations,* Modern Library Edition (New York: Random House, 1994), 361.

20. Which is why the best entertainers make truly astronomical amounts of money. See Robert La Franco and Ben Pappas, "The Top 40," *Forbes,* 21 September 1998, 220–246.

21. Bureau of Labor Statistics, "Relative Importance of Components in the Consumer Price Index, 1997," *BLS Bulletin #2499,* April 1998.

22. Prices for the higher echelon offerings tend to increase not only because customers desire them more highly, but because those companies offering them may have lower relative productivity gains over time, and create their offerings less efficiently. This is to be expected, as efficiency and productivity are tightly bound with the forces of commoditization. Until competition becomes more intense, there is little incentive for experience stagers to lower their costs.

23. Recall also the late economist Julian Simon's famous bet with Malthusian Paul Erlich to demonstrate whether or not the earth was running out of raw materials, retold by Simon in *The Ultimate Resource 2*, 35–36. Erlich and two colleagues chose five commodities and bet that the sum of their prices would be higher in 1990 than in 1980. They lost hands down to Simon. As Simon makes clear, the prices of commodities always decrease relative to goods and services over the long term, as will the prices of commoditized goods and services relative to their noncommoditized brethren and of course to experiences.

24. Nominal GDP was used because it uses actual prices, not taking inflation into account. For, as noted earlier, the inflation deflator does not accurately reflect the shift from goods to services (much less the shift to experiences). Therefore, real GDP does not accurately show the growth in services and experiences. Furthermore, the increased prices of higher echelon offerings, also noted earlier, at least partly reflects higher demand, not just higher costs of inputs.

25. These industries were motion pictures and amusement and recreation services in both sets of statistics, as well as educational services and museums and botanical and zoological gardens solely in the employment statistics (working with government statistics is never clean!). There are certainly experience businesses (theme restaurants, some retail establishments, etc.) left in the service statistics, as they could not be broken out separately. Also note that because only a few industries are represented in the experiences breakouts, they start from a much smaller base than the industries left in the service sector. While it's true that it's easier to grow from a small base, those industries that are clearly in the experience business nonetheless grew at higher rates than the services for nearly the past forty years. For more, albeit dated, statistics on the rise of experiences, see the amazingly prescient report by James A. Ogilvy (now with the Global Business Network), "The Experience Industry: A Leading Edge Report from the Values and Lifestyle Program," Business Intelligence Program Report No. 724, Fall 1985.

26. Economist Stanley Lebergott, in *Pursuing Happiness: American Consumers in the Twentieth Century* (Princeton: Princeton University Press, 1993), makes the point, "Consumers buy bazaars full of goods, but only to create the diversified experience they ultimately seek" (p. 3) and goes on to show with a wealth of data that these goods (and services, for that matter) that enable consumer experiences have seen tremendous growth in the twentieth century. See also Virginia I. Postrel, "It's All in the Head," *Forbes ASAP*, 26 February 1996, 118.

27. Peter Guttman, *Adventures to Imagine: Thrilling Escapes in North America* (New York: Fodor's Travel Publications, 1997) describes these adventures, each of which Guttman personally experienced and photographed. The book also includes a detailed directory of outfitters to contact for each adventure.

28. Quoted in Tim Stevens, "From Reliable to 'Wow,'" *Industry Week*, 22 June 1998, 24, emphasis added. Other sources for wowing customers include Paul Levesque, *The Wow Factory: Creating a Customer Focus Revolution in Your Business* (Chicago: Irwin Professional Publishing, 1995); Tom Peters, *The Pursuit of Wow! Every Person's Guide to Topsy-Turvy Times* (New York: Vintage Books, 1994); and, in a slightly different but exemplary vein, Ken Blanchard and Sheldon Bowles, *Raving Fans: A Revolutionary Approach to Customer Service* (New York: William Morrow and Company, 1993).

29. Bernd Schmitt and Alex Simonson, in *Marketing Aesthetics: The Strategic*

Management of Brands, Identity, and Image (New York: Free Press, 1997), provide a great resource for marketing an experiential brand.

30. Both "experientialize" and "sensorialize" are not the most euphonious of words, but as Stan Davis and Bill Davidson point out in reference to the word "informationalize": "We use it because it is more self-explanatory and complete, even though cumbersome. We suspect that 'industrialize' sounded equally unnatural when it first appeared." See *2020 Vision* (New York: Simon & Schuster, 1991), 207, n. 1.

31. See Carl Quintanilla, "Planning a Vacation? Give Some Thought to Spamtown USA," *The Wall Street Journal,* 30 April 1998; and Robert Gray, "Learning from Experience," *Marketing,* 20 March 1997, 27–29.

32. So far removed are suburban and urban kids from the Agrarian Economy that just being on a farm is an experience! Indeed, staging farm experiences is the next big wave in agrimarketing. See Julie V. Iovine, "A New Cash Crop: The Farm as Theme Park," *The New York Times,* 2 November 1997, and Rick Mooney, "Let Us Entertain You," *Farm Journal,* March 1998, H-8, H-9.

33. The initial term "progression of value" and its depiction were suggested to us by Rohan Champion, now vice president of Strategy and Alliances at Federal Express, when he was vice president of New Services Strategy at AT&T.

34. Of course, each economic offering has its own set of fixed costs to which margins contribute, such as a farm for commodities, a factory for goods, an office or outlet for services, and back to a farm for this particular experience.

35. "Ogden Allied Serviced: Celebrating a Century of Service," Ogden Corporation company brochure, 1988.

36. See also Laura Bird, "Retailing: Move over Mall Rats, Wild Beasts Are Taking Your Turf," *The Wall Street Journal,* 8 July 1997. Listen to the sensations that the reporter describes: "Visitors will enter the first biome on a gnarled concrete path, passing under a leafy canopy and through a strand of ersatz redwoods. Hidden scent canisters will emit a forest fragrance. The desert biome will feature a giant fake Joshua tree, plus real Gila monsters and desert tortoises. In the coast biome, visitors can touch a starfish in a tidal pool. . . . Behind the scenes in the biomes are corridors with animal pens and a separate air-circulation system. That way, the smell of the restaurant's grilled hamburgers won't waft through the animal cages, and vice versa."

37. See Eben Shapiro, "Discovery Zone Slides into Bankruptcy Court," *The Wall Street Journal,* 26 March 1996.

Chapter 2

1. See, for example, Colin Berry, "The Bleeding Edge: If You're Looking for What's Next in Online Technology and Commerce, Just Follow the Gamers," *Wired,* October 1997, 90–97.

2. See also Amy Jo Kim, "Killers Have More Fun," *Wired,* May 1998, 140–144, 197–198, 209.

3. *The New Shorter Oxford English Dictionary,* vol. 1, A–M, s.v. "entertainment."

4. Stan Davis and Jim Botkin, *The Monster Under the Bed: How Business Is Mastering the Opportunity of Knowledge for Profit* (New York: Simon & Schuster, 1994), 125.

5. Judith Rodin, "A Summons to the 21st Century," *Pennsylvania Gazette,* December 1994.

6. Although he didn't use the term *edutainment,* Philip Kotler, professor of marketing at the Kellogg Graduate School of Management, Northwestern University, made the first foray into making education entertaining that we're aware of in "Educational Packagers: A Modest Proposal," *The Futurist*, August 1978, 239–242. There he introduced "the metaphor of classroom as *theater*" and encouraged "educational packagers" (as opposed to publishers) to be "like a Hollywood film producer" in providing a "multimedia experience" where "students are both instructed and entertained."

7. See also Barbara Bailey Kelley, "Bamboola!" *Bay Area Parent*, June 1997, 22–25.

8. Psychologist Mihaly Csikszentmihalyi refers to optimal experiences of this kind as "the process of total involvement with life I call *flow*," in *Flow: The Psychology of Optimal Experience* (New York: HarperPerennial, 1990), xi.

9. Michael Krantz dubs those producing motion-based attractions and the like the "experience industry" in "Dollar a Minute: Realies, the Rise of the Experience Industry, and the Birth of the Urban Theme Park," *Wired*, May 1994, 104–109, 140–142.

10. Interestingly, Iwerks Entertainment was founded by Don Iwerks, who worked in optics for The Walt Disney Co. for thirty-five years and whose father, Ub Iwerks, was Walt Disney's chief animator in the early years.

11. This is a slightly changed formulation from William Irwin Thompson, *The American Replacement of Nature: The Everyday Acts and Outrageous Evolution of Economic Life* (New York: Doubleday Currency, 1991), 35. It should be noted that Thompson is very much a critic of staged experiences, believing that they are replacing natural ones.

12. Professor Kotler was prescient in this regard as well, discussing escapist experiences in "'Dream' Vacations: The Booming Market for Designed Experiences," *The Futurist*, October 1984, 7–13. Tibor Scitovsky, in *The Joyless Economy: The Psychology of Human Satisfaction*, Revised Edition (New York: Oxford University Press, 1992), makes the point that many affluent people pay for increasingly comfortable lifestyles, which in fact decreases the pleasure we receive from everyday experience. Those growing up in such an environment then "are prone to take up dangerous sports and become involved in reckless adventures. Could it be that, deprived of the simple pleasures by too much comfort, they seek compensation in pleasures which accompany excitement and threat? Perhaps the increasing violence of our increasingly affluent society can be similarly explained" (p. 74).

13. John Ed Bradley, "SWM, tall, handsome, 29, professional football player, seeks beautiful, intelligent young woman to help design dream house and create family equivalent of America's Team. Must like quiet evenings at home, either cruising America Online or admiring tropical fish tank. Must spend Sundays in crowded stadiums rooting for Dallas Cowboys. Dislike of 49ers and Redskins a plus, but not required," By *Sports Illustrated*, 15 January 1996, 80–90.

14. Steve Hamm, with Amy Cortese and Cathy Yang, "Microsoft Refines Its Net Game," *Business Week*, 8 September 1997, 128.

15. MIT Professor Sherry Turkle, in *Life on the Screen: Identity in the Age of the Internet* (New York: Simon & Schuster, 1995), discusses the tendency of computer-mediated reality to encourage people to take on multiple online personas. Some people do so to the degree that RL (real life) "can be 'just one more window'" (p. 14).

16. Frank Rose, "Keyword: AOL," *Wired,* December 1996, 299.

17. Ray Oldenburg, *The Great Good Place: Cafés, Coffee Shops, Community Centers, Beauty Parlors, General Stores, Bars, Hangouts and How They Get You through the Day* (New York: Marlowe & Company, 1997).

18. In *The Theming of America: Dreams, Visions, and Commercial Spaces* (Boulder, Colorado: Westview Press, 1997), 115, Mark Gottdiener points out that many themed environments fulfill "the desire for community and pedestrian communion in public spaces, along with what is often a much-needed holiday from the normal routines of everyday life. People seem to crave this street-level intimacy—a need created by the destruction of public space in contemporary society through suburbanization and the terror of urban crime."

19. The concept of flow experiences is applied to those of the esthetic kind in Mihaly Csikszentmihalyi and Rick E. Robinson, *The Art of Seeing: An Interpretation of the Aesthetic Encounter* (Malibu, Calif.: J. Paul Getty Museum and the Getty Center for Education in the Arts, 1990).

20. The live butterflies placed in the first prototype store had the unfortunate habit of dropping onto customer's plates.

21. Quoted in Chris Niskanen, "Big Big Business," *St. Paul Pioneer Press,* 29 March 1998.

22. Michael Benedikt, *For an Architecture of Reality* (New York: Lumen Books, 1987), 4.

23. Ibid., 48. We would argue, however, that architectural masterpieces are similarly "non-real" in that they are still but constructions of our own making. If Benedikt's own definition were taken literally, the only truly esthetic experiences would occur when one is immersed solely in God's creation.

24. Ada Louise Huxtable, *The Unreal America: Architecture and Illusions* (New York: New Press, 1997), 75.

25. Ibid., 58.

26. Tom Carson, "To Disneyland," *Los Angeles Weekly,* 27 March, 2 April, 1992. Carson also quotes Charles Moore, from the book *The City Observed,* in a chapter on Disneyland, saying, "People often use Disneyland as a synonym for the facile, shallow and fake. It just doesn't wash: this incredibly energetic collection of environmental experiences offers enough lessons for a whole architectural education in all the things that matter—community and reality, private memory and inhabitation, as well as some technical lessons in propinquity and choreography."

27. Charles Goldsmith, "British Airways's [*sic*] New CEO Envisions a Marriage of Travel and Amusement," *The Wall Street Journal,* 6 November 1995.

28. Other Unique Experiences periodically offered by American Express include a Customized Napa Valley Wine Country Tour, a New York Culinary Experience at the French Culinary Institute, a Country Music Extravaganza, and a Champagne Harvest at Veuve Clicquot in France. Treating these offerings as economic experiences, American Express requires a huge number of reward points be redeemed, sometimes as high as half a million, meaning $500,000 would ordinarily have been charged to the cardmember's American Express card!

29. Anthony Rooley, in *Performance: Revealing the Orpheus Within* (Longmead, England: Element Books, 1990), 108–109, delineates seven stages of any performance that seem to spiral around the sweet spot: "The arts must delight in order to attract our further attention, and lead us subtly to a more profound contemplation. This happens in seven stages during a performance as it:

"(a) delights the senses

(b) invites curiosity

(c) involves the mind

(d) encourages deeper study

(e) encourages regular practice

(f) expands love

(g) opens up knowledge"

30. Michael C. Perkins and Anthony B. Perkins, "Case by Case," *The Red Herring,* June 1996, 47.

31. Witold Rybczynski, *Home: A Short History of an Idea* (New York: Penguin Books USA, 1986), 66.

32. Ibid., 62.

Chapter 3

1. A look at the origin of our English word *theme* explains this relationship between *theme* and *place.* John Ayto, *Dictionary of Word Origins* (New York: Arcade Publishing, 1990), 527, tells us the "Greek *théma* denoted etymologically 'something placed,' hence a 'proposition' (it was formed from the base **the-,* source of *tithénai* 'place, put' and distant relative of English *do*). English acquired the word via Latin *théma* and Old French **teme* as *teme,* but soon reverted to the Latin spelling." Experiences occur in places, and the best of those places are themed.

2. James Champy, *Reengineering Management* (New York: Harper Business, 1995), 56–57. See also I. Jeanne Dugan, "The Baron of Books," *Business Week,* 29 June 1998, 108–115.

3. Quoted in Bob Thomas, *Walt Disney: An American Original* (New York: Hyperion, 1994), 11.

4. Ibid., 13.

5. Ibid., 247.

6. Ibid., 246.

7. For a great article on the art of storytelling applied to "new media" such as CD-ROMs and the World Wide Web—but generally applicable beyond that—see

Brent Hurtig, "The Plot Thickens," *New Media,* 13 January 1998, 36–44.

8. As the designer of Bamboola, Randy White, says, "Storyline-based themes are powerful. They draw guests into a fanciful, imaginary world and have the potential to touch the eye, mind and heart of visitors." In "Beyond Leisure World: The Process for Creating Storyline-Based Theming," *FEC Magazine,* November–December 1998.

9. Mark Gottdiener, *The Theming of America: Dreams, Visions, and Commercial Spaces* (Boulder, Colo.: Westview Press, 1997), 144–151. In *Marketing Aesthetics: The Strategic Management of Brands, Identity, and Image* (New York: Free Press, 1997), 137–139, Bernd H. Schmitt and Alex Simonson recommend that corporations use as a source of themes the five cultural domains of the physical world; philosophical/psychological concepts; religion, politics, and history; the arts; and fashion and popular culture. They also suggest (on pp. 129–135), that companies relate themes—which they define as "the content, the meaning, the projected image of an identity" (p. 124)—to their mission, vision, objectives, and strategies; core capabilities; legacy; corporate or brand personality; and values. For existing corporations, we think it's especially important to honor the legacy of the business.

10. Schmitt and Simonson, *Marketing Aesthetics,* 128–129.

11. For more on Mike Vance's "Kitchen of the Mind," see Mike Vance and Diane Deacon, *Think Out of the Box* (Franklin Lakes, N.J.: Career Press, 1995), especially 96–97 and 103–109.

12. Henry M. Morris with Henry M. Morris III, *Many Infallible Proofs: Evidences for the Christian Faith* (Green Forest, Ark.: Master Books, 1996), 118. Morris further points out that each of the three entities of the tri-universe are themselves trinities: space has three dimensions; matter can be energy, motion, or phenomena; and time has past, present, and future.

13. So good is Lori's faithful recreation of the 1950s diner that about all that intrudes on the illusion are the drinks offered on the menu and the earrings on the waiters and the tattoos on the waitresses. It still is, after all, located in San Francisco.

14. Schmitt and Simonson, *Marketing Aesthetics,* 172–185.

15. *Roget's International Thesaurus,* 4th ed., rev. Robert L. Chapman (New York: Harper & Row, 1977), xvii–xxiv. Never purchase a thesaurus in dictionary form; the categorized version is the only way to go.

16. Steven E. Prokesch, "Competing on Customer Service: An Interview with British Airways' Sir Colin Marshall," *Harvard Business Review* 73, no. 6, November–December 1995, 104.

17. Ibid.

18. CEO Betts and his team orchestrated such an engaging experience that in February 1997 the Walt Disney Co. itself honored East Jefferson with its "Mouscar" Award—a takeoff on the Oscar that had never before been bestowed outside of Disney. Betts quipped that "It no longer bothers me when people refer to the hospital as 'a Mickey Mouse operation.'"

19. Regarding mechanics, there is a significant discussion in the services marketing literature on "servicescapes," a term coined by Arizona State University professor Mary Jo Bitner to describe the physical surroundings of (what are generally thought of as) service providers. It is very similar to what Carbone calls "mechanics clues." See, for example, Mary Jo Bitner, "Consumer Responses to the Physical Environment in Service Settings," in *Creativity in Services Marketing,* ed. M. Venkatesan, Diane M. Schmalensee, and Claudia

Marshall (Chicago: American Marketing Association, 1986), 89–93; Mary Jo Bitner, "Servicescapes: The Impact of Physical Surroundings on Customers and Employees," *Journal of Marketing* 56, no. 2 (Spring 1992): 57–71; Kirk L. Wakefield and Jeffrey G. Blodgett, "The Importance of Servicescapes in Leisure Service Settings," *Journal of Services Marketing* 8, no. 3 (1994): 66–76; and, for an entire book dedicated to the subject with numerous excellent articles, John F. Sherry, Jr., ed., *ServiceScapes: The Concept of Place in Contemporary Markets* (Lincolnwood, Ill.: NTC Business Books, 1998). Perhaps the first article in this vein was Philip Kotler, "Atmospherics as a Marketing Tool," *Journal of Retailing* 49, no. 4 (Winter 1973): 48–64.

20. Donald A. Norman, *Turn Signals Are the Facial Expressions of Automobiles* (Reading, Mass.: Addison-Wesley, 1992), 19.

21. Tom Huth, "Homes on the Road," *Fortune,* 29 September 1997, 307, emphasis added.

22. As Alvin Toffler predicted long ago in *Future Shock* (New York: Bantam Books, 1970), 226, consumers would one day "begin to collect experiences as consciously and passionately as they once collected things."

23. Robert Frank, "Music: A British Nightclub Empire Rocks around the World," *The Wall Street Journal,* 20 July 1998.

24. Leonard L. Berry, *On Great Service: A Framework for Action* (New York: Free Press, 1995), 10.

25. Ibid., 91.

26. Anthony Rooley, in *Performance: Revealing the Orpheus Within* (Longmead, England: Element Books, 1990), 103–104, points out that "The five senses form two distinct levels: smell, taste, and feeling belong to the body and are the lower senses, providing essential information for good functioning; sight and hearing feed the mind."

27. One could say that British Airways and other airlines do charge customers for entering their "place," but here the "just" is important. Even though they control the entire immersive environment of an airplane, they don't charge *just* for getting on it but for the service of transporting people from one city to another. Interestingly, Israeli airline El Al *does* have an offering it calls the Flight to Nowhere, where it charges large groups the equivalent of about $85 to fly on a plane, eat dinner and dessert, sing songs, and watch movies. According to El Al spokesman Nachman Kleiman, "You don't necessarily have to go to London or Paris to have a good time." Associated Press, "Israeli Airline Offers 'Flight to Nowhere,'" *The Daily Tribune* (Hibbing, Minnesota), 29 December 1997.

28. One of the reasons that Planet Hollywood, Rainforest Cafe, and other theme restaurants are having trouble is that they do not charge admission. Because the entire experience is paid for by consumers through the price of their meals, they impute a higher value to the food, which does not (indeed, cannot) live up to their expectations. A cheeseburger has to be awfully good to justify a $8.95 price tag; with a $5 admission fee, however, a $3.95 burger doesn't have to be nearly as good—as long, of course, as the experience itself is worth $5.

29. Quotations and information from Joshua Levine, "Zap-Proof Advertising," *Forbes,* 22 September 1997, 146–150.

30. Ozlem Sandikci and Douglas B. Holt discuss this phenomenon in "Malling Society: Mall Consumption Practices and the Future of Public Space," in Sherry, *ServiceScapes,* 305–336, calling it "product foreplay." They even suggest

(333–334) that the "evolution of the mall" will be for mall operators "to sell this space to consumers" as "mall development is driven by the need to commodify [i.e., sell as something of value] social experience."

31. "Niketown Comes to Chicago," Niketown Chicago Press Release, 2 July 1992, cited in Sherry, "The Soul of the Company Store: Niketown Chicago and the Emplaced Brandscape," in his *ServiceScapes,* 109–146.

32. In nearly every mall in America, developers fail to capture revenue for the experience that occurs before store doors open every morning; namely, senior citizens valuing the space as a place to walk. They should charge admission for the escapist value created for guests.

33. Numbering among the Diamond Exchange fellows and visiting fellows are the coauthors of this book.

34. Many of the discoveries of the Diamond Exchange can be found in the provocative book by Diamond Exchange visiting fellow Larry Downes and its executive director, Chunka Mui, *Unleashing the Killer App: Digital Strategies for Market Dominance* (Boston: Harvard Business School Press, 1998).

Chapter 4

1. For more on Mass Customization, see Stanley M. Davis (who coined the term), *Future Perfect* (Reading, Mass.: Addison-Wesley, 1987), also available in a tenth anniversary edition from the same publisher; B. Joseph Pine II, *Mass Customization: The New Frontier in Business Competition* (Boston: Harvard Business School Press, 1993); B. Joseph Pine II, Bart Victor, and Andrew C. Boynton, "Making Mass Customization Work," *Harvard Business Review* 71, no. 5, September–October 1993, 108–119; (for manufacturers only) David M. Anderson, *Agile*

Product Development for Mass Customization (Chicago: Irwin Professional Publishing, 1997); and Bart Victor and Andrew C. Boynton, *Invented Here: Maximizing Your Organization's Internal Growth and Profitability* (Boston: Harvard Business School Press, 1998).

2. There are at least six different types of modularity (as well as myriad ways of implementing each type, depending on a company's particular circumstances); see Pine, *Mass Customization,* 196–212. Other good resources on this topic include Karl T. Ulrich and Steven D. Eppinger, *Product Design and Development* (New York: McGraw-Hill, 1995); G. D. Galsworth, *Smart, Simple Design: Using Variety Effectiveness to Reduce Total Cost and Maximize Customer Selection* (Essex Junction, Vt.: Omneo, 1994); Toshio Suzue and Akira Kohdate, *Variety Reduction Program: A Production Strategy for Product Diversification* (Cambridge, Mass.: Productivity Press, 1990); Ron Sanchez and Joseph T. Mahoney, "Modularity, Flexibility, and Knowledge Management in Product and Organization Design," *Strategic Management* 17, December 1996; Marc H. Meyer and Alvin P. Lehnerd, *The Power of Product Platforms: Building Value and Cost Leadership* (New York: Free Press, 1997); and Carliss Y. Baldwin and Kim B. Clark, "Managing in an Age of Modularity," *Harvard Business Review* 75, no. 5, September–October 1997 84–93. The six types of modularity discussed in *Mass Customization* are based on earlier work by Ulrich and one of his students.

3. Frank W. Davis, Jr., and Karl B. Manrodt, in *Customer-Responsive Management: The Flexible Advantage* (Cambridge, Mass.: Blackwell Business, 1996), 82–88, make the important point that with Mass Customization, resources are *dispatched,* not scheduled.

4. Quoted in Clayton Collins, "Five Minutes with J. D. Power III," *Profiles,* October 1996, 23.

5. Add up all the sacrifice existing across all these dimensions—each designed for the average—and one begins to understand why airline travel generally provides such an unpleasant experience. The biggest sacrifice customers encounter, of course, is arriving at an airport terminal when where they want to be is home, at a hotel, or some other specific destination. A sacrifice impossible to eliminate, short of a *Star Trek*–like transporter. Virgin Airways at least reduced it through its program of picking up and dropping off upper-class passengers in limousines—a much better experience than the antics required to get in and out of the typical airport. Airlines could further reduce this sacrifice by allowing passengers to act *as if* they were already at their destinations—by providing onboard check-in with rental cars and hotels, along with transferring bags directly to the final destination.

Chapter 5

1. "Customer Service Takes Off at British Airways," *Demand Logistics: The Magazine of Industri-Matematik International,* Spring 1997, no page numbers. See also Colleen Frye, "The Supply Chain's Missing Link," *Software Magazine,* October 1997, 8–9.

2. Dorothy Leonard and Jeffrey F. Rayport, "Spark Innovation through Empathic Design," *Harvard Business Review* 75, no. 6, November–December 1997, 104.

3. For more on Ross Controls, see Steven W. Demster and Henry F. Duignan, "Subjective Value Manufacturing at Ross Controls," *Agility and Global Competition* 2, no. 2, Spring 1998: 58–65.

4. Customers experience a third form of sacrifice when they miss out on articles outside of their normal interest area that they would, nonetheless, enjoy reading. Information providers could handle this with a "serendipity" algorithm that could, for example, deliver today an interesting article—on art, science, architecture, or any other subject matter—that those interested in such areas found most relevant yesterday. MIT Media Lab head Nicholas Negroponte, in *Being Digital* (New York: Alfred A. Knopf, 1995), 152–154, discusses such personal filters.

5. For more information on learning relationships, see B. Joseph Pine II, Don Peppers, and Martha Rogers, "Do You Want to Keep Your Customers Forever?" *Harvard Business Review* 73, no. 2, March–April 1995, 103–114. Robust details on one-to-one marketing can be found in Peppers and Rogers' fine books, *The One to One Future: Building Relationships One Customer at a Time* (New York: Currency Doubleday, 1993), and *Enterprise One-to-One: Tools for Competing in the Interactive Age* (New York: Currency Doubleday, 1997). All marketers and anyone else concerned with how their companies should adapt to a world filled with interactive technologies should read these books.

6. Of course, as with the old learning curve, the path followed is never as smooth as that pictured.

7. For more information on these four approaches, see the original article on which this section is based: James H. Gilmore and B. Joseph Pine II, "The Four Faces of Mass Customization," *Harvard Business Review* 75, no. 1, January–February 1997, 91–101.

8. For more on Lutron, which practices collaborative and cosmetic as well as adaptive customization, see Joel S. Spira and B. Joseph Pine II, "Mass Customization," *Chief Executive,* no. 83 (March 1993): 26–29, and Michael W. Pessina and James R. Renner, "Mass Customization at

Lutron Electronics—A Total Company Process," *Agility and Global Competition* 2, no. 2 (Spring 1998): 50–57.

9. For a discussion of the benefits of adaptive over collaborative customization, see Eric von Hippel, "Economics of Product Development by Users: The Impact of 'Sticky' Local Information," *Management Science* 44, no. 5 (May 1998): 629–644.

Intermission

1. Quoted in Steven E. Prokesch, "Competing on Customer Service: An Interview with British Airways' Sir Colin Marshall," *Harvard Business Review* 73, no. 6, November–December 1995, 106.

2. T. Scott Gross, *Positively Outrageous Service: New and Easy Ways to Win Customers for Life* (New York: MasterMedia Limited, 1991), 5–6. Gross defines positively outrageous service as "unexpected service delivered at random. . . . It is a memorable event and is so unusual that the customer is compelled to tell others." See also Gross, *Positively Outrageous Service and Showmanship: Industrial Strength Fun Makes Sales Sizzle!!!* (New York: MasterMedia, 1993), which discusses "signature showmanship" and "retail theater." For more on eatZi's, see Christopher Palmeri, "The Wow! Factor," *Forbes,* 18 May 1998, 156–160. Apparently, Macaroni's has since been expanded into the restaurant chain Romano's Macaroni Grill, losing its wonderful customer surprise in the process of becoming a chain.

3. Perhaps Continental does practice customer surprise for its top mileage customers without publicizing it to the rest of the world (which would only set expectations for frequent fliers that don't fly frequently enough to rate this level of customer surprise!), as Delta has done. See Nancy Keates, "The Nine-Million-Mile

Man," *The Wall Street Journal,* 24 July 1998.

Chapter 6

1. Michael Shurtleff, *Audition: Everything an Actor Needs to Know to Get the Part* (New York: Walker and Company, 1978), 162–164.

2. Selling shares to the public in 1998, the Cleveland Indians Baseball Co. stock prospectus (p. 4) explains: "Fans at Jacobs Field are offered a customer-focused experience in an attractive, comfortable environment featuring a variety of amenities, concessions and merchandise options and a courteous, well-trained staff."

3. George F. Will, *Men at Work* (New York: Macmillan Publishing Co., 1990), 6.

4. Others go even further by taking Shakespeare's proclamation that "All the world's a stage" to heart. For example, musician and sculptor Anthony Rooley, in *Performance: Revealing the Orpheus Within* (Longmead, England: Element Books, 1990), 2–3, expresses "a philosophical view which understands that from birth to death, our entire 70-year span (or whatever is our allotted length) is nothing, but nothing, other than a play, a performance. Each of us plays a part, or a series of parts, more or less willingly, more or less consciously, more or less capably. Every action, interplay of relationships, pursuits of all kinds can be seen as 'performance.'"

5. Preston H. Epps, trans., *The Poetics of Aristotle* (1942; reprint, Chapel Hill, N.C.: University of North Carolina Press, 1970), 13–29.

6. Books could be written interpreting Aristotle's *Poetics*—and scores have been. We take this brief exposition primarily from Richard Hornby, *Script to Performance: A Structuralist Approach* (New York: Applause Books, 1995), 79–91.

7. Peter Brook, *The Empty Space* (New York: Touchstone, 1968), 9.

8. Brenda Laurel, *Computers as Theatre* (Reading, Mass.: Addison-Wesley, 1993), xviii.

9. Ibid., 32–33.

10. Erving Goffman, *The Presentation of Self in Everyday Life* (New York: Anchor Books, 1959), 18.

11. Ibid., 73–74. Goffman's ideas were used to analyze the noncustomer work situation in labor negotiations in Raymond A. Friedman, *Front Stage, Backstage: The Dramatic Structure of Labor Negotiations* (Cambridge, Mass.: MIT Press, 1994).

12. A number of articles in the services literature use the "dramaturgical perspective" to analyze service work. Although theatre is used more as a metaphor than a model, this line of inquiry provides a great wealth of information along these lines. See in particular Stephen J. Grove, Raymond P. Fisk, and Mary Jo Bitner, "Dramatizing the Service Experience: A Managerial Approach," *Advances in Services Marketing and Management* 1 (1992): 91–121; S. Grove and R. Fisk, "Impression Management in Services Marketing: A Dramaturgical Perspective," *Impression Management in the Organization,* ed. R. Giacalone and P. Rosenfeld (Hillsdale, N.J.: Lawrence Erlbaum Associates, 1989), 427–438; J. Czepiel, M. Solomon, and C. Curprenant, eds., *The Service Encounter: Managing Employee/Customer Interaction in Service Businesses* (Lexington, Mass.: Lexington Books, 1985); Christopher Lovelock, *Product Plus: How Product + Service = Competitive Advantage* (New York: McGraw-Hill, 1994), 86–96; Ron Zemke, "Service Quality Circa 1995: A Play with Many Acts," in *The Quality Yearbook 1995,* ed. James W. Cortada and John A. Woods (New York: McGraw-Hill, 1995), 119–126; Carl Sewell and Paul B. Brown, *Customers for*

Life: How to Turn That One-Time Buyer into a Lifetime Customer (New York: Pocket Books, 1990), 113–117; T. Scott Gross, *Positively Outrageous Service and Showmanship* (New York: MasterMedia Limited, 1993), 89–106; and Sam Geist, *Why Should Someone Do Business with You . . . Rather than Someone Else?* (Toronto: Addington & Wentworth, 1997), 86–116.

13. Richard Schechner, *Performance Theory* (New York: Routledge, 1988), 30 n. 10. While limiting his analysis to theatre, and to a lesser degree the related activities of ritual, play, games, sports, dance, and music (the seven "public performance activities of humans," p. 10), in this endnote Schechner cites Goffman and recognizes that "performance is a 'quality' that can occur in any situation rather than a fenced-off genre. . . . Or, as John Cage has argued, simply framing an activity 'as' performance—viewing it as such—makes it into a performance." We wholeheartedly agree.

14. Ibid., 72.

15. Ibid.

16. Ibid., 70.

17. Ibid., 72.

18. Thus the importance of understanding both the *product* and *representation* that together constitute any offering, and yield the four approaches to customization discussed in Chapter 5.

19. Schechner, *Performance Theory,* 72.

20. Ibid., 71.

21. Michael Chekhov, *On the Technique of Acting* (New York: HarperPerennial, 1991), 71.

22. Eric Morris, *Acting from the Ultimate Consciousness: A Dynamic Exploration of the Actor's Inner Resources* (Los Angeles: Ermor Enterprises, 1988), 152.

23. Ibid., 153.

24. Julius Fast, in *Subtext: Making Body Language Work in the Workplace* (New York: Viking, 1991), 3–4, provides a fuller delineation: "The subtext in any exchange is a mixture of many different elements. In part, it is composed of each person's body language, posture, hand movements, eye contact, how he or she handles space, and the ability to use subtle touch at the right moment. The way we use our voices also influences how our words are interpreted."

25. The Project on Disney, *Inside the Mouse* (Durham, N.C.: Duke University Press, 1995), 110–111, emphasis added. Despite, or because of, its strikingly critical examination of Disney offerings from a leftist political perspective, the authors of this book, Karen Klugman, Jane Kuenz, Shelton Waldrep, and Susan Willis, provide a wealth of insights about the inner workings of Disney.

26. For her outline of the "Elements of an Action," including the "Magic If," see Sonia Moore, *The Stanislavski System* (New York: Penguin Books, 1984), 25–45.

27. Michael Kearns, *Acting = Life: An Actor's Life Lessons* (Portsmouth, N.H.: Heinemann, 1996), 75.

28. Moore, *Stanislavski Revealed,* 30.

29. Ibid., 83.

30. Kearns, *Acting = Life,* 42.

31. Ibid., 45. Although the acting literature abounds with admonishments to infuse performances with intention, we particularly like Kearns's formulation and his straightforward description of its application.

32. Laura Johannes, "Where a Woman Lives Influences Her Choice for Cancer Treatment," *The Wall Street Journal,* 24 February 1997.

33. Note that the key for doctors here is to get patients to properly consider the alternatives, not to get them to choose a particular alternative. As Michael Kearns says in *Acting = Life,* 43, "Many actors confuse result with intention. When I ask for an intention, I'm invariably given a result word: happy, sad, tragic, overjoyed, jealous, angry. Those are emotions that result from playing an intention; they are not intentions. . . . An actor who attempts to play resentful, hurt, or ecstatic is acting a result and it's bad acting, usually accentuated by mugging (there's a lot of this on sitcoms). An actor who plays an intention, allowing the emotions to emerge naturally, is on the road to good acting."

34. Quoted in Edward Felsenthal, "Lawyers Learn How to Walk the Walk, Talk the Talk," *The Wall Street Journal,* 3 January 1996.

35. Richard B. Schmitt, "Judges Try Curbing Lawyers' Body-Language Antics," *The Wall Street Journal,* 11 September 1997.

36. Barb Myers retired in 1997. She was replaced not by machine but by her former understudy, Joyce Lewis, who will be making memories for a new generation of Penn students.

Chapter 7

1. While not always explicitly pointed out in the text, this description of an actor at work exemplifies the following elements of theatre:

- As If
- Charting
- Costuming
- Cut 95 percent
- Dragging out
- Exiting all the way off
- Intention
- Making an entrance
- Props
- Roles and Characterization
- Subtext: body language, props, costumes

Note that some techniques (such as the use of props) appear multiple times. If you're reading this note prior to reading the vignette, we encourage you to look for exactly where Linda uses each one.

2. Anthony Rooley, in *Performance: Revealing the Orpheus Within* (Longmead, England: Element Books, 1990), 50, urges performers to use this technique before beginning any performance:

Another procedure is to use the eyes. Extend your sightlines to the far corner of the room, right to the dimly-lit recesses and encircle the audience with your vision. Moving further in, towards oneself, the eyes might meet those of another individual, perhaps someone who is ready to smile in recognition of this moment's importance, or someone who needs a little reassurance that it is all right to relax. Then the eyes of the front row, who are there because they choose to be there—sitting on the front row is a very conscious choice. These people deserve careful attention and a smile perhaps (certainly better, in most instances, than a stern encounter).

3. John Rudin, *Commedia dell'Arte: An Actor's Handbook* (London: Routledge, 1994), 51. See also *Scenarios of the Commedia dell'Arte: Flaminio Scala's Il Teatro delle favole rappresentative,* trans. Henry F. Salerno (New York: Limelight Editions, 1996).

4. See in particular Edward de Bono, *Serious Creativity: Using the Power of Lateral Thinking to Create New Ideas* (New York: HarperBusiness, 1992).

5. A good guide to improvisational techniques is Brie Jones, *Improve with Improv: A Guide to Improvisation and Character Development* (Colorado Springs: Meriwether Publishing, 1993).

6. *Commedia dell'Arte* was also performed on a raised (outdoor) platform, but without the formality of a proscenium, much less a written-out script.

7. One of the best platform theatre books is by playwright and director David Mamet, *True and False: Heresy and Common Sense for the Actor* (New York: Pantheon Books, 1997).

8. "Prepping the Chief for the Annual Meeting or Other Event Can Mean Practice," *The Wall Street Journal,* 20 March 1997. See also Quentin Hardy, "Meet Jerry Weisman, Acting Coach to CEOs," *The Wall Street Journal,* 21 April 1998.

9. William Grimes, "Audio Books Open Up a New World for Actors," *Cleveland Plain Dealer,* 9 January 1996. See also Rodney Ho, "King of Audio-Book Narrators Makes 'Readers' Swoon," *The Wall Street Journal,* 10 April 1998.

10. "California Dream$," *Forbes,* 16 December 1996, 114. Note that while most broadcast television relies on matching theatre, live productions are pure platform.

11. The term "jumpcut" has become somewhat of a pejorative in the entertainment industry, due to many directors overusing the technique to hide flaws in the script and/or in actor performances.

12. Richard Dyer MacCann, ed., *Film: A Montage of Theories* (New York: E. Dutton & Co., 1966), 23.

13. Quoted in Jeffrey M. Laderman, "Remaking Schwab," *Business Week,* 25 May 1998, 128.

14. Thomas W. Babson, *The Actor's Choice: The Transition from Stage to Screen* (Portsmouth, N.H.: Heinemann, 1996).

15. Sally Harrison-Pepper, *Drawing a Circle in the Square: Street Performing in New York's Washington Square Park* (Jackson: University Press of Mississippi, 1990), 140.

16. Bim Mason, in *Street Theatre and Other Outdoor Performances* (London: Routledge, 1992), says "One of the aims of this book is to show how much craft and expertise there is involved in this area of work" (p. 4). He also points out (p. 5) how much street theatre there is in real life: "There is plenty of drama outdoors and an element of performances starts to occur if the participants become conscious of spectators and 'play up' to them. For example, the demolition of houses in Barcelona . . . was watched by a large group of locals, so the bulldozer drivers began to show off their skill with exaggerated nonchalance." Work is, indeed, theatre.

17. For a terrific guide to selling that introduces many routines, see Don Peppers, *Life's a Pitch: Then You Buy* (New York: Currency Doubleday, 1995).

18. Rudin, *Commedia dell'Arte,* 23.

19. Mel Gordon, *Lazzi: The Comic Routines of the Commedia Dell'Arte* (New York: Performing Arts Journal Publications, 1983), 29, 43, 18, 23, and 18, respectively. Interestingly, such well-rehearsed routines are now labeled "comic stage business" (p. 4).

20. Tony Vera, quoted in Harrison-Pepper, *Drawing a Circle,* xiii.

21. Carl Asche, quoted in Harrison-Pepper, *Drawing a Circle,* 114.

22. For more on The Hartford's PLIC call center, see B. Joseph Pine II and Hugh Martin, "Winning Strategies for New Realities," *Executive Excellence* 10, no. 6 (June 1993): 20.

23. For how an environmental "sense and respond" capability relates to Mass Customization, see Stephan H. Haeckel and Richard L. Nolan, "Managing by Wire," *Harvard Business Review* 71, no. 5, September–October 1993, 122–132. See also Stephen P. Bradley and Richard L. Nolan, eds., *Sense and Respond: Capturing Value in the Network Era* (Boston: Harvard Business School Press, 1998).

24. The Four Forms of Theatre model derives from prior work on a Mass Customization model known as "The Product-

Process Matrix" in which the axes are Product [= performance] Change and Process [= script] Change. Then, the four quadrants become the four generic business models that any company can have; specifically:

> [Invention = improv theatre]
> [Mass Production = platform theatre]
> [Continuous Improvement = matching theatre]
> [Mass Customization = street performance]

Just as performers of work must cycle between each successive form of theatre to reach street theatre, companies must cycle from Invention to Mass Production—through the activities of *development*—then to Continuous Improvement—through the activities of *linking*—before reaching Mass Customization—through the activities of *modularization*. When mass customizers are faced with "capability failures"—customers requiring capabilities the company does not possess—they must return to Invention—through the activities of *renewal*—to create a new capability, just as street performers renew their capabilities through on-the-spot improvising. While Mass Customization provides the highest levels of customer value, it is not appropriate everywhere, just as street performance is not the appropriate form of theatre for every situation.

The Product-Process Matrix (Figure N-1), shown below, was originally developed by two University of North Carolina professors (visiting, at the time of this writing, the International Institute for Management Development in Switzerland), Bart Victor and Andy Boynton, and extended in collaboration with Joe Pine, and now enhanced and applied to theatre primarily through the efforts of Jim Gilmore. It has evolved considerably over time to become a very robust way of looking at the world of business competition. To trace that evolution, see Andrew C. Boynton and Bart Victor, "Beyond Flexibility: Building and Managing the Dynamically Stable Organization," *California Management Review* 34, no. 1 (Fall 1991): 53–66; B. Joseph Pine II, *Mass Customization: The New Frontier in Business Competition* (Boston: Harvard Business School Press, 1993), 215–221; Andrew C. Boynton, Bart Victor, and B. Joseph Pine II, "New Competitive Strategies: Challenges to Organizations and Information Technology," *IBM Systems Journal* 32, no. 1 (1993): 40–64; B. Joseph Pine II, Bart Victor, and Andrew C. Boynton, "Making Mass Customization Work," *Harvard Business Review* 71, no. 5, September–October 1993, 108–119; B. Joseph Pine II, Bart Victor, and Andrew C.

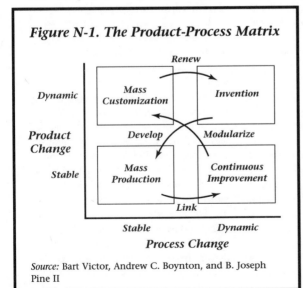

Figure N-1. The Product-Process Matrix

Source: Bart Victor, Andrew C. Boynton, and B. Joseph Pine II

Boynton, "Aligning IT with New Competitive Strategies," in *Competing in the Information Age: Strategic Alignment in Practice,* ed. Jerry N. Luftman (New York: Oxford University Press, 1996) 73–96; James H. Gilmore and B. Joseph Pine II, "Beyond Goods and Services: Staging Experiences and Guiding Transformations," *Strategy and Leadership,* May/June 1997, 10–18; B. Joseph Pine II, "You're Only as Agile as Your Customers Think," *Agility and Global Competition* 2, no. 2 (Spring 1998): 24–35; and, finally, Bart Victor and Andrew C. Boynton, *Invented Here: Maximizing Your Organization's Internal Growth and Profitability* (Boston: Harvard Business School Press, 1998). Victor and Boynton's book, while curiously eliminating the axes of the framework, provides a masterful look at how an organization must learn and leverage knowledge to make the transition to each successive business model.

25. In *Drawing a Circle,* Harrison-Pepper relates that street performers create new acts through "a process of revision, refining, and personalizing" (p. 80)—that is, flowing from improv to platform (revision), then to matching (refining), and finally to street (personalizing).

26. Ibid., 117.

Chapter 8

1. We agree with our friends Stan Davis and Bill Davidson when, in *2020 Vision* (New York: Simon & Schuster, 1991), 113, they say, *"The best place to look for the basis of organization change is in the future business, and the worst place to look is in the current organization.* The present organization, however, may be a good predictor of what will *prevent* you from developing the kind of organization you will need."

2. As James A. Ogilvy says in *The Experience Industry: A Leading Edge Report*

from the Values and Lifestyles Program (SRI International, Business Intelligence Program, Report no. 724, Fall 1985), 22, "The bad news is that marginal utility is not the only concept that won't carry over from industrial economics to the economics of the experience industry. Other familiar categories may be equally misleading. . . . [S]uch basic terms as *inventory* or even *capital* become problematic. As they say in Hollywood, 'You're only as good as your last movie.' If this saying is an accurate indication of the way value can or cannot be accrued in the experience industry, then the very concept of fixed assets calls for radical revision."

3. Edward Felsenthal, "Lawyers Learn How to Walk the Walk, Talk the Talk," *The Wall Street Journal,* 3 January 1996.

4. Jonnie Patricia Mobley, *NTC's Dictionary of Theatre and Drama Terms* (Lincolnwood, Ill.: National Textbook Co., 1992), 49. This book is an excellent resource for understanding the various terms of theatre.

5. This is not altogether different from how the mechanization of Industrial Age jobs led to the rise in the human-to-human activity of delivering services.

6. According to Charles Marowitz, *Directing the Action: Acting and Directing in the Contemporary Theatre* (New York: Applause Theatre Books, 1991), the role of director did not exist in the performing arts until the late nineteenth century. Initially, the position involved coordinating fellow actors, simply directing on- and offstage activities as an equal among peers. Gradually, directing began to include coaching actors in how to portray their respective roles. What we today know as the modern director, "men who leave their mark on material as much as they do on actors" (p. 2), did not fully emerge within the arts until the 1920s and 1930s in France and Russia. Interestingly, the rise of directing as a profession in the performing arts of these two countries coincides with the rise of professional management in the industrialized world of Britain, Germany, and the United States, as demonstrated in Alfred D. Chandler, Jr., *Scale and Scope: The Dynamics of Industrial Capitalism* (Cambridge, Mass.: Belknap Press of Harvard University Press, 1990). Directors here and there entered the world of theatre—the two sets of countries simply chose different stages. Today's Experience Economy, however, demands that the performing arts and business merge.

7. As Marowitz points out in *Directing the Action,* 6: "Too infrequently do we recognize that the central function of the man is to rethink and recreate the materials with which he works. The director who does not engage the animate and inanimate materials at his disposal and transmute them into an image of himself, is merely going through the motions. Some other title must be found for him. Call him a coordinator, a controller, a foreman, or a traffic cop, but do not confuse him with an artist of the theatre."

8. Elizabeth Weil, "Report from the Future: Every Leader Tells a Story," *Fast Company,* June–July 1998, 38. Another article from the same issue by author and publisher Harriet Rubin, "The Hitchhiker's Guide to the New Economy," profiling Douglas Adams, makes the point that "The art of the storyteller is the art of the new economy" (p. 178).

9. David Kahn and Donna Breed, *Scriptwork: A Director's Approach to New Play Development* (Carbondale, Ill.: Southern Illinois University Press, 1995), 20.

10. Gordon Shaw, Robert Brown, and Philip Bromiley, "Strategic Stories: How 3M Is Rewriting Business Planning," *Harvard Business Review* 76, no. 3, May–June 1998, 44, 47. See also Thomas A. Stewart, "The Cunning Plots of Leadership," *Fortune,* 7 September 1998,

165–166, and Rob Wilkens, "Strategic Storytelling," *Lifework,* 1, no. 5 (October 1998): 23–25.

11. A couple of good resources on scriptwriting are J. Michael Straczynski, *The Complete Book of Scriptwriting* (Cincinnati: Writer's Digest Books, 1996), and Syd Field, *Screenplay: The Foundations of Screenwriting* (New York: MJF Books, 1994). For a wonderful book on how to read scripts as literature and then turn them into engaging performances, see Richard Hornby, *Script to Performance: A Structuralist Approach* (New York: Applause Books, 1995). Interestingly, Hornby dislikes the performance theory approach of Richard Schechner because "Structure cannot be separated from substance without degenerating into triviality" (p. xv). He further calls Schechner's work "sometimes insightful and sometimes Rube Goldberg fabrication." Let us assure you that we adapted from the insightful parts.

12. Michael Hammer, "Reengineering Work: Don't Automate, Obliterate," *Harvard Business Review* 68, no. 4, July–August 1990, 104–112.

13. See also James H. Gilmore, "Reengineering for Mass Customization," *Journal of Cost Management* 7, no. 3 (Fall 1993): 22–29, and "How to Make Reengineering Truly Effective," *Planning Review* 23, no. 3 (May/June 1995): 39, as well as B. Joseph Pine II, "Serve Each Customer Efficiently and Uniquely," *Network Transformation: Individualizing Your Customer Approach,* supplement to *Business Communications Review* 68, no. 4 (January 1996): 2–5.

14. Gary Hamel and C. K. Prahalad, *Competing for the Future: Breakthrough Strategies for Seizing Control of Your Industry and Creating the Markets of Tomorrow* (Boston: Harvard Business School Press, 1994).

15. Andy Serwer, "Michael Dell Rocks,"

Fortune, May 11, 1998, 62. See also Joan Magretta, "The Power of Virtual Integration: An Interview with Dell Computer's Michael Dell," *Harvard Business Review* 76, no. 2, March–April 1998, 72–84.

16. For how Gallatin Steel mass customizes steel—a near, but not quite, commodity—see David H. Freeman, "Steel Edge," *Forbes ASAP,* 6 October 1997, 46–53. For more on how Pilkington Brothers took a laborious five-step glass-making process down to one-step float glass see James M. Utterback, *Mastering the Dynamics of Innovation: How Companies Can Seize Opportunities in the Face of Technological Change* (Boston: Harvard Business School Press, 1994), 104–120. All process and product developers should read this book.

17. Bob Thomas, *Walt Disney: An American Original* (New York: Hyperion, 1994), 264.

18. Francis Reid, *Designing for the Theatre* (New York: Theatre Art Books/Routledge, 1996), 19.

19. Felsenthal, "Lawyers Learn."

20. Angie Michael, *Best Impressions in Hospitality: Your Professional Image for Excellence* (Manassas Park, Va.: Impact Publications, 1995) provides a good resource in this area.

21. In Michael Holt, *Costume and Make Up* (New York: Schirmer Books Theatre Manuals, 1988), 7, this classic manual on costuming lays out the importance of these cues: "Costume is part of the actors' apparatus. It helps them to create their characters. Every item of clothing sends signals of one kind of another to the audience. As soon as the actors appear, even before they speak, the audience will have gleaned a great deal of information. They can see by the shape and colour of the costume whether a character is to be welcomed or feared. The whole image is composed of signs that

they will react to both consciously and unconsciously."

22. Charles Goldsmith, "British Air's New No-Frills Carrier, Go, to Battle Its Discount Rivals," *The Wall Street Journal,* 22 May 1998.

23. Quoted in Toni Mack, "High Finance with a Touch of Theater," *Forbes,* 18 May 1998, 146.

24. Erik Hedegaard, "Fools' Paradise," *Worth,* June 1998, 76.

25. Ibid.

26. Pauline Menear and Terry Hawkins, *Stage Management and Theatre Administration* (New York: Schirmer Books Theatre Manuals, 1988), 7.

27. Julian Fast, *Subtext: Making Body Language Work in the Workplace* (New York: Viking, 1991), 13.

28. Leonard A. Schlesinger and James L. Heskett, "Breaking the Cycle of Failure in Services," *Sloan Management Review* 32, no. 3 (Spring 1991): 26.

29. Given that this section is written from the perspective of the auditors, we refer aspiring actors who wish to perform well at auditions to Michael Shurtleff, *Audition: Everything an Actor Needs to Know to Get the Part* (New York: Bantam Books, 1978).

30. The Project on Disney, *Inside the Mouse* (Durham, N.C.: Duke University Press, 1995), 214–215.

31. Mark Winegardner, *Prophet of the Sandlots: Journeys with a Major League Scout* (New York: Prentice Hall Press, 1990), 97.

32. Robert L. Benedetti, *The Director at Work* (Englewood Cliffs, N.J.: Prentice-Hall, 1985), 87.

33. Mobley, *NTC's Dictionary of Theatre and Drama Terms,* 4.

34. Philip Kotler and Joanne Scheff, *Standing Room Only: Strategies for Marketing the Performing Arts* (Boston: Harvard Business School Press, 1997).

35. Ibid., 13.

Chapter 9

1. As Lisa Miller reports on the phenomenon of spiritual directors in *The Wall Street Journal,* "Americans have long hired people to care for their children, their bodies and their finances. Now, they're hiring personal trainers for their souls." In "After Their Checkup for the Body, Some Get One for the Soul," 20 July 1998.

2. Interestingly, boot camps, flight simulators, business games, and virtual reality training tools all purposefully commoditize experience in order to change people. By having them go through simulations of real-world experiences over and over and over again, their reactions become second nature, greatly increasing their ability to react to fast-changing, often life-threatening situations quickly. As Tom Orton, cofounder of Modis Training Technologies in Mesa, Arizona, told *Industry Week*, users of his company's semiconductor plant simulator "feel as though they've already been there and done that" ("25 Winning Technologies," 15 December 1997, 52).

3. We anticipate the day when the proliferation of FedEx packages, faxes, and e-mail restore the receipt of good old U.S. mail as a memorable experience, much like a trip to a farm has become.

4. David Bacon, quoted in Susan Warren, "Parents Are on a Kick for Tae Kwon Do as a Disciplinary Art," *The Wall Street Journal,* 3 October 1997.

5. Tim W. Ferguson, "Let's Talk to the Master," *Forbes,* 23 October 1995, 142.

6. Mark Wolfenberger, quoted in Nikhil Hutheesing, "Reducing Sticker Shock," *Forbes,* 3 November 1997, 151.

7. Quoted in David Kirkpatrick, "This Tough Guy Wants to Give You a Hug," *Fortune,* 14 October 1996, 178.

8. Quoted in J. P. Donlon, "The P&G of Prisons," *Chief Executive,* May 1998, 28–29.

9. Kairos, a nonprofit Christian ministries organization based in Orlando, Florida, specifically targets this recalcitrant prison population through a series of annual events that aim to change prisoners' hearts, beginning with the most hardened leaders. Understanding exactly how tough this is, Kairos employs platform theatre where its workers script and rehearse every word spoken over a three-day period.

10. Donlon, "The P&G of Prisons," 29.

11. Quoted in Sara Terry, "Genius at Work," *Fast Company,* September 1998, 176.

12. Each of the four S's in the 3-S Model still apply. First, customer satisfaction relative to expectations: how well did the transformation elicitor achieve my aspirations? Then, customer sacrifice: what gaps exist between what the customer should truly aspire to and what the customer was able to achieve? Third, customer surprise: transcending customer aspirations by eliciting change along a dimension the customer never expected. And finally, customer suspense: heightening the anticipation the customer has for what dimension the elicitor will help change next.

13. See Leif Edvinsson and Michael S. Malone, *Intellectual Capital: Realizing Your Company's True Value by Finding Its Hidden Brainpower* (New York: Harper-Business, 1997).

14. Skandia, *A Proposal for a Competence Insurance Plan* (Stockholm, Sweden: Skandia, 1996), 6.

15. And when something happens to the patient that could possibly lead to a lawsuit, one of MMI's approaches is to encourage the caregiver to actually meet with the family—something to which most lawyers would strenuously object—to explain, not apologize for, what happened. This cathartic experience often satisfies the family to the point where they do not file a suit.

16. As pointed out in Chapter 6, Brenda Laurel makes the point in *Computers as Theatre* (Reading, Mass.: Addison-Wesley, 1993), xviii, that human-computer interfaces should be "designed experiences." In "Interface Design: Diversity in Your Audience," *Interactivity,* February 1997, 69, Eric Justin Gould, principal of MONKEY media, an interface design and production studio, goes even further by encouraging interface designers to think of the transformative power of technology: "When you bring new technology into someone's life (be it cutting-edge hardware or just a new way of interacting), you can't help but have an effect on them. To respect a culture is to consider, during the design process, what influence your product might have on the people who interact with it." Exactly.

17. In a syndicated *Chicago Tribune* column by Jim Mateja, printed as "OnStar Diagnostic System Brings Aid with a Call" in the *St. Paul Pioneer Press,* 25 October 1997, OnStar's chief engineer, Walt Dorfstatter, says "We look at remote diagnostics as giving motorists instant peace of mind."

18. Stan Davis and Bill Davidson, *2020 Vision* (New York: Simon & Schuster, 1991), envision a "bio-economy" in which companies focus on how to use bioengineering, among other things, to change the human species. They foresee (p. 195) that given the trajectory of technological progress, "food, clothing, machinery, and any tangible good may be biologically monitored, maintained, and improved. By the time that the bio-economy arrives, the company that manufactures refrigerators may want to be in the food preservation and enhancement business rather than in refrigeration."

19. Yumiko Ono, "Marketers Walk Thin Line, Selling Food Products with Medicinal Lure," *The Wall Street Journal,* 23 September 1996. See also Joseph Weber, "Now, Campbell's Makes House Calls," *Business Week,* 16 June 1997, 144–146.

20. Associated Press, "New Margarine May Spur Healing-Food Trend," *St. Paul Pioneer Press,* 22 July 1998.

21. Björn Wolrath, "Competence Insurance—An Insurance Innovation in Its Time," in *A Proposal for a Competence Insurance Plan,* 10.

22. Hillel M. Finestone and David B. Conter, "Acting in Medical Practice," *The Lancet* 344, no. 8925 (17 September 1994): 801.

23. Mark DePaolis, "Doctors Can Act as If All the World's a Stage," *Minneapolis Star-Tribune,* 27 January 1995.

24. See, for example, Gregory W. Lester and Susan G. Smith, "Listening and Talking to Patients: A Remedy for Malpractice Suits?" *The Western Journal of Medicine,* March 1993; Jerry E. Bishop, "Studies Conclude Doctors' Manner, Not Ability, Results in More Lawsuits," *The Wall Street Journal,* 23 November 1994; Daniel Goleman, "All Too Often, The Doctor Isn't Listening, Studies Show," *The New York Times,* 13 November 1991.

25. Milton Mayeroff, *On Caring* (New York: HarperPerennial, 1971), 1–2.

26. C. William Pollard, "The Leader Who Serves," *Strategy & Leadership,* 25, no. 5 (September/October 1997): 50.

27. C. William Pollard, *The Soul of the Firm* (New York: HarperBusiness and Grand Rapids, Mich.: ZondervanPublishingHouse, 1996), 130. The last of Pollard's twenty-one principles of leadership (p. 166) demonstrates the power of a serving attitude: "We have all been created in God's image, and the results of our leadership will be measured beyond the workplace. The story will be told in the changed lives of people." Make no mistake: such serving yields no mere service but rather a caring transformation.

Chapter 10

1. Jeremy Rifkin, *The End of Work: The Decline of the Global Labor Force and the Dawn of the Post-Market Era* (New York: G. Putnam's Sons, 1995), xvi.

2. Ibid., xvii. Part of Rifkin's "solution" is to put a value-added tax "on the entertainment and recreation industries, which are among the fastest-growing sectors of the economy." The reason: because "Few of the nation's poor can afford home computers, cellular phones, and expensive trips to theme parks, resorts, and casinos" (p. 271). It's axiomatic that the economy gets less of whatever gets taxed, so this would seem to be the economic equivalent of cutting off one's nose to spite one's face—taxing experiences when that's where the new jobs will be created. It's also not surprising that someone who doesn't trust market mechanisms would look to target the fastest-growing economic sector for sources of revenue for more government programs and regulations.

3. Ibid., 247.

4. For GDP data, the transformation industries that could be separated cleanly from the government-gathered service sector were health, legal, and social services. For industry employment data, these three plus engineering and management services were counted as transformations. As with experiences, there are certainly transformation businesses (fitness centers, some education venues, personal trainers of all kinds, etc.) left in the service statistics, as they could not be broken out separately. Also note again that because only a few industries are represented in the transformation breakouts, it starts from a much smaller base than the industries left in the service sector. By 1996, however, those industries clearly identified as experiences or transformations were almost 10 percent of GDP and almost 20 percent of employment (more industries could be identified in the latter data). These sectors are clearly already adding up to a large portion of the economy, with transformations (because of healthcare) even larger than experiences.

5. Indeed, prior to a reprieve forced by political pressure in 1994, healthcare spending grew consistently in double digits over the previous decade, far outpacing most any other industry. Now that the political pressure has lessened, it appears to be heading upward again.

6. *The Digest of Education Statistics 1996,* (Jessup, Md.: National Center for Education Statistics, 1997), Table 309 (http://nces.ed.gov/pubs/d96/D96T309.html). As with the recent reduction in the price increases in healthcare, the education statistics are affected by politics. In particular, the increasing amount of student aid available from the government in various forms makes it easier for colleges and universities to increase their tuition commensurately.

7. Virginia I. Postrel, "It's All in the Head," *Forbes ASAP,* 26 February 1996, 118. To give her full credit, Postrel further states that "Increasingly, people aren't just buying goods and services. They're buying experiences."

8. *The New Shorter Oxford English Dictionary,* vol. 2, N–Z, ed., s.v. "Wisdom."

9. There are other versions of this sort of intelligence progression, such as Haeckel's Hierarchy, named after Stephan H. Haeckel of the IBM Advanced Business Institute, which includes intelligence itself as an echelon between information and knowledge. See Vincent P. Barabba and Gerald Zaltman, *Hearing the Voice of the Market: Competitive Advantage through Creative Use of Market Information* (Boston: Harvard Business School Press, 1990), 37–58.

10. The word *computer* originally referred to the people that made calculations for weapons delivery during World War II.

11. For example, a special issue on "Knowledge and the Firm" was published by *California Management Review* 40, no. 3 (Spring 1998).

12. Diane Senese, in "The Information Experience," *Information Outlook,* October 1997, 29–33, discusses how "information professionals" can "enjoy a unique role in preparing [their] corporations for the experience economy" when they "re-imagine [their] roles" as helping corporate customers in "experiencing knowledge."

13. Michael Schrage writes of the need to view technology from the standpoint of its effect on relationships, as opposed to information, in *No More Teams! Mastering the Dynamics of Creative Collaboration* (New York: Currency Doubleday, 1995).

14. John Dalla Costa, *Working Wisdom: The Ultimate Value in the New Economy* (Toronto: Stoddart Publishing Co., 1995), 24.

15. Taichi Sakaiya, *The Knowledge-Value Revolution, or A History of the Future* (Tokyo: Kodansha International, 1991), 20–21.

16. Ibid., 235.

17. Ibid., 57–58.

18. As consultant and author Robert H. Schaffer says, "For a consulting assignment to be considered successful, delivering a report with the 'right solutions' or installing a new system is not sufficient. The project must actually yield measurable bottom-line results for the client and, equally important, the client must develop the ability to sustain those benefits." From Ian White-Thomson and Robert H. Schaffer, "Getting Your Money's Worth," *Chief Executive,* November 1997, 41. See also Robert H. Schaffer, *High-Impact Consulting: How Clients and Consultants Can Leverage Rapid Results into Long-Term Gains* (San Francisco: Jossey-Bass Publishers, 1997).

19. Quoted in Thor Valdmanis, "Consultants Opt for Stakes in Clients' Firms," *USA Today,* 21 April 1998.

20. Erving Goffman, *The Presentation of Self in Everyday Life* (New York: Anchor Books, 1959), 20.

21. Harold Clurman, *On Directing* (New York: Collier Books, 1972), 154–155.

22. Samuel Hughes, "Lucid Observations," *The Pennsylvania Gazette,* October 1996. One of the places within a place Dr. Lucid furnished for student-actors to rehearse was the Hill House Pit Stop, a student-run convenience store that competed with the likes of WaWa Food Markets, located within Hill House and managed by one of the authors in his junior year.

23. This section is based on James H. Gilmore and B. Joseph Pine II, "Beyond Goods and Services: Staging Experiences and Guiding Transformations," *Strategy & Leadership* 25, no. 3 (May/June 1997): 18. These four universal elements—origination, execution, correction, and application—derive from the same framework behind Figure 7-1, the Four Forms of Theatre, known as the Product-Process Matrix (see Chapter 7, n. 24). The figure-eight pattern in this framework is a fractal, a pattern detectable at any level of analysis, where the level of analysis used here is the most general.

24. Henry Petroski, *The Evolution of Useful Things* (New York: Vintage Books 1992), 86.

25. Gary Hamel and C. K. Prahalad, *Competing for the Future* (Boston: Harvard Business School Press, 1994), 133–134. Note that the words of Jesus they quote are not found in the Acts 1:8 passage they cite but in Mark 16:15.

Encore

1. Peter Haynes and Dolly Setton, "McKinsey 101," *Forbes,* 4 May 1998, 130–135.

2. This articulation of the Progression of Economic Value was inspired by James Brian Quinn in *Intelligent Enterprise: A Knowledge and Service Based Paradigm for Industry* (New York: Free Press, 1992), who on p. 7 used the exact formulation given here for goods, except in choosing the word "product" instead.

3. Issues have arisen already from the demand some individuals place on perpetuating biological life. See Andrew Kimbrell, *The Human Body Shop: The Engineering and Marketing of Life* (New York: HarperCollins, 1993), and Margaret Jane Radin, *Contested Commodities: The Trouble with Trade in Sex, Children, Body Parts, and Other Things* (Cambridge, Mass.: Harvard University Press, 1996), for thoughtful preludes to what lies ahead. Let us point out that these issues concern what *should* be permissible to buy and sell, not what *can* be. While statecraft and other nonmarket forces may strive to restrict the supply of such economic commerce, only individual soul searching and changed human hearts will eradicate the demand.

4. Ephesians 2:8 (King James Version).

Index

● ●

Credits

● ●

EVERY BUSINESS A STAGE, and all our thoughts and words merely play to bring this reality to light. Many men and women have exited and entered our working lives, each playing a part in this particular written production. Like so many speeches on Oscar night, the following credits are sure to leave out someone who deserves proper thanks. Still, we do want to acknowledge those who have lent their hands, heads, and hearts to this endeavor.

First, the infancy of the ideas in this book emerged about a year after Joe left IBM, while Jim was still working at CSC Consulting & Systems Integration. While speaking on the subject of Mass Customization at the IBM Advanced Business Institute, Joe shared the oft-mentioned point that mass customizing a good automatically turns it into a service. An astute audience member raised his hand and asked, "You say companies can mass customize services as well. Into what does customization turn a service?" To which Joe intuitively replied, "Mass Customization automatically turns a service into an *experience*." Instantly, Joe recognized the significance of his response, and later that evening he called Jim. "Guess what I said today!. . . Now let's go figure out what it means." After many months of thinking, reading, and discussing, we concluded that experiences were indeed distinct economic offerings, just like goods and services. So to that unknown IBMer we owe a very large debt for asking the question that demanded not only an immediate answer, but ultimately this entire book.

We are also indebted to CSC and the IBM Advanced Business Institute, particularly Dave DeRoulet, Gary Cross, and Roger Kallock at the former and Al Barnes at the latter, for supporting (both intellectually and financially) our research into first Mass Customization and then the Experience Economy. Our colleagues at Diamond Technology Partners, with whom we've been Diamond Fellows the past few years, have also provided great support, particularly Mel Bergstein, Jim Spira, Barry Uphoff, Chap Kistler, and Chunka Mui. Diamond's Rachel Parker scoured the depths of government statistics and helped us interpret just how the shift through successive economies played out in the numbers. Thank you, Rachel—for going to school on the data when we were unwilling!

People at a number of companies loved these ideas while they were still being formulated, invited us to work with their organizations, and applied them in their relationships with their own customers. In particular we'd like to thank ARAMARK (especially Lynn McKee), Scudder Kemper Investments (especially Mark Casady and Lin Coughlin), Hillenbrand Industries (especially Fred Rockwood, Chris Ruberg, Brad Reedstrom, Brian Leitten, and Rob Washburn, among others), en•able (Mort Aaronson), Lutron Electronics (Joel Spira and Mike Pessina), CompuCom (Ed Anderson), Chem-Station (George Homan and Russ Gilmore), UCLA Executive Education (Jim Aggen, Grace Siao, and again Al Barnes), Penn State Exec Ed (Al Vicere, Gini Tucker, Maria Taylor, and Bob Prescott, among others), and the U.S. Chamber of Commerce's Institutes for Organization Management (Maggie Elgin and Nancy Turnbull). Rohan Champion, now with Federal Express, deserves special mention for pushing his former employer, AT&T, to shift beyond its commoditized services, and it was Rohan himself who first thought of expressing experiences and transformations in the form of a progression of value.

A number of individuals soldiered the discoveries we made along the way and influenced how we extended our thinking, including Jim Utterback of the MIT Sloan School of Management; Shlomo Maital of MIT and Technion University; Marvin Zonis of the University of Chicago; David Reed, an independent entrepreneur formerly of Lotus and Interval Research; Mark Dehner of Dehco; Jim Rogers of IBM; Lew Carbone of Experience Engineering; Stephan Haeckel of the IBM Advanced Business Institute; Randy White of White Hutchinson; Larry Keeley of the Doblin Group; Dave Wright of General Motors/HE Microwave; David Anderson and Stephen Fraser at GATX Corporation; Hugh Martin of The Hartford; Alan Hald of MicroAge; John Sviokla of Diamond Technology Partners and Jeffrey Rayport of the Harvard Business School; Tim Gallwey (author of the *Inner Game* books); and Mark Hatch of Avery Dennison. Our respective fathers, Haydn Gilmore and Bud Pine, both reviewed drafts of the manuscript and provided valuable encouragement and feedback, and Julie Pine helped formulate the first description of how each economic offering differed from the others.

We must also do justice to a number of thinkers and authors who were amazingly prescient in identifying some of the trends we discovered, some long before us and all unbeknownst to us until we started researching the emerging Experience Economy. Back in 1970, futurist Alvin Toffler included a chapter in *Future Shock* on "The Experience Makers." Even before that, in 1959, sociologist Erving Goffman, in *The Presentation of Self in Everyday Life,* applied the principles of theatre to work and social situations. In the 1970s marketing professor Phil Kotler of Northwestern University foresaw how education and travel would become more and more experiential. More recently, professors Mary Jo Bitner of the Arizona State University, Raymond Fisk of the University of New Orleans, and Stephen Grove of Clemson University have done the most in researching and promoting within academia the notion of experiential environments (which Dr. Bitner calls "servicescapes") and taking a dramaturgical perspective on service offerings. In many ways, the best writers on services point to the shift to experiences, most notably Chris Hart, Christopher Lovelock, Leonard Berry, Earl Sasser, James Heskett, and Leonard Schlesinger. Brenda Laurel, formerly of Interval Research and now head of game developer Purple Moon, applied drama to computer interactions in her wonderful book *Computers as Theatre.* Jay Ogilvy of the Global Business Network wrote *The Experience Industry,* a 1985 report for SRI International, demonstrating that demand for "vivid experiences" already drove marginal growth in the U.S. economy. There are surely others that we should be mentioning, and we hope that they receive due recognition for their parts in predicting and describing the rise of the Experience Economy.

A number of people, while they did not necessarily write or discuss with us views directly related to the subject of this book, significantly influenced our thinking about a range of issues that could not help but manifest themselves as we wrote. These wise saws include Stan Davis, Edward de Bono, Joel Barker, Don Peppers and Martha Rogers, Michael Schrage, Peter Drucker, George Gilder, James Brian Quinn, Taichi Sakaiya, Virginia Postrel, Larry Downes and Chunka Mui (again—again), Donald Norman, David Gelernter, Henry Morris, James Boice, and R. C. Sproul. And we learned most of what we know about theatre and how to apply its principles to work from the writings of such performing arts authors as David Mamet, Peter Brook, Richard Schechner, Richard Hornby, Michael Kearns, Michael Shurtleff, Eric Morris, Thomas Babson, Anthony Rooley, Charles Marowitz, David Kahn and Donna Breed, Harold Clurman, and Sally Harrison-Pepper, through whose work we gained a greater understanding of street performance—that form of theatre which Jim has venerated since his more youthful days of watching a pantaloon named Robert Armstrong perform on the streets of San Francisco as Butterfly Man.

Of course, the idea of this book would have quickly faced mere oblivion without a number of people contributing across a wide range of disciplines. Our agent, Rafe Sagalyn, helped find us exactly the right publisher and provided guidance at many important junctures in the writing. Many at Harvard Business School Press enthusiastically supported us from the beginning. Nick Phillipson first rallied enthusiasm for the project. Our wonderful editor, Kirsten Sandberg, pointed out the many deficiencies in early drafts and pushed and cajoled us to make each draft better. Also, Sarah Merrigan and Morgan Moss greatly improved the final manuscript through their meticulous editing. And Carol Franco, head of the Press, has been an unswerving champion of our ideas ever since her involvement in publishing *Mass Customization* many years ago. So much of what we've thought has been published first in the *Harvard Business Review* that we want to thank our longtime editor, Steve Prokesch—who is now with the Boston Consulting Group but still provides us with valuable feedback on the side—Tom Richman, Cathy Olofson, Regina Fazio Maruca, and, of course, Nan Stone. Personal editing assistance with the manuscript and industry analysis were provided by, respectively, freelancers Robin Schoen and Chris Roy, while Word Plus Project Support of Cleveland created the original graphics for many of the figures; our thanks to Ruthanne Fait, Petra Haut, and Tim McCluskey.

Of course, we would have been sans figures, sans manuscript, sans business, sans everything were it not for our managing partner Doug Parker, who handles so many of the day-to-day aspects of running our business, and took on even more thankless tasks in order to provide the time, energy, and focus we needed to write. He also marshalls all of the marketing activities that keep us in business. We owe Doug a great debt of gratitude. Scott Lash, also of Strategic Horizons LLP, has performed many tasks essential to completing this work, including researching a number of the companies we highlight.

And thank you to our families—Julie, Rebecca, and Elizabeth Pine, Beth, Evan, and Anna Gilmore—for living through our fixation on all things experiential and giving us the time to write, and to our parents—Marilou and Norman Burnett and Bud Pine, and Haydn and Marlene Gilmore and the late Jean Gilmore—for their loving support and guidance throughout our lives. Finally, we acknowledge the providential work of a triune God, who placed all these people in our footpaths and gave us the curiosity and capabilities to discover what He first made clear.

About the Authors

●　●

B. Joseph Pine II and **James H. Gilmore** are cofounders of Aurora, Ohio-based Strategic Horizons LLP, a thinking studio dedicated to helping businesses conceive and design new ways of adding value to their economic offerings. They work with management teams to grasp the nature of the emerging Experience Economy and envision their role in it—whether it be staging experiences, guiding transformations, or mass customizing any economic offering. Pine & Gilmore are frequent speakers at professional society and trade association conferences, as well as executive education programs of individual companies. They have written numerous articles on business strategy and innovation, frequently as coauthors, for such publications as the *Harvard Business Review, The Wall Street Journal, Strategy & Leadership, Context, The Journal of Cost Management, CIO,* and *Chief Executive, among others. Pine & Gilmore have appeared on Good Morning America, ABC News, CNBC,* and the *American Business Journal* and are frequently quoted in such publications as *Forbes, Fortune, Business Week,* the *New York Times, Business 2.0, Information Week,* and *USA Today.*

Mr. Pine wrote the award-winning *Mass Customization: The New Frontier in Business Competition* (Boston: Harvard Business School Press, 1993). He is a faculty leader in the Penn State Executive Education Program, a member of the Executive Education faculty at the UCLA Anderson Graduate School of Management, an adjunct faculty member with the IBM Advanced Business Institute, and frequently guest lectures at the MIT Sloan School of Management. Prior to cofounding Strategic Horizons, Mr.

Pine held numerous positions with the IBM Corporation and contributed to its Rochester, Minnesota's facility winning the Malcolm Baldrige National Quality Award. He graduated from Sloan at MIT.

Mr. Gilmore began his career with Procter & Gamble after which he spent more than ten years consulting with Cleveland Consulting Associates and Computer Sciences Corporation, heading CSC Consulting's process innovation practice. Mr. Gilmore is a certified instructor in the lateral thinking methodologies of Dr. Edward de Bono and a member of both the Creative Education Foundation and the Creative Thinking Association of America. He also serves on the faculty of The Institutes for Organization Management for the U.S. Chamber of Commerce and works with for-profit and non-profit enterprises to foster innovative thinking. Mr. Gilmore is a graduate of the Wharton School of the University of Pennsylvania.